The
Photographer

The Photographer

Emmanuel Guibert · Didier Lefèvre · Frédéric Lemercier

Translated by Alexis Siegel

First Second

New York & London

Introduction

by ALEXIS SIEGEL

UNTIL THE EVENTS OF SEPTEMBER 11, 2001, Afghanistan had been off the radar of nearly all Americans for many years. *The Photographer* takes us back to 1986 and brings us along on a journey through that war-torn nation. In the process, it illuminates many of the challenges that Americans have been struggling to understand since 9/11.

A turning point, in a strategic place

We discover Afghanistan through the eyes and camera of photojournalist Didier Lefèvre, who is admittedly naïve about the geopolitical complexities that he is stumbling into. The story begins in 1986 in Peshawar, Pakistan, where Didier kicks himself for not being savvier about all the intrigue swirling around him as he prepares to cross into Afghanistan—although it would have taken a particularly effective crystal ball to understand the situation completely.

As it turns out, Didier's innocence, openness, and eagerness to learn make him an ideal guide for us as readers. His reportage has a depth of honesty that comes from a passion for service—service to his art, first and foremost, and, second, to the mission that he has agreed to be part of: a humanitarian expedition of Doctors Without Borders/Médecins Sans Frontières (MSF). That sincerity about his work even leads Didier to make a high-risk decision, against all advice and common sense, on how to conclude his stay in Afghanistan.

At the time of this story, most Westerners saw Afghanistan simply as one of the regional theaters of the Cold War, a place where local resistance movements, backed by the CIA and by various groupings from around the Muslim world, fought the Soviet Army and its Afghan Communist allies. But we now know that it was a key turning point in the Cold War—a military overreach by the Red Army that exposed fissures in the

70-year-old Communist system, brought about the breakup of the Soviet Union, and paved the way for America's moment as the sole global superpower.

Afghanistan had been a strategic crossroads ever since the days of the Silk Road, when the valleys of the Hindu Kush were a key passage point for trading caravans shuttling between China, the Middle East, and Europe. China borders Afghanistan to its east, while Iran lies to its west, and Pakistan to its south and east. To its north are three of the five Central Asian "Stans" (Tajikistan, Uzbekistan, and Turkmenistan) that were part of the Soviet Union at the time of Didier's story (Kyrgyzstan and Kazakhstan being the other two).

During the days of the British Raj in India, the British and Russian spheres of influence collided in Afghanistan. Britain's attempt to dominate this mountainous, sparsely populated country led to protracted guerrilla wars. Afghanistan's complex ethnic and tribal makeup, as well as its history of internal strife, made it notoriously hard to control. But, because of its strategic position, foreign meddling in its affairs continued, amplifying domestic conflicts. The country finally gained full independence in 1919, establishing itself as a neutral buffer zone between neighboring empires. Afghanistan then experienced a period of stability as a monarchy, and even as a democratic parliamentary monarchy starting in the mid-1960s and continuing until a series of coups began in 1973. Against a backdrop of rising Soviet influence, power struggles between rival Marxist groups developed, and in December 1979 the Soviet Union decided to invade the country to support the faction it favored.

Hints of trouble to come

Beyond boycotting the 1980 Olympic Games in Moscow, there was little the United States and the West could do openly about the Soviet invasion of Afghanistan without risking a dangerous escalation. Local Afghan resistance movements, which formed up in the countryside into a myriad of groups, often with competing agendas, were left to fend for themselves against the Soviet army, one of the most powerful in the world. Their prospects seemed dim. However, some four years into the conflict these groups were still putting up a tenacious fight, and they began to attract outside attention. Behind the scenes, the CIA and several other players organized covert assistance to the Afghan fighters, known as mujahideen (fighters in the jihad, or holy war).

One of the Arab players who began to rise to prominence at that time was Osama bin Laden. He came from one of the wealthiest families in Saudi Arabia: his father, originally a poor immigrant from Yemen, had built a vast construction empire with close ties to the Saudi royal family. Osama set about using the oil wealth of the Arab world to liberate the Muslim country of Afghanistan from the Soviets. By making generous donations, he gained considerable influence within the Afghan refugee camps in Pakistan (at the time the Afghan refugee population, numbering over 4 million, was the largest in the world), and he supported Pakistan-based fighters. Bin Laden's project was facilitated by the CIA, through the Pakistani secret service, the Inter-Services Intelligence. This was not the only dangerous alliance that the logic of the Cold War led the United States and its allies to entertain, but it is probably the one that has had the most grievous consequences for America.

Foreshadowing trouble that would come later, a member of the MSF team explains to Didier that their mission has to seek protection from warlords*; otherwise its members would be at the mercy not only of bandits, but also of Wahhabi fundamentalists, who have infiltrated the region of Nuristan. Wahhabism is the deeply conservative interpretation of Sunni Islam that is dominant in Saudi Arabia, and this passage refers to the violent, militant element within it (not yet organized into Al Qaeda, the founding of which is generally dated around 1988). The worldview of these extremists centered on an all-out war between Muslims and non-Muslims, thus even health workers from the West could become targets.

Life under the Taliban

As difficult as the situation in Afghanistan was at the time of Didier's story, we now know that it took a turn for the worse in the following years. The Soviet Union's eventual withdrawal from Afghanistan in 1989 did not lead to harmonious sharing of power. Instead, the unstable anti-Soviet Afghan alliance dissolved, and

---

* This is one instance where Didier's account is inaccurate regarding one important detail: he recalled that the warlord's protection was bought with a baksheesh, a bribe. In fact, Aider Shah was acting out of gratitude and respect for the work that had been done in his region in the 1960s by Jacques Fournot, an engineer with the United Nations Development Program, and the father of Juliette Fournot, the leader of the MSF expedition. See the Portraits section at the end of book for more about this.

fighting resumed among the many different factions: ethnic Tajiks and Uzbeks in the north, Pushtuns in the south, and minorities like the Hazara, a Shiite group, plus political, tribal, and personal rivalries within each of the groups and parties. Afghanistan became a failed state between 1991 and 1996, to the point that many Afghans, even liberal-minded ones, welcomed the eventual victory of the Taliban: they saw that faction's control over most of the country as the only way of restoring law and order and eliminating drug-financed warlordism.

Because the Taliban movement was not monolithic, many hoped that the more pragmatic elements within it would prevail, as they did for a time and in some provinces. However, the government in the capital city of Kabul came more and more under the ideological sway of foreign elements, particularly Al Qaeda, and drifted toward increasingly repressive policies that caused dismay around the world. Women and girls were denied any professional or educational opportunity. Club-wielding thugs from the "Ministry of the Prevention of Vice and Promotion of Virtue" enforced a long list of prohibitions, from music to chess. And the unique giant Buddhas of Bamiyan Valley, which had stood for 1,500 years as one of the great wonders along the Silk Road, were dynamited in 2001.

The Taliban did curb opium production, but this was achieved only through authoritarian control, without creating viable alternative livelihoods for farmers. This meant that the drug economy promptly bounced back after the fall of the Taliban, and today 90 percent of the world's opium comes from Afghanistan. Crop substitution remains a daunting challenge to this day, for multiple reasons. Much of the country's good agricultural land is heavily contaminated by landmines, which continue to maim and kill farmers and their families. With arable land so limited, the opium poppy is not only far more profitable than perishable crops; once harvested, it can also be stored when the roads are unsafe.

Probably no American needs reminding that it was the Taliban's harboring of Al Qaeda at the time of the attacks of September 11, 2001, that led to their downfall at the hands of the US and its allies of the Northern Alliance. This coalition (also known as the United Islamic Front for the Salvation of Afghanistan), dominated by ethnic Tajiks and Uzbeks, had just lost its foremost leader, Ahmad Shah

Massoud, a hero of the resistance to the Soviets and a leader of truly national stature. He is referred to a few times in the course of this story, since he was based in Panjshir Valley, next to Badakhshan, where the MSF team worked. Massoud, "The Lion of Panjshir Valley," was murdered by Al Qaeda suicide bombers posing as journalists, on September 9, 2001, two days before the attacks on New York and Washington.

The humanitarian mission

Long before these events, in the fall of 1986, the MSF team that we follow in *The Photographer* set out to

build a hospital, and also to staff one that had been set up by the previous mission. It was a dangerous expedition. The team ran the risk of being bombed or captured by Soviet forces or of running afoul of rivalries among the various factions of the Afghan resistance. Incredibly, the whole endeavor was helmed by a young French woman. This unexpected leader, Dr. Juliette Fournot, has a fascinating discussion with Didier on her work and the meaning of gender in Afghanistan, which is bound to make many readers question their assumptions about Afghan society.

Dr. Fournot, who had firsthand knowledge of the country and culture and fluent command of its Dari Persian language* thanks to having spent her teenage years in Afghanistan, had assembled an exceptional team to do important work, against long odds, to help alleviate some of the Afghan population's suffering. Sadly, we learn from the historical update in the Profiles section at the end of the book that those odds lengthened in subsequent years, with international and national aid workers becoming targets of attack. Finally, after the murder of five of its staff in Baghdis province in June 2004, MSF considered the risks too extreme and pulled out of the country, although the organization is currently seeking to return given the deteriorating humanitarian situation.

---

* Afghan Persian, known as Dari, is a close relative both of Tajik and of Iranian Persian (sometimes called Farsi). The lettering of the Persian-language dialogue in *The Photographer* was done by none other than Marjane Satrapi, the acclaimed Iranian author of the graphic novel and animated film *Persepolis.*

Médecins Sans Frontières, as the group is known in French, was founded in 1971 by a dozen French doctors and medical journalists, several of whom had witnessed atrocities in the southern Nigerian state of Biafra during a failed secession in 1968-69. Driven by the urge to go wherever medical and humanitarian needs are greatest, MSF grew from its French beginnings into an international organization, now providing aid in nearly 60 countries. It was awarded the Nobel Peace Prize in 1999.

Witnessing an MSF mission in a war zone, as we do reading *The Photographer*, is a humbling experience. The members of the MSF team demonstrate a thorough knowledge of Afghanistan's culture and circumstances, and it is clear that an astonishing amount of preparation went into making a dangerous undertaking take shape as safely and peacefully as possible. Didier is struck by how Robert, a French doctor, can look and sound more Afghan than the Afghans, and he delights in photographing the complex negotiations for the purchases of the expedition's horses and mules, conducted in an elaborately coded sign language. The photojournalist also notes how the team defers to local hierarchy by taking hours to thoroughly examine the paralyzed arm of a regional leader, even though there is no hope of treating it.

We see the team endure many tribulations in this mission, and we hear even more recounted. We can only marvel, as Didier does, at their seemingly limitless drive and determination. When Didier feels unable to go on, either because of physical fatigue from climbing mountain peaks or from the psychological strain of seeing children injured when a village is bombed, he draws strength from the example provided by the doctors and nurses around him. What fuels them seems to be both a profound respect and love for the people of Afghanistan, and a belief in the importance of their work.

This dedication is evident both in Didier's remarkable photographs and in Emmanuel Guibert's art, which seamlessly completes the narrative around the pictures and gives them further depth and meaning. Through the alchemy of this rare collaboration, *The Photographer* ushers us into a deeper understanding of a fascinating country and a truer appreciation of humanitarian workers who risk their lives in the service of others.

*

In 2007, the life of the talented and empathetic photographer Didier Lefèvre was cut short at the age of 49, just as his work was starting to reach a wide audience.

Alexis Siegel

New York City, 2008

UZBE-
KISTAN
TAJIKISTAN
TURKMENISTAN
CHINA
IRAN
INDIA
AFGHANISTAN
PAKISTAN

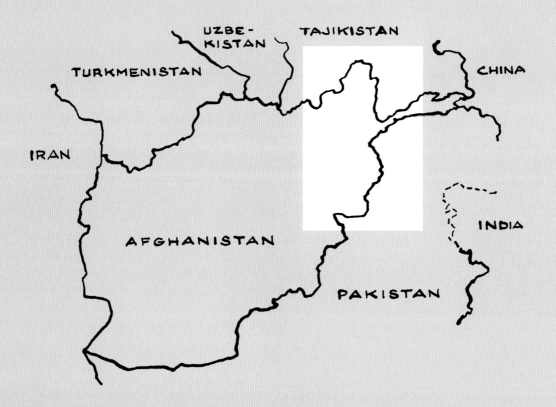

TAJIKISTAN

YAFTAL

FEYZABAD

KOKCHA

TESHKAN

BADAKH|SHAN

PAKISTAN

ANJOMAN   DEWANA   BABA

PANSHIR   BUM   BORET   CHITRAL

BARG. E. MATAL

DORUNS

KANTIWA

NURISTAN

KABUL

AFGHANISTAN

0 10 20   40   60   80   100 KM
0   10   20   40   60 MI

PESHAWAR

Part 1

I SAY GOOD-BYE TO EVERYONE. TO THE FOLKS AT MSF.

TO MY MOM, WHO IS MOVING INTO A NEW HOME IN BLONVILLE, NORMANDY.

TO MY GRANDMOTHER, AND TO HER DOG, BIENCHEN.

IN THE PARIS APARTMENT THAT MY MOM HAS JUST MOVED OUT OF, I TAKE PICTURES OF THE HI-FI SYSTEM LEFT ALL ALONE.

AND THAT'S IT. FAREWELL, PARIS.

IT'S THE END OF JULY 1986. I GET ON THE PLANE AND TAKE OFF.

WE HAVE A NIGHTTIME LAYOVER IN KARACHI, PAKISTAN, FOR ABOUT TEN HOURS.

I HEAD TO A HOTEL NEXT TO THE AIRPORT. THE COST OF THE ROOM IS INCLUDED IN THE PLANE TICKET.

A LOUSY NIGHT'S SLEEP, TOO SHORT. I TAKE TWO PICTURES OF MYSELF IN THE MIRROR. THOSE ARE MY FIRST SHOTS FROM THE TRIP.

THE NEXT DAY I LAND IN PESHAWAR, IN NORTHWEST PAKISTAN. IT'S REALLY HOT.

A WOMAN FROM MSF COMES TO PICK ME UP.

I'M SORRY, I CAN'T KISS YOU ON THE CHEEKS. IT'S FORBIDDEN HERE.

HER NAME'S SYLVIE AND SHE'S A NURSE. APPARENTLY THE AFGHANS CALL HER "BATCHA"—"THE LITTLE BOY."

I DUMP MY THINGS IN A RICKSHAW, WHICH TAKES US TO UNIVERSITY TOWN.

WE GO THROUGH WIDE STREETS BETWEEN COLONIAL-STYLE HOUSES WITH PARKS AND GARDENS, IN THE PLEASANT RESIDENTIAL NEIGHBORHOOD AROUND THE UNIVERSITY.

WE GET TO THE MSF HOUSE.

I'M GIVEN A MATTRESS IN A CORNER OF A ROOM.

IT'S LATE AFTERNOON. EVERYONE'S COMING BACK TO HAVE A DRINK AND TAKE A SHOWER. I MEET UP WITH A NUMBER OF PEOPLE I KNOW.

JULIETTE, THE HEAD OF OUR MISSION.

JOHN, A SURGEON.

ROBERT, A DOCTOR.

RÉGIS, A NURSE-ANESTHESIOLOGIST.

I'M INTRODUCED TO MAHMAD, AN AFGHAN WHO'LL BE OUR GUIDE AND INTERPRETER.

SO YOU'RE THE PHOTOGRAPHER?

5

ALL THE GUYS HAVE BEARDS. I STARTED LETTING MINE GROW IN FRANCE, BUT THE RESULTS AREN'T TOO IMPRESSIVE YET.

YUP, THAT'S ME.

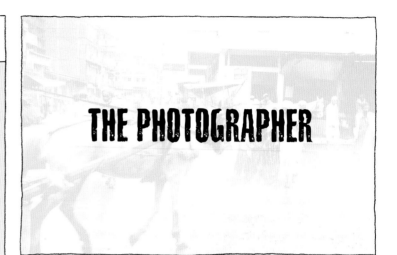

THE PHOTOGRAPHER

A story lived, photographed, and told by DIDIER LEFÈVRE

Written and drawn by EMMANUEL GUIBERT

Laid out and colored by FRÉDÉRIC LEMERCIER

CLICK.

Translated from the French by ALEXIS SIEGEL

PESHAWAR'S BEAUTIFUL—A TRUE CITY OF THE EAST, TEEMING WITH PEOPLE, NOISY, POLLUTED, WITH NONSTOP TRAFFIC: BRRRMMM, BRRRMMM...

EVERYTHING'S INTENSE: SMELLS ARE STRONG, NOISES ARE LOUD, CROWDS ARE HUGE, THE MIDDAY HOURS ARE UNBEARABLY HOT. IN WESTERN DRESS YOU SIMPLY CAN'T COPE.

ROBERT AND RÉGIS IMMEDIATELY TAKE ME TO A TAILOR.

HE TAKES MY MEASURE-MENTS. BY THE NEXT DAY, HE'LL MAKE ME A FULL SET OF CLOTHING, INCLUDING PANTS, A VERY LONG SHIRT, A VEST, A HAT, A SCARF, SHOES, AND THE FAMOUS AFGHAN BLANKET CALLED A PATOO. HERE PEOPLE DON'T WEAR UNDERWEAR.

HE MAKES THREE OF EACH ITEM SO I'LL ALWAYS HAVE A CHANGE OF CLOTHES. IT COSTS PEANUTS AND THERE ARE A NUMBER OF BENEFITS TO DRESSING IN THE FLOWING AFGHAN STYLE. FIRST, I'LL BE COMFORTABLE.

SECOND, I'LL CONFORM TO ISLAMIC STANDARDS OF DECENCY BY WEARING LONG CLOTHING THAT CONCEALS THE BODY WELL.

THIRD, I'LL BLEND INTO THE CROWD.

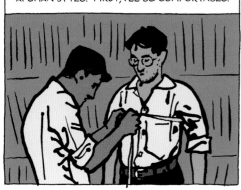

IN THE MSF HOUSE, WE SPEND MOST OF THE TIME FILLING AND SEALING BOXES.

MY MOM MOVED LAST WEEK.

WHERE'D SHE GO?

BLONVILLE, IN NORMANDY.

THAT'S GOOD—NICE AND COOL AROUND THERE.

YOU HAVE TO FILL EACH BOX PERFECTLY, NOT LEAVING THE TINIEST BIT OF EMPTY SPACE: WITH THE BATTERING THOSE BOXES WILL TAKE DURING THE EXPEDITION, THE CONTENTS OF A PACK OF PILLS COULD ARRIVE CRUSHED TO A FINE POWDER IF THEY WERE TO SHIFT EVEN SLIGHTLY.

IN CASE A BOX FALLS INTO A RIVER (THIS DOES HAPPEN), EVERYTHING HAS TO BE CAREFULLY WRAPPED IN A WATERPROOF TARP.

THEN WRAPPED IN BURLAP CLOTH, SEWN UP, TIED UP.

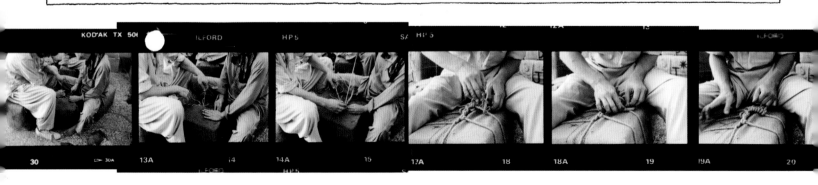

FINALLY, EACH BOX IS NUMBERED AND STORED.

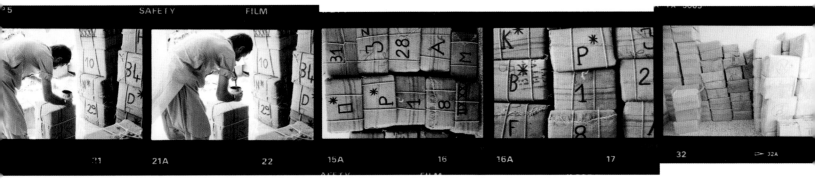

IT TAKES DAYS. AFGHAN STAFFERS HELP US. SOMETIMES WE GET BREAKS.

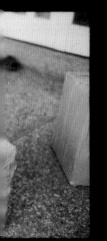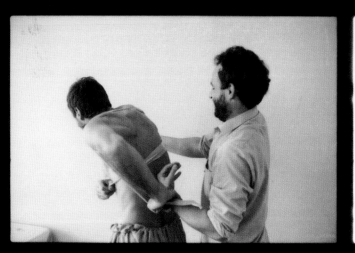

I GET HAZED. THEY WRAP ME FROM HEAD TO TOE IN PACKING TAPE AND SHOOT DOZENS OF PICTURES OF ME WITH MY OWN CAMERA.

ONE NIGHT A BLACKOUT HITS UNIVERSITY TOWN...

THE AIR CONDITIONING STOPS. WITHIN MINUTES THE TEMPERATURE CLIMBS TO 120°F.

HERE WE GO: A PAKISTANI INTERLUDE.

THE FOLLOWING MONTH WE'LL BE IN AFGHANISTAN. FOR WEEKS PEOPLE HAVE BEEN WARNING ME THAT IT'LL BE TOUGH. I'M 29, IN GOOD SHAPE. I'VE DONE PLENTY OF HIKING IN MY LIFE. I'M PRETTY RESILIENT AND I CAN PUT UP WITH A LOT.

BUT THIS WILL INVOLVE CROSSING FIFTEEN MOUNTAIN PASSES OVER 16,000 FEET HIGH, ON FOOT.

PASS ME THE BOTTLE, PLEASE.

AFGHANISTAN IS AT WAR. ON ONE SIDE YOU HAVE THE INVADING SOVIET FORCES AND THE ARMY OF THE COMMUNIST GOVERNMENT IN KABUL, AND ON THE OTHER ARE THE MUJAHIDEEN, THE RESISTANCE.

IN THE MIDDLE ARE THE HUMANITARIAN ORGANIZATIONS.

EVERYTHING I DRINK I SWEAT OUT IN SECONDS.

BLOCK UP YOUR PORES, THEN.

MSF HAS HIRED ME TO DO PHOTO-REPORTAGE ON A CARAVAN THAT'S GOING INTO THE REGION OF BADAKHSHAN IN NORTHERN AFGHANISTAN, NEAR THE CITY OF FEYZABAD.

JULIETTE, JOHN, ROBERT, RÉGIS, MAHMAD, AND OTHERS HAVE BEEN PREPARING THE EXPEDITION FOR MONTHS. THE AIM IS TO REACH A SMALL FIELD HOSPITAL IN ONE VALLEY AND GO CREATE ANOTHER ONE FARTHER ALONG.

HAND ME THAT BOTTLE AGAIN FOR A SEC.

WE HAVE TO PUT TOGETHER THE CARAVAN, BUY THE DONKEYS AND HORSES, AND HIRE THE ESCORT. THAT WILL BE THE WORK OF THE NEXT MONTH. AFTER THAT, WE'LL SET OFF.

IF WE COULD TAKE VEHICLES AND GO ON THE ROADS, THAT TRIP WOULD BE A DAY'S EXPEDITION. BUT THE ROADS ARE HELD BY THE GOVERNMENT ARMY AND THE RUSSIANS.

CUTTING THROUGH THE MOUNTAINS AND GOING AROUND SENTRY POSTS WILL TAKE US THREE WEEKS, IF ALL GOES WELL.

YOU BASTARD, YOU FINISHED IT OFF.

YUP.

WILL I BE UP TO IT?

AS A DOCTOR, I HAVE TO DRINK MORE THAN YOU.

IN HUMANITARIAN MISSIONS, THE FIRST GUY WE SACRIFICE IS THE PHOTOGRAPHER.

ALLAH BLESS DIESEL GENERATORS.

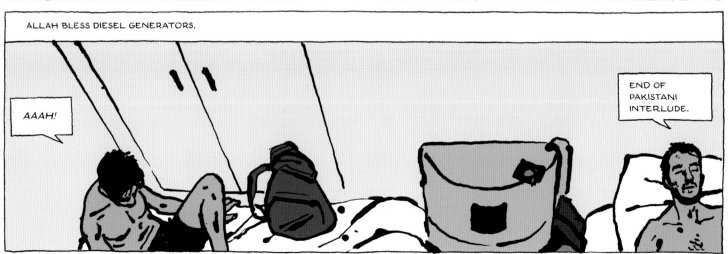

AAAH!

END OF PAKISTANI INTERLUDE.

11

GOING THROUGH PESHAWAR, I REALIZE THAT THE WAR IN AFGHANISTAN IS GLOBAL, BECAUSE THE ENTIRE WORLD IS HERE.

FIRST OF ALL, IT'S TEEMING WITH AFGHANS. A RICKSHAW DRIVEN BY AN AFGHAN AND LOADED DOWN WITH FIVE OTHER AFGHANS PROVIDES A PRETTY GOOD SUMMARY OF THE SITUATION: PESHAWAR IS OVERFLOWING WITH AFGHANS.

THERE ARE REFUGEES ALL OVER THE PLACE. THEY LIVE IN HUGE CAMPS SURROUNDING THE CITY. THEY DO EVERY IMAGINABLE JOB.

DID HE PAINT HIS RICKSHAW HIMSELF?

I'LL ASK HIM.

NO, HE SAYS A FRIEND OF HIS PAINTED IT. HE'S A TAJIK, SO HE ORDERED A PORTRAIT OF MASSOUD WITH "THE LION OF PANJSHIR VALLEY" AS THE CAPTION.

SUPERB.

THE HEAD OF MASSOUD HAS BEEN STUCK ON THE BODY OF RAMBO, WITH A HUGE MACHINE GUN AND BLOOD ALL OVER THE PLACE.

VÉRONIQUE, FROM REUTERS:

AT FIRST, YOU ALWAYS GIVE THEM TOO MUCH.

YOU HAVE A GOOD TRIP AND YOU PULL OUT FIVE BILLS, THE GUY'S HAPPY, HE BEAMS A BIG SMILE, TAKES THE CASH AND SPLITS. YOU PAID TOO MUCH.

THE NEXT TIME, YOU ASSESS THINGS MORE CAREFULLY: ONE BILL. AGAIN, THE GUY'S HAPPY, DOESN'T HAGGLE. CHANCES ARE YOU OVERPAID AGAIN.

AFTER A FEW DAYS, YOU GIVE THE RIGHT PRICE. YOU GOTTA CATCH THE KNACK OF IT, BECAUSE NO MATTER WHERE YOU ARE, ANY CHANCE THEY GET TO SCREW YOU, THEY WILL.

THE HORSE AND DONKEY MARKETS ARE INSIDE THE REFUGEE CAMPS.

WE CHOOSE THE ANIMALS THAT WE'LL BE TAKING ALONG: ABOUT A HUNDRED DONKEYS AND TWENTY HORSES.

MSF HAS SOME TRUSTED AFGHAN OVERSEERS.

THIS GUY, FOR EXAMPLE, IS ONE OF THEM—A REALLY BURLY MAN, A PALAWAN. THE STRENGTH OF THESE GUYS IS UNBELIEVABLE. SO IS THE RESPECT THEY ENJOY IN AFGHANISTAN.

THEY ARE OFTEN PLAYERS OF BUZKASHI, THE NATIONAL SPORT. IT'S PLAYED ON HORSEBACK. THE PLAYERS FIGHT OVER A DECAPITATED CALF WEIGHING 80 TO 100 POUNDS, WHICH THEY HOLD UP AT ARM'S LENGTH.

AND SPEAKING OF THOSE ARMS, THEY DON'T NARROW AT THE WRIST AT ALL. THEY'RE TREE TRUNKS.

I WATCH NEGOTIATIONS. THE SELLER AND BUYER GRAB EACH OTHER'S HANDS. A SORT OF UMPIRE PRESIDES OVER THE EXCHANGES. TO KEEP THE NEGOTIATION SECRET, THE MEN SOMETIMES COVER THEIR HANDS WITH A CLOTH. THEN THEY TALK BY MOVEMENTS AND PRESSURE OF THE FINGERS. ONE MAN'S FINGERS OFFER SUMS, THE OTHER MAN'S FINGERS ACCEPT OR REFUSE THEM. IT'S A CODE AMONG THEM, A LANGUAGE, WITH LOOKS AND FACIAL EXPRESSIONS ADDING A FURTHER LAYER. AT TIMES, YOU SEE ONE OF THEM TEAR AWAY HIS HAND BECAUSE THE PROPOSAL THAT WAS JUST MADE IS INTOLERABLE. FIELD DAY FOR A PHOTOGRAPHER.

JULIETTE INTRODUCES ME TO THIS BOY. HE IS THE SON OF THE WAKIL, A SORT OF REPRESENTATIVE OF BADAKHSHAN, THE REGION WHERE WE'RE GOING.

HE'S JUST A KID, BUT SINCE HIS FATHER IS A BIGWIG, HE ALREADY HAS THE RANK OF COMMANDER.

ESSALAAM.

SALAMA-LEYKOOM.

OUR CARAVAN WILL BE DIPLOMATICALLY CORRECT, WITH PEOPLE FROM THE TWO VALLEYS WHERE WE ARE GOING, YAFTAL AND TESHKAN. THIS IS ABDUL JABAR, FROM TESHKAN.

ESSALAAM.

SALAMA-LEYKOOM.

AND NAJMUDIN, FROM YAFTAL. THEY ARE THE TWO GROUP LEADERS. I EXPECTED THEM TO CRUSH MY HAND, BUT NO, THEY MERELY TOUCH IT.

ESSALAAM.

SALAMA-LEYKOOM.

ARE YOU PLEASED WITH YOUR PURCHASES?

YES, I THINK WE'LL HAVE SOME GOOD ANIMALS.

BUT BUYING THEM'S NOT ENOUGH. WE'LL HAVE TO MAKE SURE THAT THE ANIMALS WE BOUGHT ARE THE ONES THAT GET BROUGHT TO THE BORDER. WE'LL KEEP OUR EYES PEELED.

AND WE'LL ALSO HAVE TO CHECK THAT WE CAN RIDE THEM. SO DO ME A FAVOR AND GET ON THIS ONE.

RIGHT NOW?

RIGHT NOW.

HE'S A NICE LITTLE HORSE, BUT NERVOUS. HE DOESN'T OBEY AT ALL.

HE DOESN'T WANT TO GO WHERE I WANT HIM TO.

AND WHEN HE DECIDES TO HEAD SOMEWHERE, HE GETS THERE FAST.

STOP HIM! STOP HIM!

WHOA!

WHOA!

HOLD IT!

TOO BAD YOU'VE GOT YOUR HANDS FULL, 'CAUSE THAT WAS SOME PHOTO OP.

WHAT A LITTLE BASTARD!

JULIETTE IS FULLY UP TO HER TASK, WHICH ISN'T EASY. WE TALK A LOT AND SHE TRIES TO BRIEF ME ON WHAT TO EXPECT AHEAD.

MAHMAD DOES, TOO. A LOVELY GUY, WITH A REALLY SOFT MANNER. HE TEACHES ME ACCELERATED AFGHAN PERSIAN 101.

I'M IMPRESSED BY THE EASE WITH WHICH JOHN, ROBERT, AND RÉGIS INTERACT WITH AFGHANS (WELL, MAYBE JOHN IS A BIT LESS IMPRESSIVE: ALTHOUGH HIS PERSIAN IS QUITE FLUENT, HE SPEAKS IT WITH A THICK AMERICAN ACCENT).

WHEREAS ROBERT COULDN'T BE CLOSER TO THE REAL THING—THE LOOK, THE ATTITUDES, THE FLUENCY WITH THE LANGUAGE, IT'S ALL THERE.

ROBERT, I CAN'T BELIEVE HOW WELL YOU SPEAK!

WELL, YEAH, BEEN AT IT FOR A WHILE NOW, SO I MANAGE. I EVEN KNOW THEIR DIRTY JOKES.

IN THE STREET, IN SHOPS, IT'S A PLEASURE TO WATCH THEM AT WORK.

17

IN THE PREVIOUS MISSIONS, ALL THE MSF MEMBERS HAVE BEEN GIVEN AN AFGHAN NAME. JULIETTE IS JAMILA, ROBERT IS MALIK, RÉGIS IS WALID, SYLVIE IS LATIFA, AND SO ON.

WE HAVE TO GIVE DIDIER A NAME.

WE COULD JUST CALL HIM "CHAPANDOZ."

HAHA

HAHAHA

HAHAHA

HAHA

TRANSLATION, PLEASE?

IT MEANS "THE HORSEMAN."

AH, YES, GREAT.

JULIETTE TURNS TOWARD THE PALAWAN AND SAYS TO HIM IN PERSIAN, "FIND A NAME FOR DIDIER."

HE LOOKS AT ME FOR A SHORT WHILE WITH THE SQUINTING LOOK OF SOMEONE CONCENTRATING.

AND THEN, WITH A SMILE AND A SURPRISINGLY SOFT VOICE FOR A GUY THAT SIZE, HE SAYS:

AHMADJAN MEANS "THAT DEAR AHMAD" AND THE NAME IS AN INSTANT HIT.

VERY GOOD.

SUITS YOU PER- FECTLY.

EVEN BET- TER THAN DIDIER.

THANKS, THANKS.

IN THE FOLLOWING DAYS, THE AFGHANS START CALLING ME "AHMADJAN," BUT THEY DO IT AFGHAN-STYLE, MEANING THAT THEY OFTEN CALL OUT TO ME IN A KIND OF CHANT.

WAAAHMADJAN

WOOOAAAHMADJAN

WAAAHMADJAN

18

MAHMAD:

YOU HAVE TO LEARN THE FORMAL SALUTA-TIONS; THAT'S VERY IMPORTANT. WHEN YOU PASS SOMEONE, EVEN WAY UP IN THE MOUNTAINS, THEY'LL SAY THEM AND YOU'LL HAVE TO SAY THEM TOO.

OKAY.

SO THERE'S "AS SALAAM WA ALEIKUM," THAT YOU KNOW.

MAY PEACE BE WITH YOU.

"SALAMALEYKOOM," YES.

AND YOU REPLY "WA ALEIKUM ES SALAAM."

"ALEYKOOM SALAM."

IT'S LIKE HELLO, BASICALLY.

YOU SAY IT ALL THE TIME. IF YOU ENTER A HOUSE OR A ROOM, EVEN AN EMPTY ONE, AS YOU PASS THE THRESHOLD, YOU SAY IT, "AS SALAAM WA ALEIKUM," OR "ESSALAAM" FOR SHORT.

AND DON'T FORGET TO TAKE OFF YOUR SHOES.

"MANDA NA BAASHI."

"MANDANABOSHEE."

"MAY YOU NOT BE TIRED."

"ZENDA BAASHI."

"ZENDABOSHEE."

"MAY YOU STAY ALIVE."

"DJUR BAASHI."

"DJOORBOSHEE." ALWAYS "BOSHEE."

YES. IT MEANS "MAY YOU STAY HEALTHY."

NOW, LISTEN CAREFULLY: "CHETOAR ASTIN."

TCHOO WHAT?

"CHETOAR ASTIN."

"TCHOOTOOR ASTEEN."

ROLL THE "R": "CHETOARRR ASTIN."

"TCHOOTOORRR ASTEEN."

THAT'S "HOW ARE YOU?"

"TCHOOTOORRR ASTEEN."

THAT'S IT.

KHUB ASTIN?

RUBASTEEN?

ARE YOU WELL?

YES, I'M WELL, BUT I'LL NEVER REMEMBER ALL THIS.

SURE YOU WILL. YOU'LL BE HEARING IT ALL THE TIME AND IT'LL STICK.

LET'S GO ON.

ROBERT:

SO MAHMAD TAUGHT YOU "SALLY MY LAY COME" AND THE WHOLE SHEBANG?

YES.

THOSE GOOD MANNERS ARE ALL VERY WELL, BUT I HEARD THAT RECENTLY, IN BADAKHSHAN, A SWISS JOURNALIST PASSED A GROUP OF AFGHANS...

AND THE JOURNALIST SAID, WITH A BIG SMILE, "HELLO, HELLO, PEACE BE WITH YOU, ZENDABOSHEE, MANDANABOSHEE," THIS, THAT AND THE OTHER.

THEN A GUY CAME OUT FROM THE GROUP, WALKED TOWARD HIM, AND—BAM!—PUNCHED HIM IN THE FACE!

HE WAS A SUDANESE GUY WHO HAD COME TO FIGHT THE JIHAD. HE COULDN'T UNDERSTAND PERSIAN, BUT HE KNEW AN INFIDEL WHEN HE SAW ONE.

OUCH!

THAT SAID, THE "AS SALAAM WA ALEIKUM" BUSINESS HAS BECOME SECOND NATURE TO ME, TO THE POINT THAT EVEN IN FRANCE I SAY IT UNDER MY BREATH WHENEVER I GO INTO A PLACE.

JULIETTE:

YOU KNOW THAT FOR MSF THE RULE IS TO TREAT ALL THE WOUNDED, REGARDLESS OF WHAT SIDE THEY'RE ON.

WE OFFERED IT TO THE RUSSIANS, BUT THEIR ANSWER WAS NYET. SO WE CAN ONLY TREAT AFGHANS.

ABOUT THE RUSSIANS, I WAS THINKING ABOUT SOMETHING LAST NIGHT...

IT'S WEIRD: SINCE WE WERE KIDS, THE SOVIETS HAVE ALWAYS BEEN THE BAD GUYS, THE BOGEYMEN. THE RED ARMY IS ALWAYS THIS LOOMING THREAT.

AND RIGHT NOW I CAN'T REALLY THINK ABOUT IT AS SOMETHING TANGIBLE. I DON'T KNOW HOW TO PUT IT... I'M LESS WORRIED ABOUT THE RUSSIANS THAN ABOUT HOW TOUGH THE ROAD WILL BE.

WELL, OUR PLAN IS TO AVOID THE RUSSIANS.

AND AS FOR THE ROAD, TELL YOURSELF THAT YOU'LL BE DISCOVERING THE MOST BEAUTIFUL COUNTRY IN THE WORLD. I'M NOT KIDDING.

IT'S TRUE.

20

MAHMAD:

THE ENEMY IS HELICOPTERS.

PLANES ARE AWFUL, BUT THEY FLY PAST YOU, AND BY THE TIME THEY RETURN YOU HAVE A CHANCE OF HIDING.

WHILE A HELICOPTER WILL FLY OVER YOU, STOP, HOVER— LOOKING FOR YOU, SEEKING YOU. IT'S HORRIBLE.

IF YOU'RE IN A PLACE WHERE IT'S HARD TO HIDE, YOU DIVE UNDER YOUR PATOO. THE PATOO IS THE AFGHAN BLANKET.

YES, I KNOW, I HAVE ONE. IT'S BROWN.

COLOR OF EARTH.

YOU DON'T MOVE AND YOU MAKE SURE NOTHING'S STICKING OUT. YOU CLENCH YOUR FISTS WITH THE THUMB INSIDE, LIKE THAT. YOU KNOW WHY?

NO.

BECAUSE THE HELICOPTER WILL SPOT ANYTHING SHINY. EVEN A FINGERNAIL.

DAYS GO BY. THE TEAM GOES OVER TO TAL, ABOUT 20 MILES FROM PESHAWAR.

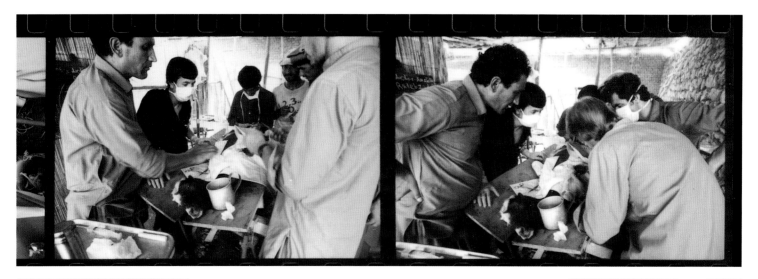

AFGHAN TRAINEE NURSES ARE BEING TAUGHT SURGERY, BY PRACTICING ON GOATS.

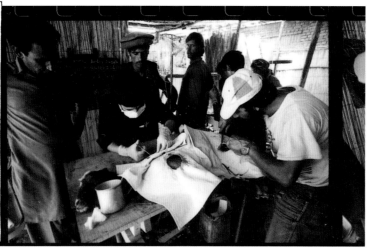

BACK TO PESHAWAR.

I SAID THE CITY IS TEEMING WITH AFGHANS. IT'S ALSO TEEMING WITH ADVENTURERS, MERCENARIES, POTHEADS, AND FUNDAMENTALISTS COMING TO PICK UP SOME TRAINING IN WAR.

I MEET A LOT OF WEIRD CHARACTERS THAT LEAVE YOU SCRATCHING YOUR HEAD. FOR EXAMPLE, THIS GUY, A PATHOLOGICAL LIAR WHO SHOWS UP FOR DINNER ONE EVENING AT THE MSF HOUSE.

HE'S YOUNG, WITH A MARINE-TYPE CREW CUT, AND IS WITH ANOTHER KID WHO IS COMPLETELY DEVOTED TO HIM (I'M TOLD HE GETS A NEW ONE FOR EACH TRIP).

HE FIRST INTRODUCES HIMSELF AS A PHOTOGRAPHER, BUT PRETTY QUICKLY EXPLAINS THAT WHAT HE'S AFTER IS PICKING UP A GUN AND GETTING TO SEE SOME ACTION.

THE BIG THING IS HATRED OF COMMUNISM. IT ATTRACTS MILITARY TRAINERS FROM ALL OVER THE WORLD. THEY COME TO TRAIN THE AFGHANS AND WHOEVER WANTS TO FIGHT THE RUSSIANS— SAUDIS, SUDANESE, ALGERIANS, AND SO ON.

RÉGIS:

I HEAR THERE'S EVEN A JAPANESE GUY WHO'S BUSY TEACHING MARTIAL ARTS TO THE MUJ'.

DOZENS OF SO-CALLED NGOS USE THE COVER OF HUMANITARIAN ACTIVITIES TO PURSUE ESPIONAGE, WAR, OR DIPLOMACY. SOME HAVE A PRETTY SIMPLISTIC VIEW OF THINGS: THEIR JOB CONSISTS OF LOADING BAGS FULL OF BANKNOTES ONTO DONKEYS, CROSSING INTO AFGHANISTAN, AND DISTRIBUTING THE MONEY IN VILLAGES. A PRETTY CRUDE FORM OF ASSISTANCE.

THERE'S PLENTY OF MONEY SLOSHING AROUND IN PESHAWAR.

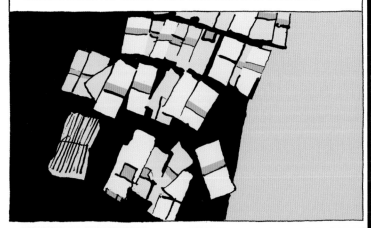

THAT'S OUR MONEY, THE CASH FOR THE EXPEDITION. ENOUGH FOR EVERYONE TO LIVE ON FOR THREE MONTHS IN AFGHANISTAN. OUR PALAWAN COUNTS IT UP. THEN, LIKE EVERYTHING ELSE, IT GETS WRAPPED IN PLASTIC AND, ON THE DAY WE START OUT, SHARED OUT AMONG US.

IT'S ALL A JUMBLE OF THINGS THAT I SEE, HEAR, FEEL, GUESS AT, BUT HAVE TROUBLE ANALYZING. I'M NOT DETACHED ENOUGH, AND MY KNOWLEDGE OF INTERNATIONAL POLITICS IS TOO LIMITED. I WALK AROUND, TAKE MY PICTURES, WAIT FOR THE DAY OF DEPARTURE. I FIND IT INTERESTING TO BE IN THE THICK OF THIS GIANT MESS OF A BAZAAR.

THERE'S ONE PLACE THAT SUMS UP THE SITUATION PRETTY WELL: THE AMERICAN CLUB. JOHN BRINGS US THERE ONE EVENING.

IT'S A BEAUTIFUL, WELL GUARDED HOUSE WITH A BEAUTIFUL GARDEN, IN A BEAUTIFUL NEIGHBORHOOD.

TO GET IN, YOU HAVE TO BE AMERICAN OR ACCOMPANIED BY AN AMERICAN. THE RESTAURANT IS DOWNSTAIRS.

WHEN WE FEEL LIKE EATING WESTERN FOOD, WE'LL GO TO THE AMERICAN CLUB. SINCE MY ARRIVAL, I'VE EATEN AFGHAN, PAKISTANI, EVEN A BIT OF CHINESE. THAT EVENING, IT'S AMERICAN PIZZA, STEAK WITH FRIES, AND SO ON. EVERYTHING IS IMPORTED.

BUT SINCE THIS IS AN ISLAMIC COUNTRY, PEOPLE COME MOSTLY FOR THE BOOZE. AND THAT'S SERVED UPSTAIRS, AT THE BAR.

AT THE RESTAURANT, YOU CAN INVITE MUSLIMS. SO, THEORETICALLY, THEY DON'T SERVE ALCOHOL.

BUT AN AFGHAN PROBABLY WON'T WANT ANYONE TO KNOW HE'S BEEN INVITED TO THE AMERICAN CLUB, BECAUSE RIGHT AWAY THERE'LL BE RUMORS THAT HE'S GETTING PLASTERED.

WE HEAD UPSTAIRS.

AND, YES, UP THERE IS A REAL, LARGE BAR, ABSOLUTELY PACKED WITH PEOPLE. IT HAS BEER, WHISKY, SODA, DART GAMES. A PRICEY PLACE.

WE ELBOW OUR WAY TO A SPOT AND ORDER.

24

NOBODY INTRODUCES THEMSELVES WITH "HI, I'M SO-AND-SO, CIA" OR "HI, I'M SUCH-AND-SUCH, KGB," BUT IT'S OBVIOUS THAT THE PLACE IS CRAWLING WITH SPIES.

SO I CAN'T HELP WONDERING IF EVEN JOHN, WHO IS GOING FROM GROUP TO GROUP GREETING EVERYONE, ISN'T ALSO DOING A BIT OF INTELLIGENCE WORK ON THE SIDE.

ANYWAY, THERE'S ENOUGH MATERIAL HERE FOR TEN LE CARRÉ NOVELS.

RÉGIS:

THIS MISSION WE'RE ABOUT TO GO ON, I ALREADY DID IT TWO YEARS AGO.

AND I KNOW PERFECTLY WELL WHY I'M GOING BACK. I'M GOING BACK BECAUSE I'LL BE PRACTICING SURGERY IN A PLACE WHERE PEOPLE HAVE ABSOLUTELY NO ACCESS TO HEALTH CARE. AND I FIND THAT DEEPLY FULFILLING.

SO FULFILLING THAT IT'S UNLIKELY I'LL EVER GO BACK TO A CUSHY ANESTHESIOLOGIST'S JOB AT A FANCY HOSPITAL IN BORDEAUX.

SO, I DON'T KNOW... WHEN I STOP WORKING FOR MSF, MAYBE I'LL GO FOR SOMETHING TOTALLY DIFFERENT.

LIKE WHAT?

LIKE GOING BACK TO SCHOOL TO LEARN ANOTHER TRADE. I'D LIKE TO KNOW HOW TO MAKE WINE, FOR INSTANCE.

BUT THAT'S CUSHY, TOO.

OH NO, I DON'T THINK SO. NOT AT ALL.

LATER IN THE EVENING I MEET A SHORT, WIRY MAN IN HIS SIXTIES, WITH A SEVERE LOOK ON HIS FACE. I FIND HIM INTRIGUING. WE TALK.

A STRONG GERMANIC ACCENT. HIS MANNER IS ICE-COLD BUT, WEIRDLY ENOUGH, WE CLICK.

IN THE RICKSHAW HEADING BACK:

WHO WAS THAT SHORT GUY YOU WERE TALKING TO? GERMAN?

NO, FROM ALSACE. HE'S A JOURNALIST. EVER HEARD OF THE "MALGRÉ-NOUS"?

NO.

THAT'S WHAT THEY CALLED THE FRENCH PEOPLE OF ALSACE CONSCRIPTED BY THE GERMAN ARMY DURING WWII AND SENT TO FIGHT ON THE RUSSIAN FRONT.

HE WAS ONE?

YES. SENT TO FIGHT IN SIBERIA AT 14. HE TOLD ME ABOUT IT.

WOW.

THE ALSATIAN TAKES A LIKING TO ME. HE INVITES ME INTO HIS ELEGANT AND IMMACULATELY TIDY APARTMENT. WE TALK FOR A LONG TIME.

A FASCINATING GUY. A PHOTOGRAPHER. A COLLECTOR OF LEICAS.

I HAVE FIFTEEN.

FIFTEEN!

JUST GOT BACK FROM NEW YORK, WHERE I LEFT MY LEICA TELEPHOTO LENS IN A HOTEL ROOM. IT'S A 280—ARE YOU FAMILIAR WITH THOSE?

NOT ONLY AM I FAMILIAR WITH THEM, BUT I'M SURE THAT IF I HAD ONE AND HAPPENED TO LEAVE IT IN A HOTEL ROOM, I WOULDN'T BE AS CALM ABOUT IT AS YOU ARE.

YOU'RE ALSO NOT MY AGE.

A 300-MILLIMETER WITH AN APERTURE OF 2.8, THAT'S TWELVE GRAND, SIR.

I KNOW THAT. I'LL HAVE TO MAKE SURE I CALL THE HOTEL TO ASK THEM TO KEEP IT IN THEIR SAFE FOR ME.

HE WORKS FOR THE GERMAN MAGAZINES *DER SPIEGEL* AND *STERN*. HE HAS MASSIVE RESOURCES AND UNUSUAL METHODS.

I'M GOING TO SHOW YOU SOMETHING.

HE WAS THE FIRST WESTERNER, FOR EXAMPLE, TO HAVE GONE AMONG THE KHMER ROUGE IN CAMBODIA WITH THE DELIBERATE INTENT OF GETTING HIMSELF CAPTURED.

DO YOU KNOW THESE LITTLE VIDEO 8 CAMCORDERS?

YES. ANY GOOD?

VERY CONVENIENT.

I TAKE A GOOD STOCK OF THEM INTO AFGHANISTAN AND HAND THEM OUT TO MUJAHIDEEN COMMANDERS.

SIX MONTHS LATER I GO PICK UP THE TAPES. HAVE A LOOK.

WHAT HE SHOWS ME ARE FILMS OF EXECUTIONS OF RUSSIAN PRISONERS. BADLY FILMED, BUT UNCENSORED.

YOU'VE NEVER SEEN ANYTHING LIKE IT, RIGHT?

NO.

ALL THE MONEY, LOGISTICS, AND CONNECTIONS THAT THIS MUST HAVE REQUIRED LEAVES ME SPEECHLESS. THE IMAGES LEAVE ME SPEECHLESS, TOO.

HE TELLS ME ABOUT HIS AMERICAN WIFE, A DOCTOR FOR UNICEF. SHE WAS PREVIOUSLY POSTED IN MAPUTO, MOZAMBIQUE. SHE IS NOW INSIDE AFGHANISTAN.

HE SHOWS ME A PICTURE OF A BEAUTIFUL YOUNG WOMAN. IT'S TRUE THAT, FOR HIS AGE, HE'S IN UNBELIEVABLY GOOD SHAPE.

GOOD LUCK.

THANK YOU, SIR. GOOD-BYE.

THERE HAS TO BE SOME POLITICAL AGENDA BEHIND THAT MAN. ALL HIS MONEY COULDN'T POSSIBLY COME FROM JOURNALISM.

PRO-AFGHAN PEOPLE ARE SUPPOSED TO BE ANTI-COMMUNIST, BUT HE ALSO SAID THAT HE LIKES THE COMMUNIST GUERRILLAS IN THE PHILIPPINES (WHERE HE ALSO HAS A HOUSE).

HE MIGHT ALSO BE A SOVIET SPY, WHO KNOWS... I BLAME MYSELF FOR BEING TOO NAÏVE TO FIGURE THESE THINGS OUT.

THE MONTH OF AUGUST IS DRAWING TO A CLOSE. I CONTINUE TAKING MY WANDERER'S PICTURES, HAPHAZARD PICTURES, MORE OR LESS AIMLESSLY—PESHAWAR IN AUGUST.

PATHAN

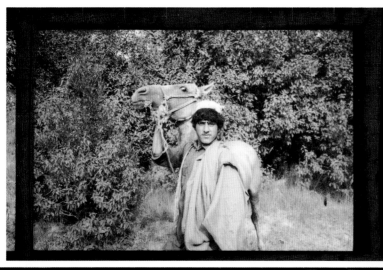

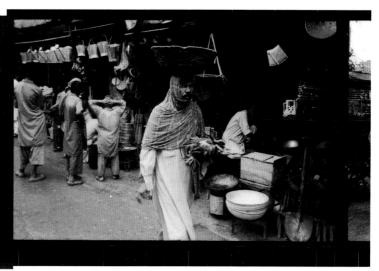

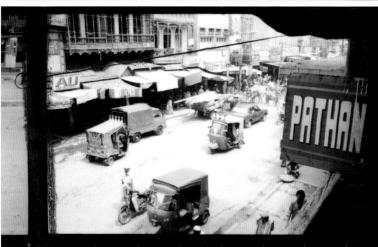

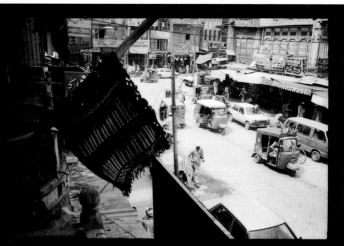

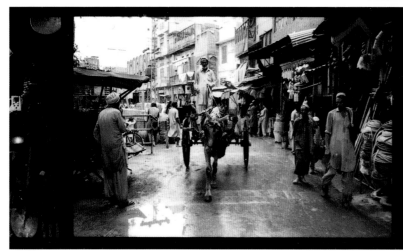

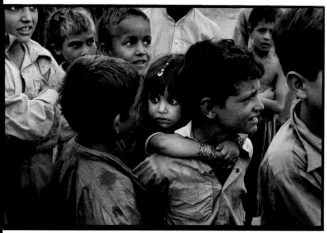

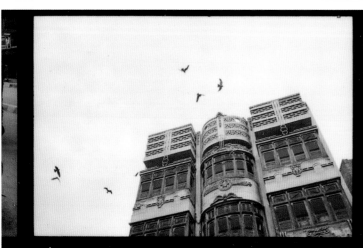

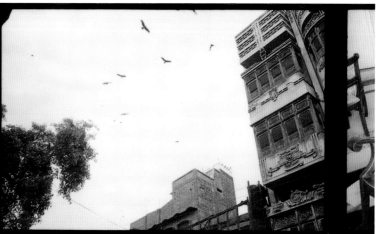

AND THEN IT'S TIME TO LEAVE.

FIRST, THE CARAVAN IS ASSEMBLED, WITH ABOUT A HUNDRED DONKEYS, SOME TWENTY HORSES, AND ROUGHLY A HUNDRED MEN, INCLUDING SOME FORTY ARMED FIGHTERS.

I'LL EXPLAIN THE SYSTEM OF CARAVANS:

THEY DELIVER WEAPONS IN AFGHANISTAN AND RETURN EMPTY TO PAKISTAN TO PICK UP MORE WEAPONS, CONTINUOUSLY, AS LONG AS THE TRACKS ARE USABLE.

OUR CARAVAN WILL BE AMONG THE FIRST MAJOR ONES TO LEAVE, IN AUGUST, AND ONE OF THE LAST TO RETURN, IN NOVEMBER, BEFORE THE WINTER—WHICH MOST OF THE CARAVANS WILL SPEND IN PESHAWAR, WHERE TEMPERATURES ARE MILDER THAN IN THE MOUNTAINS.

AS SOON AS THE SNOW MELTS AND THE MOUNTAIN PASSES CAN BE CROSSED, THE CARAVANS WILL SET OUT AGAIN.

BECAUSE THE ROADS ARE CONTROLLED BY THE RUSSIANS, THE JOURNEY IS ALL OFF-ROAD.

ALL THIS ORGANIZATION IS MANAGED BY PESHAWAR'S AFGHAN COMMUNITY, UNDER THE BENEVOLENT GAZE OF THE PAKISTANI AUTHORITIES.

PAKISTAN, AS THE REAR BASE OF THE RESISTANCE, TURNS A BLIND EYE TO THE CONSTANT TO-AND-FRO OF THE CARAVANS.

WESTERNERS, THOUGH, AREN'T SUPPOSED TO GO THROUGH—BUT THE NET ISN'T VERY TIGHT, SO, SHORT OF FLINGING YOURSELF INTO CUSTOMS AGENTS' ARMS, YOU CAN GET THROUGH WITHOUT TOO MUCH TROUBLE.

OBVIOUSLY, IF THEY CATCH YOU THEY'LL THROW YOU IN JAIL.

HAPPENED TO FRIENDS OF MINE: A WEEK IN JAIL.

NOT THE END OF THE WORLD, BUT STILL NOT VERY PLEASANT, AND, ABOVE ALL, A WASTE OF TIME AND MONEY (YOU HAVE TO GREASE PALMS TO GET OUT).

IDEALLY, MSF WOULD'VE WANTED TO SET UP ONLY UNARMED CARAVANS, BUT THE ONLY VIABLE SOLUTION, TO PROTECT YOURSELF FROM RACKETEERS AND KIDNAPPERS, AND ALSO FROM SOVIET ARMY HELICOPTERS, IS TO JOIN THE ARMS CARAVANS.

SO WE HAVE A PRETTY SUBSTANTIAL ESCORT: FORTY AK-47S AGAINST WOULD-BE THIEVES, AND TWO OR THREE SHOULDER-FIRED MISSILES AGAINST THE HELICOPTERS.

BUT THE BOTTOM LINE IS THAT WE HAVE TO CROSS THE BORDER IN SEPARATE GROUPS—THE AFGHANS UNOFFICIALLY AND US, THE MSF PEOPLE, ILLEGALLY.

WE'LL MEET UP ON THE OTHER SIDE, IN AFGHANISTAN, AT AN AGREED LOCATION.

I WATCH THE TRUCKS BEING LOADED. WE ARE HEADING TO CHITRAL, UP NORTH—IT'S PRONOUNCED "TCHATROL." FIRST COME THE EQUIPMENT AND PROVISIONS. WE BUILT UP A MASSIVE STOCK OF DRIED FRUIT IN THE PREVIOUS DAYS.

THEN COME THE DONKEYS, WHO ARE BRUTALLY SHOVED IN BY PUSHING THEM FROM THE BACK AND PULLING THEM BY THE EARS.

LAST COME THE HORSES, IN STAGGERED ROWS. THOSE ARE REAL STALLIONS, NOT GELDINGS, AND THEY EXPRESS THEIR DISAPPROVAL VIOLENTLY.

WE HAVE TO EXPECT THAT ONE OR TWO OF THEM WILL BE DEAD ON ARRIVAL IN CHITRAL, AND THE OTHERS WILL HAVE BEEN BITTEN OR BATTERED BY KICKS.

AND THE CARAVAN SETS OFF.

OVER A WEEK LATER IT'S OUR TURN TO LEAVE PESHAWAR FOR CHITRAL. BEFORE GOING, I STOLE A POCKET EDITION OF STEVENSON'S *TRAVELS WITH A DONKEY IN THE CEVENNES* FROM THE MSF HOUSE. CARRIED IT OFF IN MY BAG.

YOU'LL SEE, CHITRAL'S AMAZING. IT'S RIGHT AT THE FOOT OF THE MOUNTAINS.

ARE WE SLEEPING THERE TONIGHT?

NOT IN CHITRAL ITSELF. CLOSE BY, IN A VILLAGE CALLED GUERMSHESHMA, WHICH MEANS "HOT-WATER SPRINGS."

OH YEAH, WE FORGOT TO MENTION—THE MISSION IS CANCELED AND MSF IS SENDING US TO A SPA FOR THREE MONTHS.

IN GUERMSHESHMA WE ARE PUT UP IN A VERY NICE ABANDONED HOUSE WITH AN INDOOR POOL OF NATURAL SPRING WATER. THAT'S WHERE WE HAVE TO WAIT FOR OUR SMUGGLER, WHO'LL LET US KNOW WHEN IT'S TIME TO CROSS THE BORDER.

THE PLACE IS CAPTIVATING. OF COURSE WE ALL BATHE IN THE POOL. (BY THAT I MEAN ALL WESTERNERS. IT'S OUT OF THE QUESTION FOR MAHMAD AND THE FEW AFGHANS ESCORTING US TO SHARE A BATH WITH US, EVEN THOUGH WE STRICTLY SEPARATE MEN AND WOMEN).

THE WATER IS VERY HOT. BECAUSE THE WEATHER IS COOLER IN GUERMSHESHMA THAN IN PESHAWAR, THE SENSATION IS PLEASANT.

WE ALL BUY CHADRI, THOSE LONG ROBES WORN BY AFGHAN WOMEN THAT COMPLETELY CONCEAL THE FACE AND BODY. THEY WILL HELP US REACH THE BORDER WITHOUT ATTRACTING ATTENTION.

JULIETTE AND THE NURSES POSE FOR ME IN THEIR CHADRI.

I START READING THE STEVENSON BOOK. HE TOO IS BUSY WITH PREPARATIONS.

A NIGHT GOES BY. THEN A DAY. JULIETTE BRUSHES HER HAIR. JOHN TAKES NOTES. WE TALK, WE SLEEP IN THE HOUSE WITH GRAFFITI-FILLED WALLS.

A SECOND NIGHT FALLS. THAT'S WHAT COVERING A STORY IS LIKE: PLENTY OF WAITING.

ALL OF A SUDDEN, THE SMUGGLER IS HERE.

NOW.

I SHOVE MY CAMERAS INTO A MESSENGER BAG, SLING THE BAG ACROSS MY SHOULDER, AND SLIP THE *CHADRI* OVER IT.

WE FILE INTO AN OLD PICKUP TRUCK WITH A TARP.

I WATCH THE OTHERS THROUGH THE MESH OF THE *CHADRI*. THEY LOOK LIKE GHOSTS HEADED FOR A SKI VACATION.

THE PICKUP DRIVES THROUGH THE NIGHT. I SAID COVERING A STORY INVOLVES A LOT OF WAITING, BUT WHEN THINGS HAPPEN, THEY HAPPEN VERY FAST AND ONLY ONCE. YOU HAVE TO BE ALERT NOT TO MISS THE BOAT.

I TRY TO THINK ABOUT STEVENSON'S BOOK. I'M NOT SURE I REMEMBERED TO MARK THE PAGE I WAS ON BEFORE TOSSING IT INTO THE BAG.

SUDDENLY WE STOP. WE HEAR VOICES.

THE DRIVER TALKS, NEGOTIATES. SOMEONE LIFTS THE TARP.

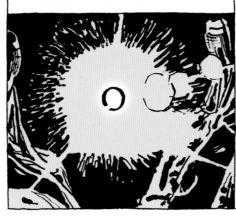

THE TARP FALLS BACK DOWN. WE MOVE ON.

AS WE NEAR THE SPOT, WE REMOVE OUR *CHADRI*.

WE ARE DROPPED OFF AT THE EDGE OF A FIELD. FROM THERE ON, WE'LL HAVE TO RUN IN THE DARK.

NOT AN EASY TASK. I HEAR SOMEONE FALL. I NARROWLY MISS FALLING, TOO.

NOTHING IN THIS FIELD OF ROCKS HINTS AT A CHANGE OF NATION. BUT THIS DARKNESS IS NO LONGER PAKISTAN.

IT'S AFGHANISTAN.

WITHOUT A PAUSE, WE LAUNCH INTO THE ASCENT OF OUR FIRST MOUNTAIN.

WE ARE ON THE BORDER MOUNTAIN, THE DEWANAH BABA—THE OLD MADMAN'S PASS. SIXTEEN THOUSAND FEET.

I'VE BEEN WARNED IT WOULDN'T BE A PICNIC. AS PROMISED, IT'S REALLY TOUGH.

ALL NIGHT LONG, WE'RE CHARGING UP AN ENDLESS MOUND OF ROCKS WE CAN'T SEE.

AS WE CLIMB THE TRAIL, WE CAN HEAR THE SOUNDS OF PEOPLE AND HORSES, WHO CATCH UP WITH US, ACCOMPANY US FOR A MOMENT, AND OUTPACE US. THERE'S A WHOLE MESS OF TRAFFIC, BUT IT'S IMPOSSIBLE TO MAKE OUT WHAT IS GOING ON.

WHILE MY MIND INSISTS I'M NOT GOING TO MAKE IT, MY FEET CONTINUE TO STEP FORWARD. IT'S GROWING COLDER. AROUND 5 AM, DAWN BEGINS TO BREAK.

I'M ASTONISHED TO REALIZE THAT WE ARE IN THE MIDDLE OF OUR CARAVAN. I RECOGNIZE NAJMUDIN, THE CHIEF OF THE YAFTAL GROUP.

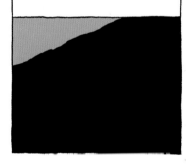

FOR ONE OF THE NURSES IN THE TEAM WHO REALLY ISN'T IN SHAPE, THE GOING IS EVEN HARDER. BUT, COMPARED TO ME, ALL OF THEM HAVE THE ADVANTAGE OF ALREADY HAVING MADE THIS TRIP.

TEETERING WITH FATIGUE AS WE REACH THE PASS, I'M WONDERING WHAT THE HELL I'M DOING THERE. AND AS USUAL, I ANSWER MY QUESTION BY TAKING PICTURES.

AT LAST, IT'S DOWNHILL.

MAN, WE'RE REALLY SPRINTING!

THAT'S 'CAUSE WE'RE FOLLOWING AFGHANS.

AN AFGHAN HAS A MOTOR HERE. GOES STRAIGHT AHEAD. NEVER STOPS.

THE DEWANAH BABA ISN'T BEING BOMBED BY THE RUSSIANS. THE WAR IS FARTHER AWAY. WE PASSED IT AT NIGHT TO CROSS THE BORDER UNDETECTED. ONCE WE REACH BADAKHSHAN, WE'LL HAVE TO GO THROUGH BOMBED PASSES AND ZIGZAG AROUND "ENEMY" POSTS. WE'LL HAVE TO MOVE AT NIGHT AND BE VERY DISCREET, FOR OBVIOUS REASONS.

WE HAVE OUR FIRST REST. WE HIT THE GROUND. I PHOTOGRAPH OUR POOR FEET.

WELL, WE WARNED YOU, RIGHT?

YES, BUT YOU HAVE TO DO IT TO BELIEVE IT.

YOU ALREADY LOST SOME WEIGHT LAST NIGHT AND YOU'RE GOING TO LOSE MORE. ALL YOUR SURFACE FAT WILL MELT AWAY. IN EIGHT DAYS YOU'LL BE LEAN AS A BROOMSTICK.

AND I'LL BE DEAD THEN?

NO, BECAUSE INTERESTING STUFF HAPPENS. YOUR BODY REACTS TO PROTECT YOU. IT DROPS SOME BALLAST, BUT IT ALSO GIVES YOU EXTRA SUPPORT.

FOR EXAMPLE, BECAUSE WE'RE CONSTANTLY AT HIGH ALTITUDES, IT'S GOING TO MANUFACTURE MORE RED BLOOD CELLS, SO YOU GET MORE OXYGEN.

SO, IN FACT, THE MORE TIME GOES BY THE MORE YOU'LL BE ABLE TO WALK AND THE LESS TIRED YOU'LL BE.

REALLY?

WHAT HE ISN'T TELLING YOU IS THAT ON AVERAGE RED BLOOD CELLS TAKE 120 DAYS TO GET PRODUCED. SO THE WHOLE OF YOUR THREE MONTHS IN AFGHANISTAN WILL BE GRUELING, BASICALLY.

OKAY, BUT ONCE HE'S BACK IN PARIS HE'LL BE ABLE TO CLIMB THE STAIRS TO MONTMARTRE INSTEAD OF TAKING THE FUNICULAR.

VERY FUNNY!

BUT SERIOUSLY, WITHOUT HAVING TO WAIT 120 DAYS, YOU CATCH THE WAY OF IT.

AND CAN'T WE USE A BIT OF DOPING, LIKE EAST GERMAN FEMALE SWIMMERS?

SURE. I HAVE SOME DRIED FRUIT IF YOU WANT.

AND I SHOULD HAVE A PIECE OF AFGHAN CHEESE.

THE REGION WE ARE ENTERING IS CALLED NURISTAN. IT'S AN UNUSUAL PLACE. IT HASN'T TAKEN PART IN THE WAR. AFGHANS FROM OTHER PROVINCES AREN'T CRAZY ABOUT THE NURISTANI, WHO HAVE ONLY BEEN MUSLIM FOR A CENTURY. THE PEOPLE FROM OUR CARAVAN HAVE NOTHING GOOD TO SAY ABOUT THEM.

THEY HAVE A REPUTATION OF BEING BANDITS, OF ATTACKING CARAVANS AND HOLDING TRAVELERS FOR RANSOM.

I CAN'T SAY IF IT'S BECAUSE OF WHAT WE'VE HEARD OR BECAUSE IT'S TRUE, BUT WHEN WE PASS SOME OF THEM, THEY DO LOOK UNSAVORY.

IN AN ARMED CARAVAN LIKE OURS WE'RE OKAY, BUT IF WE'D BEEN AMBLING THROUGH THE PLACE ON OUR OWN, WE'D HAVE BEEN WORRIED.

OUR FIRST REAL STOPOVER, AT THE END OF THE AFTERNOON, IS IN A VILLAGE WITH A FAMILIAR NAME: PESHAWARAK. THERE WE MEET UP WITH THE DONKEYS AND THEIR HANDLERS.

I NOTICE WITH CONCERN THAT MY HIGH-QUALITY WATERPROOF HIKING BOOTS ARE COMING UNSEWN BECAUSE OF ALL THEIR RUBBING AGAINST ROCKS.

JOHN:

HANG ON, I'VE GOT SOMETHING FOR SEWING UP THICK LEATHER.

JOHN TEACHES ME HOW TO USE THIS CONTRAPTION WITH A HANDLE, WHERE THE THREAD IS SLIPPED INSIDE THE NEEDLE. I SEW MY SHOES BACK UP.

WE SLIP INTO THE AFGHAN RHYTHM: BEDTIME AT 7 PM. I SLEEP OUTDOORS, ON A ROOF, TUCKED INTO MY SLEEPING BAG.

IN THE VERY EARLY DAWN, AROUND 4:30 AM, THE DIN OF PRAYERS, ANIMALS, ABLUTIONS IN THE RIVER WAKES ME UP.

JULIETTE CALMLY BRUSHES HER LONG HAIR BEFORE TYING IT UP AND HIDING IT UNDER HER HAT. A HORSE GROOM FROM OUR ESCORT, WHO HAS NEVER SEEN A WOMAN BRUSH HER HAIR, WATCHES HER SURREPTITIOUSLY.
HE'S A COUNTRY GUY. IN RURAL AFGHANISTAN, A MAN WITHOUT MEANS DOESN'T HAVE A WIFE.

IN THE VILLAGE THERE'S A TEAHOUSE, CALLED A *CHAYRANA*, WHERE WE HAVE A BREAKFAST THAT LIVES UP TO THE REPUTATION OF NURISTAN: NOT GOOD.

NAJMUDIN:

احمد جان، غزام دیر، وتشیر به بدخشان بسیار در غذا من غذای جانانای غذای غرد .

WHAT DID HE SAY?

HE SAID THAT WHEN YOU'RE IN HIS HOME REGION OF BADAKHSHAN YOU'LL EAT WELL.

WE SET OFF AND, MERCIFULLY, IT'S FLAT TERRAIN. PART OF THE WAY IS ON HORSEBACK. I DO REASONABLY WELL. I EVEN MANAGE TO TAKE PICTURES BETWEEN MY HORSE'S EARS.

THE NURISTANI HAVE A DISTINCTIVE FEATURE THAT YOU NOTICE RIGHT AWAY: THE WOMEN WORK AND THE MEN DON'T LIFT A FINGER. THE WOMEN ARE IN THE FIELDS WITH HUGE HUTCHES LOADED WITH DOZENS OF POUNDS OF STUFF, WHILE THE MEN SIT AROUND BY THE SIDE OF THE PATHS WATCHING THEM.

AT A SECOND STOP IN A VILLAGE JULIETTE GATHERS TOGETHER THE MAIN LEADERS AND TAKES STOCK: HOW MUCH GROUND WILL WE COVER BEFORE NIGHTFALL? HOW LONG WILL WE WALK? WHO WILL LEAD THE WAY? WHEN WILL WE REACH THE NEXT PASS?

WHAT JULIETTE IS PULLING OFF IS IMPRESSIVE, BECAUSE THE ODDS CERTAINLY AREN'T IN HER FAVOR.
FOR AN AFGHAN, A CHIEF IS A STRONG FIGURE. THERE'S NO WAY A WOMAN CAN BE A CHIEF.
AND YET THEY ALL UNDERSTAND THAT JULIETTE IS THE BOSS.

YOU KNOW, I'M USED TO IT NOW, AND THEY ARE, TOO.

YEAH, BUT HOW WAS IT AT FIRST?

AT FIRST, I SURPRISED ALL OF THEM WITH MY KNOWLEDGE OF THEIR LANGUAGE. AND I'D GENERALLY TAKE ADVANTAGE OF THAT SURPRISE TO ASSERT MYSELF.

PLUS, I KNOW THEIR TRADITIONS. YOU'LL NEVER SEE ME REACH OUT MY HAND TO THEM, STARE AT THEM, OR DO ANYTHING THAT COULD HUMILIATE THEM.

AND I TRY TO SPEAK CALMLY AND WITH AUTHORITY. THERE'S A CERTAIN TONE I USE, WHICH MEANS, "OKAY, I'M A WOMAN, BUT I'M THE LEADER." OVERALL, IT WORKS PRETTY WELL.

AMAZING!

THIS CORNER OF NURISTAN IS MAGNIFICENT, WITH ALPINE SCENERY AND PLENTY OF RIVERS AND TORRENTS.

WE SPEND THE FOLLOWING NIGHT IN THE OPEN. A FEW GUYS FROM THE ESCORT HAVE MINOR AILMENTS AND WANT CONSULTATIONS. ROBERT AND RÉGIS EXAMINE THEM.

SEEING THAT, ALL THE OTHERS SHOW UP AND GET IN LINE. THEY ASK FOR PILLS THAT THEY STORE CAREFULLY IN THE FOLDS OF THEIR TURBAN OR HAT. I PHOTOGRAPH ALL THAT WITH THE FLASH.
I DON'T LIKE THE FLASH.

THE NEXT DAY, AS WE'RE APPROACHING BARG-E-MATAL DAWLAT:

YOU'RE GOING TO MEET AIDER SHAH, THE HEAD HONCHO OF THE AREA.

HE'S A GOOD GUY?

HE'S A SMUGGLER OF PRETTY MUCH ANYTHING THAT CAN BE SMUGGLED, BEGINNING WITH DRUGS, BUT HE PROTECTS US. JULIETTE BUYS OUR SAFETY FROM HIM AND HE ANSWERS FOR OUR HEADS IN THE REGION. OTHERWISE, WE WOULDN'T GET THROUGH.

BECAUSE OF THE BANDITS?

WELL, IT'S COMPLICATED. NURISTAN IS INFILTRATED BY WAHHABI FUNDAMENTALISTS WHO DON'T LIKE TO SEE US AROUND HERE AND WOULDN'T MIND SLITTING OUR THROATS.

SO WE GIVE AIDER SHAH A GOOD BAKSHEESH, HE SLIPS US UNDER HIS LONG BEARD, AND WE CAN GO THROUGH.

YOU'LL SEE, HE HAS AN AMAZING BEARD.

AND WHO ARE THESE WAHHABI FUNDAMEN- TALISTS?

A BUNCH OF LOSERS.

AIDER SHAH WELCOMES US INTO HIS HOME, SERVING TEA AND BREAD. HE HANDS US A FEW RECOMMENDATION LETTERS THAT WILL FACILITATE OUR PROGRESS THROUGH NURISTAN. THE ATMOSPHERE BETWEEN THE AFGHANS IS CORDIAL, BUT NOT EFFUSIVE.

NAJMUDIN IS IN A CORNER OF THE ROOM, SEATED ON A CHAIR NEXT TO A TABLE. IT'S WORTH NOTING, BECAUSE TABLES AND CHAIRS ARE RARE IN THE VICINITY. HE'S FOLLOWING THE DISCUSSIONS, SEEMING DETACHED. ON HIS HEAD HE'S WEARING A CHAPKA TAKEN FROM THE RUSSIANS. NEXT TO HIM A VASE OF PLASTIC FLOWERS ADDS A POETIC TOUCH TO HIS AK-47.

HE'S HANDSOME, THIS NAJMUDIN. MORE THAN HANDSOME, IMPRESSIVE.

44

I GO OUT. KIDS ARE DOING HEADSTANDS. THERE'S NO WAR HERE.

A SHORT PRAYER BEFORE LEAVING. I DON'T DARE STAND IN FRONT OF THEM, SO I ALWAYS MAKE SURE I'M TO THE SIDE OR BEHIND THEM. CHILDREN AREN'T SO CONCERNED.

I HAVE A THEORY.

THAT'S NICE. WHAT IS IT?

IT HASN'T BEEN TESTED OUT STATISTICALLY TO BE A HUNDRED PERCENT RELIABLE YET, BUT IT'S GETTING THERE.

GO AHEAD, TELL ME.

THE THEORY IS THAT IN AFGHANISTAN NICE GUYS LOOK LIKE NICE GUYS AND BAD GUYS LOOK LIKE BAD GUYS.

HAHA! YOU'RE ONTO SOMETHING.

TAKE NAJMUDIN, FOR INSTANCE: HANDSOME GUY, A CLEAR LOOK IN HIS EYES, AN OPEN FACE AND A FORTHRIGHT ATTITUDE. YOU CAN ALWAYS COUNT ON HIM.

CONVERSELY, LOOK AT THAT MUJ' FROM YAFTAL THERE, HE REALLY HAS THE FACE OF A CROOK.

YEAH, THAT ONE'S AN ASSHOLE. I DON'T LIKE HIM.

BUT THE TWO AFGHANS WHO BEST ILLUSTRATE THE THEORY ARE YOU AND ME. BECAUSE WE'RE BOTH PHYSICALLY ATTRACTIVE AND MORALLY FLAWLESS.

TRUE. WELL, IN MY CASE, AT LEAST.

WE PASS A HORSE.
IT'S DYING.

THE ONLY HORSES
AFGHANS HAVE ANY
CONSIDERATION FOR ARE
BUZKASHI HORSES. THOSE
GET PAMPERED.
BUT CARAVAN HORSES GO
THROUGH MARTYRDOM.

THEY'RE OVERLOADED,
YANKED HERE AND THERE,
SUBJECTED TO FREEZING
COLD, AND WOUNDED BY
STONES.

THEY COLLAPSE FROM EXHAUSTION AND GET ABANDONED ON THE SIDE OF THE ROAD. THE TRAILS ARE LITTERED WITH DEAD HORSES AND DONKEYS.

CAN'T WE PUT HIM DOWN?

NO. SUPPOSEDLY, IT'S SO THEY HAVE A CHANCE OF MAKING IT.

BUT THAT ONE'S NEVER GOING TO MAKE IT! IT'S DYING!

I KNOW.

LOOK, THE MUJ' HAVE MARKSMANSHIP CONTESTS SHOOTING AT ROCKS, BUT THEY WON'T FINISH OFF HORSES. THAT'S THE WAY IT IS. YOU WON'T CHANGE IT.

AND I CAN'T STOP EVERY TIME I SEE ONE TO GIVE IT A SHOT OF MORPHINE. BUT IF YOU WANT, YOU CAN ASK TO BORROW AN AK-47 AND STICK A FEW BULLETS INTO HIM.

ME? BUT I'VE NEVER SHOT AT ANYTHING.

I POINT CAMERAS, NOT GUNS.

FARTHER ON, A NURISTANI SELLS US HIS CHEESE IN A NET. IT'S A COOKED HARD CHEESE.

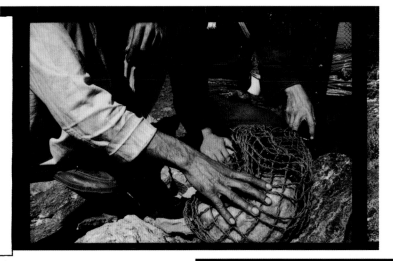

IT'S FUNNY TO SEE SIDE BY SIDE A GUY FROM NURISTAN AND ONE FROM BADAKHSHAN. THEY'RE REALLY VERY DIFFERENT.

WHO ARE THEY?

NORTHERNERS ESCAPING FROM THE FIGHTING.

THEY'RE GOING TO SEEK REFUGE IN PAKISTAN.

POOR THINGS! THEY STILL HAVE A WAY TO GO.

A NEW PASS RISES UP IN FRONT OF US: THE PAPROK. THERE'S A DONKEY THAT REFUSES TO MOVE. IT TAKES SEVEN GUYS TO CONVINCE HIM OTHERWISE. HE GETS PULLED, PUSHED, BEATEN, AND STUNG.

THE DONKEY HANDLERS YELL.

RRRAK TSSS TSSS
RRRAK TSSS TSSS

YEH! YEH!

IT'S ANOTHER STEEP CLIMB. ONCE AGAIN, THE SEAMS OF MY BOOTS ARE GETTING WORN DOWN BY THE ROCKS AND COMING UNDONE. I CURSE THEM.

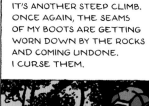

THERE ARE SOME VERY NARROW PASSAGES WITH STEEP DROPS. NOBODY FALLS.

49

YOU HAVE TO WALK WITH YOUR GAZE LOCKED IN FRONT OF YOUR FEET. AS SOON AS YOU LOOK UP, YOU STUMBLE. IT'S EXHAUSTING.

AS WE CLIMB, WE SEE THE VEGETATION CHANGE AND BECOME SPARSER.

MIDWAY UP THE MOUNTAIN, WE PAUSE. A LAMB PURCHASED IN BARG-E-MATAL WILL PROVIDE US WITH KEBABS.

THE MUJ' ASK ME FOR MY POCKET KNIFE AND GIVE IT BACK TO ME ALL DENTED. I LIKED THAT KNIFE.

WE SETTLE THERE FOR THE NIGHT. I SEW UP MY SHOES AGAIN. ONE OF US (I CAN'T SEE WHO FROM WHERE I AM) TAKES OUT SOME STUFF AND AROUSES THE CURIOSITY OF THE MUJ'.

YOU CAN'T OPEN A BAG WITHOUT HAVING TEN OR TWELVE MUJ' PEEKING INTO IT.

AT BEDTIME, LIKE EVERY NIGHT, THEY PROMISE US THAT THEY'LL BE QUIET THE NEXT MORNING: "WE WON'T WAKE YOU UP."

AT 4 AM ONE OF THEM BELLOWS OUT A CALL TO PRAYER.

FIFTEEN OF THEM STEP OVER ME TO GO JOIN HIM.

ANOTHER ONE, WHILE SADDLING UP HIS HORSE, DROPS HIS STRAP ON MY FACE AND PART OF HIS LOAD ON MY FEET.

THE PAPROK PASS IS AT THE HEART OF NURISTAN. THE RUSSIANS DON'T RISK COMING NEAR HERE. WE CAN CROSS IT BY DAY WITHOUT FEAR OF GETTING BOMBED.

I HAVEN'T YET TALKED ABOUT A TALL DUTCH DOCTOR NAMED RONALD, AKA NURUDIN, A REAL GIANT. I HAVEN'T MENTIONED HIM BECAUSE HE AND I DON'T TALK MUCH.

THE MUJ' FIND HIS SIZE INTRIGUING. THEY WANT TO KNOW IF HE'S AS STRONG AS HE IS TALL. EVERY EVENING, NAJMUDIN CHALLENGES HIM AT ARM WRESTLING.

EVERY EVENING RONALD LOSES, BECAUSE NO ONE IS STRONGER THAN NAJMUDIN.

BUT EVEN IF NAJMUDIN HAD BEEN A WIMP, RONALD WOULD HAVE BEEN WELL ADVISED TO LET HIM WIN. YOU DON'T WANT TO HUMILIATE A MUJ' ON THE SUBJECT OF PHYSICAL STRENGTH—A FEW WESTERNERS WHO DIDN'T KNOW THAT ENDED UP AT THE BOTTOM OF A CLIFF. I TAKE PICTURES OF BIG RONALD AS HE CROSSES THE PASS, WRAPPED IN HIS PATOO.

THE LIGHT IS VERY CLEAR THAT DAY, AND AN AMAZINGLY CRISP, CLEAN AIR FILLS YOUR LUNGS. EVEN EXHAUSTION AND THE BACKDROP OF WAR CAN'T CANCEL OUT A FEELING OF INTENSE JOY.

SEEING THE SUN, THOSE MOUNTAINS, AND JOHN WITH HIS BACKPACK WALKING WITH A HIKER'S STRIDE, YOU COULD SWEAR THIS IS PEACETIME.

WE PASS A RIVER. NAJMUDIN, AS REGULAR AS A METRONOME, OVERSEES THE DONKEYS' CROSSING.

RRRAK TSTSS

A BIT FARTHER, THE MUJ' LINE UP FOR THEIR PAY.

JULIETTE HANDLES IT LIKE A TROOP REVIEW. THE AFGHAN CURRENCY, AFGHANIS, CHANGES HANDS.

WE THEN HEAD TOWARD A SMALL TOWN CALLED PORUNS.

DID YOU SEE THAT OLD-TIMER WE JUST PASSED, WITH THE KID ON HIS BACK?

YES. I TOOK A PICTURE OF HIM.

TYPICAL OF COUNTRIES AT WAR.

THE GENERATION OF FATHERS GOES TO FIGHT AND ONLY GRANDFATHERS AND MOTHERS REMAIN TO TAKE CARE OF THE YOUNG ONES. AND SINCE THE WOMEN RARELY LEAVE THEIR HOME OR VILLAGE, IT'S THE OLD MEN WHO WALK THEM AROUND AND TRAVEL WITH THEM.

BY THE WAY, DO YOU KNOW WHAT THEY'RE CALLED, THOSE OLD MEN?

NO.

THE BABAS, MEANING THE WHITE BEARDS.

AH, YES, I DID KNOW! AS IN "DEWANAH BABA."

IT'S WEIRD, BUT IF I'M NOT MISTAKEN THAT SAME WORD, "BABA," THAT THE AFGHANS USE FOR OLD MEN IS THE ONE RUSSIANS USE FOR OLD LADIES.

MUST BE WHAT CAUSED THE CONFLICT.

AS SOON AS WE COME INTO PORUNS, WE'RE WELCOMED BY THE LOCALS. AN OLD LADY IS SICK, THEY ASK US TO OPERATE ON HER. WE CLIMB UP ON A TERRACE.

THEY LAY THE OLD LADY DOWN. THE DIAGNOSIS DOESN'T TAKE LONG: HER LEFT FOOT IS DEFORMED BY A CANCEROUS TUMOR.

THE MSF TEAM TURN HER COT INTO AN OPERATING TABLE. RÉGIS ANESTHETIZES HER. THEN, AS HER CHILDREN LOOK ON, SHE IS SLOWLY AND CAREFULLY OPERATED ON.

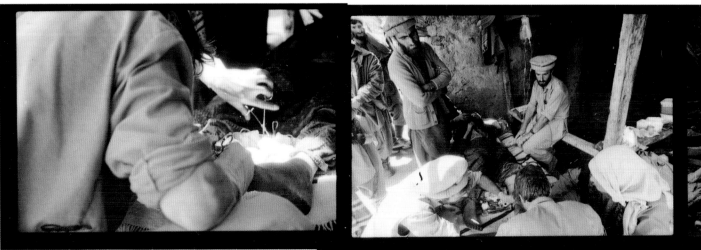

UP TO NOW, I'VE ONLY OBSERVED CONSULTATIONS. IT'S THE FIRST SURGERY ON THE TRIP. I'M STRUCK BY THE SERIOUSNESS AND CONCENTRATION OF EACH OF THE PARTICIPANTS. GUYS LIKE RÉGIS AND ROBERT, WHO THE REST OF THE TIME ARE A HILARIOUS STAND-UP COMEDY DUET, TAKE ON A LARGER-THAN-LIFE STATURE. I'M DEEPLY IMPRESSED.

THEY KEEP THE OLD LADY UNDER OBSERVATION FOR A FEW HOURS. HER FAMILY IS GIVEN MEDICATION AND INSTRUCTIONS FOR HER TREATMENT.

SYLVIE, DOES THE OLD LADY HAVE A CHANCE OF MAKING IT?

NO, NONE AT ALL.

YOU KNOW, THERE'S A CYNICAL SAYING THAT SURGEONS' PATIENTS DIE CURED. OBVIOUSLY, NOBODY'S INTERESTED IN DYING CURED. BUT DYING TREATED IS SOMETHING ELSE.

SOMETIMES PEOPLE DIE IN OUR HANDS, DURING THE OPERATION, AND THERE'S NOTHING WE CAN DO. BUT THE FAMILY STILL THANKS US.

THEY THANK US BY SAYING: "HE WAS SICK, OR HE WAS WOUNDED, AND YOU TREATED HIM, YOU PREPARED HIM TO MEET ALLAH. THANK YOU."

FOR US, WHO COULDN'T SAVE HIM, THAT'S HARDLY A CONSOLATION. BUT TO THEM IT'S VERY IMPORTANT THAT HE DIED TREATED.

AND YOU KNOW, WHEN YOU GIVE A DEAD CHILD BACK TO ITS MOTHER— THAT'S HAPPENED TO ME—AND, IN RETURN, SHE SLIPS A HANDKERCHIEF WITH A FEW WALNUTS INTO YOUR HAND...

...AND SHE SAYS, "THANK YOU, THANKS TO YOU HE IS READY TO MEET ALLAH"...

MUST BE HEARTBREAKING.

SURE IS.

I'VE OFTEN HAD PEOPLE WE'D TREATED SAY TO ME, WITH A VERY SAD LOOK: "IT'S REALLY TOO BAD YOU'RE NOT MUSLIM! WE'LL BE IN DIFFERENT HEAVENS."

AS WE LEAVE PORUNS, THE BABA WE SAW EARLIER HAS BECOME MUCH YOUNGER. HE'S NOW 12 OR 13 YEARS OLD, BUT IS STILL CARRYING THE SAME BABY ON HIS BACK.

WE REACH ANOTHER PASS, THE SIM. UNDER AN OLD ROCK WITH A GAPING MOUTH, WE TAKE A BREAK.

AND YOU, AHMADJAN, DON'T YOU HAVE BLISTERS?

NO. IT'S BAD ENOUGH THAT MY BOOTS KEEP COMING UNSEWN.

WELL, I'LL TRADE YOU MY BLISTERS FOR YOUR SHOES.

THAT REMINDS ME OF SOMETHING FROM MILITARY SERVICE.

IT WAS IN THE... WHAT WAS IT, AGAIN? THAT LITTLE BOOKLET FOR SOLDIERS... THAT THEY GAVE YOU...

THE MANUAL.

AH, YES, THE SOLDIER'S MANUAL.

I REMEMBER THAT IN THE SOLDIER'S MANUAL, THERE WAS A QUESTION: "WHAT ARE AN INFANTRYMAN'S FEET?"

AND THE ANSWER WAS...

"THEY ARE AN OBJECT OF CONSTANT CARE."

HAHAHA!

HOW POETIC!

WE GIVE OURSELVES A TREAT. THE STANDARD RATION OF TEA IS REPLACED BY A GULP OF INSTANT SOUP WITH CROUTONS.

A BIT HIGHER UP, IN A VILLAGE IN RUINS, WE PASS ANOTHER BABA. HE'S WEARING GOGGLES FROM A RUSSIAN HELICOPTER PILOT. I TAKE HIS PORTRAIT.

DOESN'T THE BABA REMIND YOU OF SOMEONE?

YES, BUT I CAN'T PUT MY FINGER ON IT.

POLNAREFF.

YEAH, MICHEL POLNAREFF, THAT POP SINGER WITH THE WILD GLASSES!

"C'EST UNE POUPÉE..."

"QUI FAIT NON, NON, NOOOON, NON..."

AT FIRST, I'D DUTIFULLY FILL MY CANTEEN AT EACH BREAK AND I'D LUG IT AROUND FULL. BUT THERE'S SO MUCH RUNNING WATER EVERYWHERE THAT I GIVE IT UP. I OFTEN DRINK DIRECTLY FROM THE RIVER. THE WATER IS VERY PURE.

SINCE I'M TALKING ABOUT DRINKING, LET'S TALK ABOUT PEEING. IN AFGHANISTAN, IT'S OUT OF THE QUESTION TO PEE STANDING UP—ONLY ANIMALS PEE STANDING UP AND SPLATTER THEIR PAWS. WE AREN'T ANIMALS, SO WE SQUAT. SOMEONE WHO PEES STANDING UP WOULD AT BEST FACE DERISION, AND AT WORST WOULD BE SHUNNED AS WORTHLESS. IN JEANS, OF COURSE, IT WOULD BE IMPOSSIBLE TO SQUAT, BUT IN AFGHAN GARB, WITH THE VERY WIDE PANTS, YOU MANAGE. YOU SQUAT, THEN YOU LIFT UP AND PUSH ASIDE THE PANTS SO YOU DON'T PEE ALL OVER YOURSELF.

POOP INVOLVES ANOTHER TABOO: UNDER NO CIRCUMSTANCES CAN YOU WIPE YOUR BEHIND WITH YOUR RIGHT HAND. THE RIGHT HAND IS RESERVED FOR FOOD. I HAVE TO ADMIT THAT I HAVE SOME TROUBLE USING MY LEFT HAND FOR THIS, SO I CHEAT. THERE'S LITTLE OR NO TOILET PAPER, AND IF YOU USE ANY YOU HAVE TO BURY IT. IN WARTIME, THE SOVIETS WHO FIND TOILET PAPER WILL KNOW THAT THERE ARE WESTERNERS IN THE AREA. THERE IS ONE SURPRISING TECHNIQUE USING ROUND ROCKS THAT WORKS PRETTY WELL. AND THE IDEAL SOLUTION STILL IS TO USE WATER.

ONCE AGAIN, I SEE THE SUN RISE. TO MAKE UP FOR THE TIME SPENT TREATING PATIENTS IN PORUNS WE WALKED A GOOD PART OF THE NIGHT. WE ARE SO EXHAUSTED WHEN WE STOP FOR A BREAK THAT EVEN THE HORSES HAVE TO LIE DOWN.

THE FOLLOWING NIGHT WE SLEEP IN THE TOWN SQUARE OF KANTIWA.

I MUST SAY THAT ONE OF THE THINGS THAT MAKES MY TREKKING EVEN MORE EXHAUSTING IS THAT I CONSTANTLY CARRY MY MESSENGER BAG ACROSS MY SHOULDERS, WITH MY FOUR CAMERAS AND SOME OF MY FILM. BUT I FEEL SAFER THAT WAY. I'M TOO FRIGHTENED THAT, IF I LEAVE MY EQUIPMENT ON A DONKEY, IT MIGHT DISAPPEAR WITH HIM DOWN A RAVINE. WHEN I SLEEP, I ALWAYS KEEP MY BAG NEAR MY HEAD.

IN THE MORNING, STILL HAZY IN MY SLEEPING BAG, I PEEK OUT AT THE USUAL COMMOTION AROUND ME. A FEW TALL MUJ' ARE TALKING THREE FEET AWAY FROM ME.

I KNOW I SHOULD TAKE A PICTURE, BUT I FEEL SO EMPTY.

I FUMBLE IN MY BAG AND WEAKLY PULL OUT THE FIRST CAMERA I FEEL.

BARELY FRAME THE PICTURE.

THERE. SO BE IT.

CLICK

HAVING WOKEN UP, I
STROLL AROUND AS THE
CARAVAN SHAKES OFF
ITS SLUMBER. I'M GLAD
TO CATCH A TYPICAL
LOCAL GESTURE THAT
I LIKE. IT'S SILENT AND
IT MEANS, "WHAT DO
YOU WANT?" IT COULD
BE VAGUELY ITALIAN.
I HAVE AN ITALIAN
GRANDMOTHER.

MY MISGIVINGS ABOUT
LOADING MY BAG ONTO A
DONKEY ARE BORNE OUT
BY SEVERAL FALLS IN THE
COURSE OF THE DAY. ONE
OF THEM IS PREVENTED
AT THE LAST SECOND BY
THE DONKEY HANDLERS.
IF THAT DONKEY HAD
FALLEN, THAT'S WHERE HE
WOULD'VE LANDED, DOWN
BELOW.

AT THE CAMP THAT EVENING, JULIETTE SHOWS ME THE GROUND WE'VE COVERED, ON A MAP.

YOU SEE, WE CROSSED THE BORDER HERE.

THEN THE DEWANAH BABA.

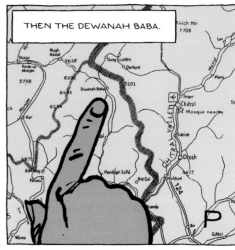

THEN WE CAME DOWN THAT WAY, HOP HOP HOP, BARG-E-MATAL, PORUNS, KANTIWA.

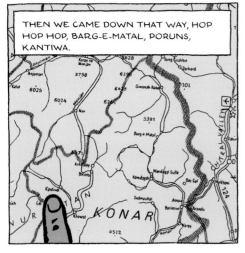

NOW WE'RE ABOUT HERE. TOMORROW WE'RE CROSSING THE POJOL. IN OTHER WORDS, WE'RE HEADING NORTH.

WHAT'S THE POJOL? ANOTHER PASS?

YES. AND YOU'LL SEE, IT'S A REAL ONE.

LATER THAT DAY.

YOU'VE GOT FIVE OR SIX PARAMETERS THAT YOU HAVE TO LEARN TO JUGGLE: DIAPHRAGM APERTURE, EXPOSURE TIME, FOCAL LENGTH, FILM SENSITIVITY... PLUS THE HANDLING OF THE CAMERA ITSELF, OF COURSE.

I THINK IT'S IMPORTANT TO LEARN TO BE A GOOD TECHNICIAN, TO PUT IN THE TIME IT TAKES TO MASTER THE TECHNIQUE. BUT THAT DOESN'T TAKE FOREVER, YOU KNOW? YOU CAN LEARN IT REALLY FAST. BASICALLY, IF YOU DECIDE TO WASTE A DOZEN ROLLS OF FILM OVER THE COURSE OF, SAY, THREE DAYS—WELL, NO, A BIT MORE, THREE WEEKS—YOU CAN KNOW THAT STUFF LIKE THE BACK OF YOUR HAND.

AND YOU DEVELOP YOUR PICTURES YOURSELF?

YES, I LEARNED TO DO THAT. IT'S REALLY PART OF THE JOB. THOUGH YOU DO FIND SOME EXCELLENT PHOTOGRAPHERS WHO NEVER PRINT THEIR OWN PICTURES. THERE ARE EVEN SOME VERY GOOD ONES WHO DON'T KNOW THE FIRST THING ABOUT TECHNIQUE.

THERE'S NO FORMULA FOR SUCCESS AS A PHOTOGRAPHER. THE MAIN THING, TO PRODUCE TECHNICALLY GOOD PICTURES, IS TO BE ABLE TO HANDLE THE CAMERA WITHOUT THINKING ABOUT IT.

YOU KNOW, FOR EXAMPLE, IF YOU HAVE AN APERTURE OF 11 WITH A SHUTTER SPEED OF 1/60TH, AND YOU DECIDE TO CLOSE THE DIAPHRAGM DOWN TO 5-6 FOR A SHALLOWER DEPTH OF FIELD, YOU'LL AUTOMATICALLY HAVE TO INCREASE SHUTTER SPEED BY TWO STOPS.

HM.

THAT BECOMES SECOND NATURE.

BUT OF COURSE BEING ABLE TO PRODUCE A TECHNICALLY GOOD PICTURE DOESN'T MEAN YOU'LL MAKE GREAT PICTURES. FOR GREAT PICTURES YOU REALLY HAVE TO TEAR YOUR EYES OUT.

I WANT TO POUR ALL MY ENERGY INTO IMPROVING MY PHOTOGRAPHY. I WANT TO TAKE GOOD PICTURES.

AND WHAT IS A GOOD PICTURE?

I DON'T KNOW.

YOU HAVE TO SEARCH FOR IT, SEARCH ALL THE TIME, ALL THE TIME.

AND NOT NECESSARILY IN WAR ZONES OR SPECTACULAR PLACES.

I HOPE TO BRING BACK GOOD PICTURES FROM AFGHANISTAN, BUT LATER ON, WHEN I GO VISIT MY MOM IN BLONVILLE, OR YOU IN BORDEAUX WHEN YOU'LL BE MAKING YOUR WINE, I WANT TO TAKE SOME EQUALLY GOOD ONES. EVEN BETTER, IF I CAN.

IMPROVING YOUR PICTURES NECESSARILY IMPLIES IMPROVING YOUR RELATIONS WITH PEOPLE.

WHAT YOU'RE SAYING, IN FACT, IS THAT TO TAKE GOOD PHOTOS YOU HAVE TO AGE WELL.

EXACTLY.

WELL, SORRY, BUDDY, BUT THE PROCESS YOU'RE DESCRIBING— THAT'S MATURING, AND IT'S WHAT WINEMAKING'S ALL ABOUT.

SO I SAY, LET'S MAKE WINE, BECAUSE WINE IS EVERYTHING YOU JUST TALKED ABOUT, BUT ON TOP OF IT YOU GET TO DRINK IT AND IT TASTES GOOD.

HAHA!

EVERY TIME I SEE HER BRUSHING HER TEETH I GET PANGS OF CONSCIENCE, BECAUSE I HAVEN'T BRUSHED MINE SINCE PESHAWAR. I'M JUST RINSING MY MOUTH IN THE STREAMS. BUT WITH THE AMOUNT OF DRIED FRUIT WE'RE EATING I KNOW THAT ISN'T SMART.

THE POJOL PASS IS INDEED A TOUGH CLIMB. FORTUNATELY WE CAN CROSS THAT ONE BY DAY, BECAUSE WE'RE STILL IN NURISTAN. THE AIR IS GETTING THIN. YOU FEEL AS IF YOUR TEMPLES ARE BEING SQUEEZED. THE ANIMALS STRUGGLE WITH THEIR LOADS.

THAT HORSE IS MAKING LONG STOPS. HE CAN'T TAKE ANY MORE; HIS EYES SEEM TO BE SAYING, "ENOUGH."

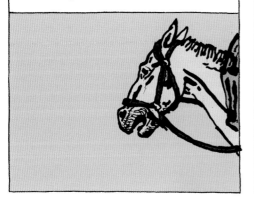

'THE ASSHOLE MUJ', THE ONE RÉGIS AND I DON'T LIKE, COMES UP TO HIM, PLACES HIS AK-47 ON TOP OF THE HORSE'S HEAD AND FIRES A VOLLEY OF SHOTS FORWARD BETWEEN HIS EARS.

THE POOR HORSE WHINNIES AND RUNS DESPERATELY FOR FIFTY YARDS BEFORE STOPPING AGAIN, PANTING. AND THE MUJ' STARTS AGAIN, AND KEEPS AT IT ALL THE WAY TO THE TOP.

HE ISN'T THE ONLY ONE DOING THAT. I'VE BEEN TOLD ABOUT THAT PRACTICE. IT'S SICKENING TO SEE. ON THE OTHER HAND, MY WESTERNER'S HOWLS OF INDIGNATION PROBABLY DON'T MEAN MUCH IN A COUNTRY WHERE KIDS ARE GETTING BLOWN UP BY LANDMINES AND PICKING UP BOOBY-TRAPPED DOLLS.

THE SUMMIT. I KNOW I'M REPEATING MYSELF, BUT THIS NAJMUDIN GUY IS INCREDIBLE. WHILE WE DO ONE CLIMB, HE DOES TEN. HE GOES TO RECONNOITER THE PASS, THEN COMES BACK DOWN TO CHECK UP ON THE CARAVAN'S PROGRESS, THEN GOES BACK UP, THEN DOWN AGAIN, NONSTOP. HE'S EVERYWHERE AT ONCE.

A BIT LOWER DOWN, WE GET SOME REST BY A SMALL LAKE. NOT FOR LONG, BECAUSE IT'S COLD AND WE HAVE TO BE DOWN BEFORE NIGHTFALL. MY MOOD FEELS A BIT SOMBER. I'M SITTING NEXT TO MAHMAD.

HOW MANY PRAYERS ARE YOU DOING A DAY AT THE MOMENT, MAHMAD?

RIGHT NOW, I'M ONLY DOING TWO, BECAUSE I'M REALLY TIRED. I DO ONE IN THE MORNING AND ONE AT NIGHT. THAT'S THE MINIMUM, BUT IT'S OKAY, WE'RE ALLOWED.

AND IN NORMAL TIMES?

WELL, NORMALLY YOU'RE MEANT TO SAY FIVE PRAYERS A DAY, BUT IF YOU'RE SICK OR TRAVELING YOU'RE NOT REQUIRED TO SAY ALL FIVE, THERE ARE EXCEPTIONS. BUT IF I CAN, I TRY TO DO THREE.

IN ANY CASE, THE TRAVELER'S PRAYER IS ALWAYS SHORTER, BECAUSE WE'RE ALWAYS RUNNING AROUND. BUT, AS YOU SAW, WE FOLLOW THE RITUAL: WE TAKE OFF OUR SHOES; IF WE DON'T HAVE A PRAYER RUG, WE USE A HANDKERCHIEF OR THE SCARF ON OUR HEADS; IF WE CAN'T DO COMPLETE ABLUTIONS, WE AT LEAST WASH OUR HANDS AND FACE. WE ADAPT TO CIRCUMSTANCES, YOU SEE.

AND YOU REALLY TURN TOWARD MECCA?

OH YES, ALWAYS. IN A MOSQUE, THAT'S EASY, BECAUSE THEY'RE ALWAYS FACING THE RIGHT WAY. IN THE MIDDLE OF NOWHERE IT'S HARDER TO FIND YOUR BEARINGS, SO SOMETIMES PEOPLE DISAGREE ABOUT WHICH WAY THEY SHOULD TURN.

DO YOU KNOW WHAT MUSLIMS' HEAVEN IS LIKE?

I CAN DESCRIBE IT TO YOU, IF YOU WANT.

NO, NOT REALLY.

LATER ON.

MAHMAD TOLD ME ABOUT PARADISE.

OH YEAH, ME TOO, SEVERAL TIMES. IT'S PRETTY PRECISE, ISN'T IT?

WHAT'S FUNNY, WITH MAHMAD, IS THAT HE'S VERY DEVOUT, BUT SINCE HE'S LIVED IN FRANCE HE ALSO HAS AN OUTSIDE PERSPECTIVE. WITH HIM, YOU CAN GET AWAY WITH JOKES THAT PUSH THE ENVELOPE A BIT, THEY MAKE HIM LAUGH. IF HE WERE A PRIEST, HE'D BE THE KIND WHO LAUGHS HEARTILY, THEN QUICKLY DOES THE SIGN OF THE CROSS IN A CORNER.

YES, THAT'S IT.

MAHMAD IS REALLY LIKED AT MSF. WHAT HE'S DOING IS BRAVE, BECAUSE HE'S NO WARRIOR. HE WOULD NEVER HURT ANYONE, BUT HE STILL WANTS TO DO HIS JIHAD. SO HE FOUND THIS THING OF BEING AN INTERPRETER FOR US.

HE'S TERRIFIED OF HELICOPTERS. I DON'T KNOW IF HE TOLD YOU...

YES. FINGER-NAILS.

YES. "TUCK IN YOUR FINGERNAILS." I SAID TO HIM, "MAHMAD, IF A HELICOPTER SHOWS UP THEY WON'T SEE MY NAILS BECAUSE I'LL HAVE BITTEN THEM OFF IN NO TIME."

AND YOU KNOW WHAT—

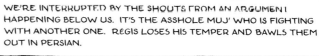

WE'RE INTERRUPTED BY THE SHOUTS FROM AN ARGUMENT HAPPENING BELOW US. IT'S THE ASSHOLE MUJ' WHO IS FIGHTING WITH ANOTHER ONE. RÉGIS LOSES HIS TEMPER AND BAWLS THEM OUT IN PERSIAN.

BRATATAT

WE FREEZE. THE MUJ' HAS JUST FIRED A BURST FROM HIS AK-47 BETWEEN THE TWO OF US. THE THREE BULLETS HAVE JUST ZINGED PAST US RIGHT THERE, ZZZZZ.

RÉGIS SEES RED. HE'S A HOT-BLOODED SOUTHERNER, RÉGIS IS, AND A RUGBY PLAYER. HE STARTS RUNNING DOWN TOWARD THE MUJ'.

I THINK TO MYSELF, "HE'S GOING TO GET HIMSELF KILLED, I HAVE TO STOP HIM," SO I FOLLOW HIM DOWN.

IN THE MOUNTAINS IT'S NOT A GREAT IDEA TO TRY TO RUN, BACK UP YOUR BUDDY IN A FIGHT, AND TAKE PICTURES AT THE SAME TIME.

DOING THAT PRETTY MUCH SETS YOU UP FOR A FALL.

FORTUNATELY, WHEN I LOOK UP I SEE THAT A FEW OTHER MUJ' HAVE ARRIVED ON THE SCENE AND HAVE TAKEN THE RIFLE AWAY FROM THE ASSHOLE MUJ'.

NAJMUDIN IS CALLED. HE LISTENS TO EVERYONE INVOLVED AND RULES THAT THE ASSHOLE MUJ' WILL GO UNARMED FOR THE REST OF THE TRIP.

MAKES YOU FEEL BETTER, NO?

YES, BUT WE'D BETTER WATCH OUT. IT'S A BIG HUMILIATION FOR THAT GUY TO HAVE HIS RIFLE TAKEN AWAY. HE COULD VERY WELL SEEK REVENGE.

WE HAVE NOW CROSSED THE POJOL PASS AND ARE HEADED TOWARD WHAT MY BUDDIES CALL *LES MONTAGNES RUSSES*—WHICH IN FRENCH MEANS BOTH "THE ROLLERCOASTER" AND "THE RUSSIAN MOUNTAINS"—BECAUSE THE RUSSIANS ARE FLYING OVER AND BOMBING THEM. FOR THE MOMENT, NO RUSSIANS IN SIGHT, JUST A SCARECROW IN A WHEAT FIELD.

IN FRONT OF ME WALKS A CARRIER OF ANTITANK SHELLS. A MAN CAN CARRY A BUNDLE OF A HALF-DOZEN OF THOSE. THE HEAVIER MISSILES ARE CARRIED BY DONKEYS, BUT SOMETIMES ONE OF THE MUJ' WILL CARRY ONE TOO, IN A BAG AND SECURED BY ROPES.

SUCH IS THE LIFE OF A ROCKET-MAN, OR SHELL-MAN: HE'LL GO PICK UP HIS BURDEN IN PAKISTAN, TRUNDLE WITH IT FOR THREE WEEKS UP AND DOWN THE MOUNTAINS, DELIVER IT, AND HEAD OFF TO GET ANOTHER ONE.

I'VE LEARNED TO TAKE CARE OF MY HORSE. WHEN WE STOP, I COVER HIM SO HE WON'T GET COLD. THEN I WAIT A LITTLE BEFORE MAKING HIM DRINK AND EAT. IT'S BETTER NOT TO FEED A HORSE IMMEDIATELY AFTER EXERTION.

THEN HE GETS HIS RATION OF *KAH* AND *JAO*—HAY AND OATS.

HE'S EVEN ENTITLED TO A CUDDLE.

DON'T FONDLE HIM TOO MUCH, HE'S NOT USED TO IT.

IT MIGHT KILL HIM.

WHILE THE HORSES MUNCH ON THEIR FODDER, THE MEN CHEW THEIR *NASWAR*. THEY'LL TAKE OUT A ROUND BOX THAT LOOKS LIKE A PILLBOX, WITH A LID THAT DOUBLES UP AS A POCKET MIRROR.

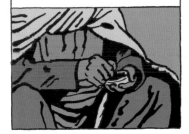

IN THE BOX IS THE *NASWAR*, A POWDERED MIXTURE OF TOBACCO, LIMESTONE, AND OTHER STUFF. THEY'LL POUR THE POWDER INTO THE PALM OF THEIR HAND, CHOP IT WITH THE LID, AND FLING IT INTO THEIR MOUTH LIKE A HANDFUL OF PISTACHIOS.

THEY'LL KEEP IT STORED AN AVERAGE OF TEN MINUTES, EITHER UNDER THE TONGUE OR BETWEEN LIP AND GUM, THEN SPIT IT OUT.

WHEN CHEWING TOBACCO IN A HOUSE, THE THING TO DO IS LIFT THE CARPET, SPIT ALONG THE WALL, AND PUT THE CARPET BACK ON TOP. A BIT OF ADVICE: BEST NOT TO SLEEP IN THAT CORNER.

NASWAR IS EXTREMELY CORROSIVE. OVER TIME, IT EATS AWAY AT GUMS AND MANY MEN'S MOUTHS ARE DEVASTATED BY IT.

AN INCIDENT HAPPENS: ON A MAKESHIFT BRIDGE, BECAUSE OF A STONE THAT HAS MOVED, A DONKEY GETS A HOOF STUCK IN A HOLE. NAJMUDIN COMES TO THE RESCUE.

HE POSITIONS HIMSELF BEHIND THE DONKEY, GRABS IT BY THE TAIL, LIFTS IT UP—INCLUDING ITS LOAD—AND PUTS IT BACK ON ITS FEET. A SLAP ON THE RUMP AND OFF IT GOES, ALL BACK IN ORDER.

I'M FAR AWAY AND THERE ISN'T ENOUGH LIGHT. I HOPE THAT THE ACTION WILL BE VISIBLE ON THE PHOTOS, OTHERWISE NOBODY WILL BELIEVE ME. NAJMUDIN PUTS THE ROCK BACK IN PLACE AND THE CARAVAN HEADS OFF AGAIN.

THE DONKEYS DON'T LIKE BRIDGES, BUT I DON'T FIND THEM TOO FRIGHTENING. THEY AREN'T ABOVE PRECIPITOUS DROPS. SURE, IT'S BETTER NOT TO FALL, BUT THEY'RE MANAGEABLE.

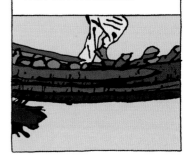

A FEW MUJ' ARE HOLDING A SHOOTING CONTEST, JUST FOR FUN. A BIRD FLIES BY, NO BIGGER THAN A CHICKADEE. ONE OF THE MUJ' TAKES AIM.

BLAM. A SINGLE SHOT.

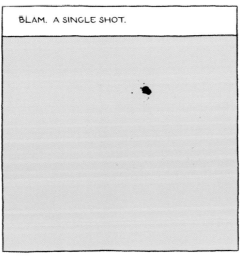

HE BRINGS THE BIRD RIGHT UP TO MY FACE TO SHOW ME THAT THE BULLET HAS ONLY TORN OFF ITS HEAD. THE LITTLE EDIBLE BODY IS INTACT.

ONCE AGAIN, WE PASS PEOPLE FLEEING. YOU COULD CALL THEM REFUGEES, EVEN THOUGH THEY'RE FAR FROM THEIR PLACE OF REFUGE. THIS GROUP IS FROM KESHEM, IN WESTERN BADAKHSHAN. THE JOURNEY THEY STILL HAVE TO GO THROUGH IS THE ONE WE'VE JUST COVERED.

THE CARAVAN IS APPROACHING THE KALOTAC PASS.

THE KALOTAC PASS IS LIKE THE STATION OF LA FOURCHE IN THE PARIS METRO—DO YOU KNOW IT?

YES, OF COURSE, IT'S UP NORTH.

HERE, ON THE LEFT YOU HAVE THE PANJSHIR VALLEY, HOME OF COMMANDER MASSOUD. ON THE RIGHT IS BADAKHSHAN, WHERE WE'RE GOING.

SO YOU CAN SAY THAT WE'RE TAKING THE SAINT-DENIS SIDE OF THE FORK, WHILE MASSOUD IS OVER THERE ON THE ASNIÈRES SIDE.

I SEE.

WE SETTLE DOWN FOR MOST OF THE AFTERNOON. WE HAVE TO GATHER OUR STRENGTH AND BE VERY CLEAR ABOUT OUR ITINERARY. THERE ARE LONG DISCUSSIONS.

I TAKE ADVANTAGE OF THE BREAK TO SHOOT PORTRAITS OF ABDUL JABAR AND HIS LIEUTENANTS. IN THE MIDST OF ALL THESE BEARDS, ONE OF JULIETTE'S EARRINGS.

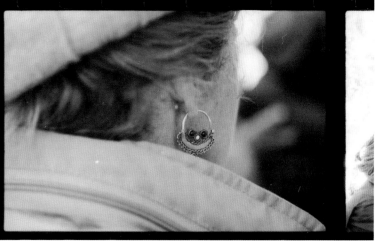

WE TRY TO CATCH RADIO FRANCE INTERNATIONALE ON OUR LITTLE SHORTWAVE RADIOS. SOMETIMES WE MANAGE, SOMETIMES NOT. THIS TIME IT'S NOT.

AT THE END OF THE AFTERNOON, THE MUJ' LISTEN TO THE BBC'S PERSIAN NEWS. LIFE STOPS IN AFGHANISTAN AT THE TIME OF THE BBC'S PERSIAN BROADCASTS.

BEFORE WE SET OFF AGAIN, THOSE WHO REQUEST IT ARE EXAMINED.

AND OFF WE GO, CLIMBING THE KALOTAC.

EVERY NOW AND AGAIN, I THINK ABOUT TINTIN. THOSE STORIES ARE REALLY SOMETHING. I OFTEN HAVE THE IMPRESSION HE'S TRAVELED THROUGH WHERE WE'RE GOING.

WE CROSS THE PASS AT NIGHT. WE STOP ON THE SIDE OF THE MOUNTAIN, IN RUINS THAT MORE OR LESS SHELTER US. WE HUDDLE AGAINST THE OLD STONES, AFTER HAVING SHARED A HARD-BOILED EGG AMONG TEN PEOPLE.

BY DAWN WE ALL FEEL AS STIFF WITH COLD AS THE HORSE'S CORPSE WE SAW THE DAY BEFORE.

WE DON'T WANT TO STAY HERE FOREVER, SO WE HAVE TO GET TO THE VILLAGE OF ANJOMAN AS QUICKLY AS POSSIBLE. WE WALK LIKE SLEEPERS AWAKENED BY AN EARTHQUAKE WHO ONLY HAD TIME TO WRAP THEMSELVES IN A BLANKET. WE KEEP AN EYE ON THE OPAQUE SKY.

THIS IS A VERY WIDE RIVER THAT ISN'T DEEP BUT HAS A POWERFUL CURRENT. AS THE CARAVAN STARTS CROSSING IT, ANOTHER DONKEY GETS INTO TROUBLE. SOME MUJ' RELIEVE HIM OF HIS PACKSADDLE AND TRY TO LIFT HIM ONTO A ROCK.

I TAKE A LOT OF PICTURES. AS I'M SHOOTING I START TO FEEL THAT A GOOD PICTURE IS WITHIN MY REACH. IT'S A BIT LIKE FISHING AND FEELING A FISH BITE. I HOLD MY BREATH EACH TIME I PRESS THE BUTTON.

I FEEL THAT, IF I'VE DONE MY JOB CORRECTLY, IT SHOULD BE THERE, AMONG THE LAST FIVE OR SIX SHOTS.

APPARENTLY, WE LOST A GUY LAST NIGHT. HE MUST'VE GOTTEN LOST WHEN WE CROSSED THE PASS IN THE DARK.

WHO WAS IT?

ONE OF THE HORSE GROOMS.

WHAT ARE WE GOING TO DO?

NOTHING. THERE'S NOTHING WE CAN DO. IF HE'S ALIVE, HE'LL HAVE TO FIND A WAY TO CATCH UP WITH US.

OUT OF NOWHERE, A GUY SELLING CAKES APPEARS. HE IS CARRYING A BAG FULL OF CAKES AND SELLS THEM TO US BY WEIGHT.

HE WANDERS AWAY AND SO DO WE.

74

WE GET A WARM WELCOME IN ANJOMAN. THERE HAS BEEN WAR HERE. RIGHT AWAY, CONSULTATIONS ARE SET UP FOR THE VILLAGERS.

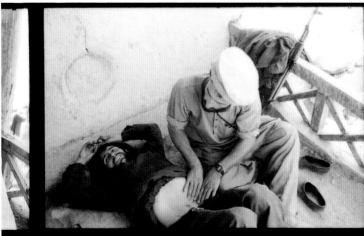

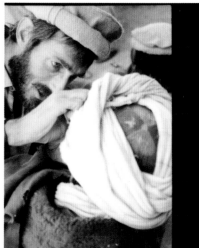

LATER ON, IN THE VILLAGE HALL, WE TALK. I HAVEN'T YET MENTIONED THAT JOHN IS AN OUTSTANDING FISHERMAN. QUITE A SPEAKER, TOO.

WHEN AFGHANISTAN IS NO LONGER A HELL OF WAR, IT'LL BE A HEAVEN FOR ANGLING.

WITH HIS FISHING ROD IN HAND, HE GIVES A DEMONSTRATION, LIKE A STREET PEDDLER.

SUDDENLY, THE DOOR OPENS. MAHMAD THROWS HIMSELF INTO THE ARMS OF THE MAN WHO HAS JUST ENTERED.

IT'S THE GUY WHO WAS FEARED LOST. EVERYONE CROWDS AROUND HIM, PRESSING HIM WITH QUESTIONS. I TAKE PICTURES AS HE TELLS HIS STORY. LAST NIGHT HE FELL BEHIND IN THE DARK. THE HAUNTED LOOK IN HIS EYES GIVES AN IDEA OF WHAT HE HAS BEEN THROUGH: THE TERROR OF BEING LOST, AT NIGHT, IN THE ICY COLD WEATHER; THE TERROR, COME MORNING, OF BEING BOMBED.

HE THOUGHT HE WAS FINISHED. EVERYONE THOUGHT HIM DEAD. HE DOES IN FACT LOOK A BIT LIKE A GHOST. TO HELP HIM RECOVER, HE IS GIVEN PIPING HOT *CHORMAZCHOY*, A REALLY OILY WALNUT TEA, AND SOME BREAD.

CHORCHOY, CHORMAZCHOY: I GOT USED TO THESE SALTED MILK TEAS. I FOUND THEM DISGUSTING AT FIRST, BUT OVERCAME MY AVERSION AND SOON COULDN'T DO WITHOUT THEM. NO SOONER HAVE YOU FINISHED YOUR BOWL THAN YOU'LL BE SERVED SOME MORE.

AT THE NEXT DAY'S BRIEFING WE DISCUSS THE TRICKY CROSSING THAT'S COMING UP; A LARGE, UNPROTECTED PLATEAU WHERE CARAVANS ARE OFTEN MACHINE-GUNNED FROM THE AIR. THAT HAPPENED TWO YEARS AGO, THE LAST TIME THE MSF TEAM CAME. A MUJ' DIED, SOMEONE RÉGIS KNEW WELL.

BECAUSE OF THE CONSTRAINTS OF THE WALKING SCHEDULE, THAT PLATEAU HAS TO BE CROSSED IN THE DAYTIME. BEFORE ENTERING IT, WE'LL SPLIT THE GROUP INTO PAIRS, LEAVING A LOT OF SPACE BETWEEN EACH OF THEM TO AVOID OFFERING TOO COMPACT A TARGET.

WE LEAVE ANJOMAN. THE BEAUTY OF THESE LANDSCAPES IS ALL THE MORE POIGNANT AS WE ARE NOW ENTERING COMBAT ZONES.

WE ENTER THE PLATEAU. IT'S TRUE THAT IT'S HUGE AND YOU HAVE NOWHERE TO HIDE. BLESSING OUR LUCK, WE SEE THE SKY IS EMPTY, TOO. THE SMALL GROUPS FORM UP AND START OUT ONE BY ONE.

NOTHING BAD HAPPENS.
WE GET THROUGH. ON
THE OTHER SIDE THERE'S
A RIVER AND THE COVER
OF A FEW TREES. THAT'S
WHERE, TWO YEARS AGO,
THEY BURIED THE MAN
WHO DIDN'T MAKE IT.

SOME MUJ' SQUAT AND
PRAY. RÉGIS JOINS THEM.
EVERYONE TAKES A
MOMENT OF RESPECTFUL
CONTEMPLATION.

Part 2

HELICOPTER! THE SHOUT MAKES ITS WAY DOWN THE CARAVAN, JUST AHEAD OF THE ENGINE HUM EVERYONE FEARS.

EVERYONE RUNS FOR WHATEVER COVER THEY CAN FIND. LUCKILY, THERE ARE PLENTY OF HIDING PLACES AROUND US.

I HIDE UNDER A ROCK LEDGE AND TRY TO SPOT THE CHOPPER IN THE PORTION OF SKY I CAN SEE.

THERE IT IS, FAR AWAY—BUT NOT AS FAR AS I'D LIKE.

PHEW! GONE.

THERE, YOU'VE BEEN INITIATED. YOU'VE SEEN RUSSIANS.

YES. PHOTOGRAPHICALLY, IT WASN'T THAT GREAT. A BIT FAR.

TELL YOU WHAT: NEXT TIME, INSTEAD OF HIDING UNDER A ROCK, CLIMB ON TOP OF IT AND WAVE AT THEM. YOU'LL GET A CLOSER LOOK.

SURE THING.

WE WERE LUCKY. WHEN THEY FLY HIGH AND IN A STRAIGHT LINE LIKE THAT, THEY'RE HEADED SOMEWHERE SPECIFIC. THEY'RE NOT ON THE HUNT.

THE DANGER HAS PASSED. THE SENTINELS RELAX. WE SET OFF AGAIN. A BIT FARTHER, WE PASS AN EMPTY CARAVAN GOING BACK TO PAKISTAN TO PICK UP WEAPONS. JULIETTE, ON HORSEBACK AND DRESSED AS A MAN, CAUSES THE USUAL STIR AMONG THE MUJ'.

A SHEPHERD CROSSES A RIVER WITH HIS SHEEP. FOR HIM THE DAY'S JOURNEY IS COMING TO AN END. NOT FOR US.

WE'RE GOING TO WALK THROUGH THE NIGHT, BECAUSE THIS IS THE REGION OF SKAZAR. SKAZAR IS THE MAIN SOVIET BASE IN THE AREA, BARRING THE ROAD INTO BADAKHSHAN. WE ARE GOING TO SKIRT FAIRLY CLOSE TO IT.

THE NIGHT IS ON OUR SIDE: A MOONLESS NIGHT, LIKE IN SUSPENSE NOVELS. ON THE OTHER HAND, WE CAN'T SEE THREE FEET AHEAD. WE'RE TWISTING OUR ANKLES AT EVERY OTHER STEP. AND STOPPING IS OUT OF THE QUESTION.

BY DAYBREAK, I'M EXHAUSTED. ALONG WITH A FEW OTHERS, I BEG FOR A HALT.

CONTINUE IF YOU WANT, I'M STOP-PING. I CAN'T TAKE ANY MORE.

ME NEITHER!

BREAK!

WHERE DID THOSE FEW FISH COME FROM? WAS IT JOHN WHO FOUND THE STRENGTH TO CATCH THEM? WE EAT THEM GRILLED ON THE END OF A STICK.

WE MOVE ONTO STEEP AND ROUGH PATHS. I FEEL COMPLETELY OUT OF SYNCH. WHILE CHANGING LENSES, I LOSE THE SUN GUARD FOR MY 105MM. THOSE THINGS ARE EXPENSIVE.

I WAS ALREADY IN A FOUL MOOD, AND THAT MAKES ME FURIOUS AT MYSELF. AND DEPRESSED.

IS THAT FIGHTING WE'RE HEARING?

NO, THAT'S MAIDAN.

BOOM BOOM

IN MAIDAN THEY HAVE DEPOSITS OF LAPIS LAZULI.

THOSE BLUE STONES?

YES. THEY'RE BLOWING UP THE MOUNTAIN WITH DYNAMITE.

WE ENTER MAIDAN, A MINING TOWN. THE HOUSES SEEM TO CRAWL UP THE MOUNTAINSIDE, ON EITHER SIDE OF A MAIN STREET. THE GROUND IS LITTERED WITH LAPIS LAZULI DEBRIS.

NO POINT LOOKING. YOU WON'T FIND ENOUGH TO MAKE YOURSELF A TIE PIN. THOSE ARE CASTOFFS, STONES THEY'VE ALREADY SORTED.

YES, LOOKS THAT WAY.

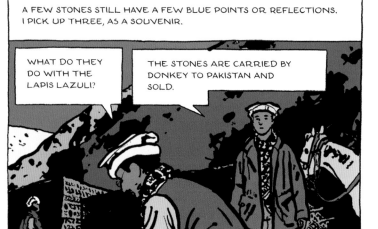

A FEW STONES STILL HAVE A FEW BLUE POINTS OR REFLECTIONS. I PICK UP THREE, AS A SOUVENIR.

WHAT DO THEY DO WITH THE LAPIS LAZULI?

THE STONES ARE CARRIED BY DONKEY TO PAKISTAN AND SOLD.

THE MONEY GOES TO THE JAMIAT-E-ISLAMI PARTY, ONE OF THE SEVEN PARTIES OF THE RESISTANCE. THAT'S THE PARTY OF MASSOUD AND OF BASSIR, THE COMMANDER WE'RE GOING TO SEE IN YAFTAL.

I KNEW THE RESISTANCE WAS MAKING MONEY FROM DOPE, BUT I HADN'T HEARD ABOUT PRECIOUS STONES.

YEAH. THEY ALSO MINE EMERALDS AND RUBIES.

88

DOES THE DYNAMITING CONTINUE AT NIGHT? I HAVE NO IDEA. I SLEEP. THE FATIGUE IS ACCUMULATING AND I NEVER SEEM TO MANAGE TO REST ENOUGH.

AS SOON AS WE'RE UP, A BIG EVENT: WE DECIDE TO WASH. NOT PIECEMEAL AS USUAL, WE'RE GOING TO HAVE A REAL BATH IN A RIVER.

THERE IS NOTHING HAPPY-GO-LUCKY ABOUT IT. THIS TAKES AS MUCH PLANNING AS A MILITARY OFFENSIVE—AN ARMED ESCORT COMES WITH US, AND GUARDS ARE POSTED AROUND THE TORRENT, WITH THEIR BACKS TURNED AND UNDER ORDERS TO TURN AWAY ANY GAWKERS.

BETWEEN THE DEPLOYMENT OF FORCES AND THE ICE-COLD WATER, THE BATH ISN'T THE MOST CAREFREE EXPERIENCE. PLUS, SEEING MYSELF NAKED FOR THE FIRST TIME SINCE GERMSHESHMA, I BARELY RECOGNIZE MY BODY.

I'M EMACIATED. BESIDES MY FACE, HANDS, AND WRISTS, WHICH ARE TANNED A DEEP BROWN, EVERYTHING ELSE IS PALLID. YOU CAN SEE EVERY MUSCLE FIBER, LIKE ON AN ANATOMICAL DRAWING.

AS I PUT ON A FRESH SHIRT, THE SMELL OF CLEAN CLOTH JUMPS OUT AT ME.

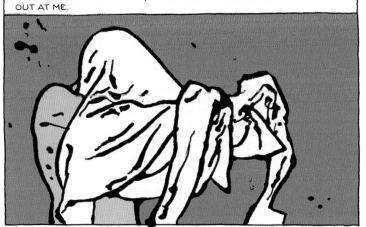

BEFORE LEAVING THE RIVER, THE MUJ' DECIDE TO FISH IN IT, BUT THEIR TECHNIQUE ISN'T MUCH LIKE JOHN'S. IT OWES MORE TO THE MINERS OF MAIDAN.

BOOM.

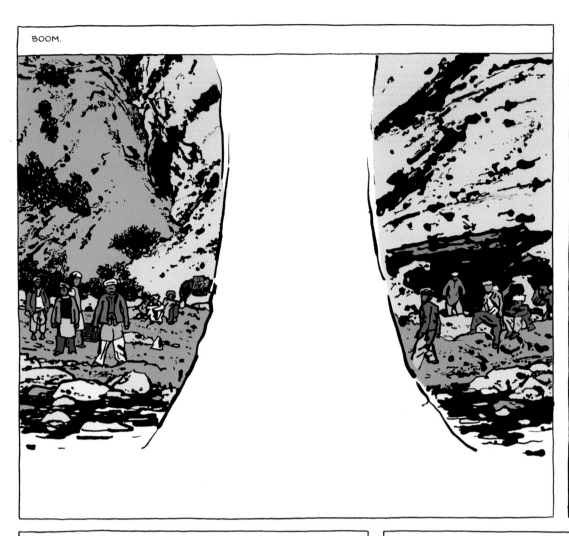

THE NUMBER OF DEAD FISH IS BEYOND BELIEF. SEVERAL THOUSAND? THEY PICK UP A DOZEN. WE SET OFF.

ONE LAST PASS SEPARATES US FROM TESHKAN: THE ARASH PASS. APTLY NAMED, SINCE THE WORD MEANS "TO RIP OUT" IN FRENCH. WE COME TO A STREAM THAT WE HAVE TO CROSS BY HOPPING FROM STONE TO STONE. LOOKS EASY ENOUGH.

BUT MY LITTLE RUN OF BAD LUCK CONTINUES. I SLIP AND TAKE A DUNKING. SO DOES MY BIG NIKON F2.

I PULL IT OUT RIGHT AWAY BUT IT'S NICELY SOAKED.

THE DIAGNOSIS: THE FILTER OF THE 20MM AND THE LIGHT METER ARE SHOT.

I FEEL ALL MY NERVOUS FATIGUE RUSH INTO THAT INCIDENT, PRODUCING NO END OF DISCOURAGEMENT. I'M FED UP.

YOU OKAY, DIDIER?

NO.

THE DYING DONKEY THAT WE PASS A BIT FARTHER ALONG DOESN'T EXACTLY CHEER ME UP.

A SHORT WAY FROM THE SUMMIT, WE WALK AMONG HERDS OF SHEEP AND GOATS LEFT TO THEIR OWN DEVICES. IN THAT WAR-RAVAGED REGION, WHERE PEASANTS HAVE BECOME SOLDIERS, THERE AREN'T ENOUGH MEN TO LOOK AFTER THE ANIMALS OR TEND THE FIELDS.

AT THE TOP OF THE PASS I TAKE A FEW GROUP PICTURES WITH MY F2 CAMERA. IT SEEMS TO BE RESPONDING MORE OR LESS NORMALLY. I DON'T KNOW WHAT TO EXPECT OF THE FILM.
IT'S SEPTEMBER 4TH, JULIETTE'S BIRTHDAY.
I HAVE TO BE SURE TO BRING BACK AT LEAST ONE GOOD SHOT. JOHN LENDS ME HIS CAMERA, WITH COLOR FILM.
THE MUJ' FROM TESHKAN, WHO ARE NEARLY HOME, POSE IN FRONT OF THE ROW OF MSF PEOPLE.
I SAY, "SMILE!"
THOSE WHO UNDERSTAND, SMILE.

ON THE WAY DOWN, IN THE VILLAGE OF RASMI, I TAKE ANOTHER GROUP PHOTO, INDOORS THIS TIME. THE MUJ' DON'T PUT DOWN THEIR WEAPONS, BUT THEY DO PUT THEIR BAGGAGE DOWN. THEY'RE BACK HOME.

DURING THE CONSULTATIONS IN RASMI, I WATCH ROBERT AS HE LISTENS TO THE PATIENTS. HIS FACE SHOWS THE STRAIN OF THE SAME EXHAUSTION I'M FEELING. YET HE KEEPS GOING. IT'S UP TO ME TO DO AS MUCH.

THERE. JUST A COUPLE MORE MILES AND WE REACH THE VALLEY OF TESHKAN, OUR JOURNEY'S FIRST DESTINATION. THE WAKIL, OR REGIONAL REPRESENTATIVE, WHOSE SON I MET IN PESHAWAR, HAS DEPLOYED HIS SECURITY DETAIL IN A GUARD OF HONOR TO WELCOME US.

HIS REUNION WITH JULIETTE IS JOYFUL. SHE SHAKES THE WAKIL'S HEALTHY HAND. THE OTHER ONE DIED WHEN A BULLET HIT HIS LEFT ARM.

IT'S ALMOST CERTAIN THAT NOTHING CAN BE DONE FOR HIS ARM, BUT SINCE HE'S THE WAKIL, WE'RE GOING TO EXAMINE HIM FOR THREE HOURS, TO MAKE IT VERY CLEAR THAT HE'S THE CHIEF.

INDEED, IN THE WAKIL'S HOUSE, AROUND CUPS OF TEA, ROBERT, RÉGIS, AND JOHN HANDLE HIS ARM WITH A GREAT DEAL OF RESPECT. THERE ARE A THOUSAND EXPLANATIONS, ALL SURROUNDING THE SAME CONCLUSION: THE WAKIL WILL NOT RECOVER THE USE OF HIS LEFT ARM.

DESPITE THE BAD NEWS, HE GIVES US A FEW RECOMMENDATION LETTERS THAT WILL ALLOW THOSE WHO ARE CONTINUING THE JOURNEY TO REACH YAFTAL.

AS WE LEAVE TESHKAN, WE'RE ALSO LEAVING BEHIND SYLVIE, ODILE, MICHEL, AND TALL RONALD, WHO ARE GOING TO RUN A SMALL AND RUDIMENTARY HOSPITAL, LOST AMONG THE FLOWERS. WE'LL PICK UP ODILE, MICHEL, AND RONALD ON THE WAY BACK. SYLVIE WILL SPEND THE ENTIRE WINTER THERE, TILL THE NEXT TEAM ARRIVES.

THE CARAVAN, HAVING SHED HALF ITS MEMBERS, SETS OFF ON THE LAST STRETCH, TESHKAN TO YAFTAL, VIA DARAIM.

WE ENTER DARAIM, WHERE THE GUARD OF HONOR, LESS MARTIAL THAN IN TESHKAN, IS COMPOSED OF BLACK SHEEP.

IT'S A BEAUTIFUL VILLAGE, AND SEEMS TO HAVE BEEN SPARED BY THE WAR. THE COMMANDER WELCOMES US WITH WONDERFUL KINDNESS.
ONE THING IS WORRYING HIM: HIS YOUNG SON'S TESTICLES ARE NOT COMING DOWN.

FOR REASONS OF MODESTY, THE BOY IS EXAMINED BEHIND A BLANKET. THE DIAGNOSIS IS NOT ALARMING. BEFORE AND AFTER THE EXAMINATION HIS FATHER IS VERY GENTLE AND CARING.

MOST OF THE AFGHAN MEN, INCLUDING THOSE WHO SEEM MOST BRUTAL, BEHAVE LIKE MOTHERS TOWARD THE CHILDREN. THEY DEMONSTRATE THEIR LOVE IN A VERY PHYSICAL AND TENDER WAY. I OFTEN SEE THEM CHECK THAT THEIR KIDS AREN'T COLD, STRAIGHTEN THEIR HATS, AND SO ON.

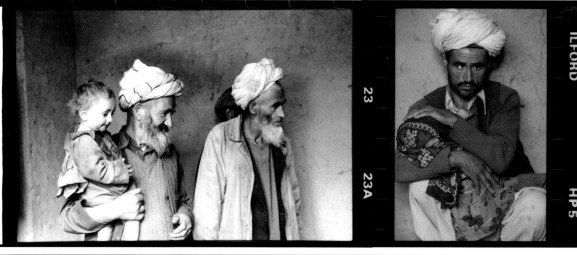

WE GO FROM THE VILLAGE HALL TO THE MOSQUE. A KORANIC CLASS HAS BEEN IMPROVISED FOR US.

SINCE THE BEGINNING OF TIME, EVERY KID WHO IS LEARNING TO READ HAS HAD THE SAME EXPRESSION.

POOR THINGS! SUCH BIG PAGES PRINTED SO SMALL!

DON'T FEEL SORRY FOR THEM, THEY'RE NOT OVERLOADED WITH READING RIGHT NOW.

I GAVE SOME MONEY TO THE COMMANDER FOR THE SCHOOL. OUT OF GRATITUDE, TO SHOW THAT HE TAKES IT SERIOUSLY, HE ORGANIZED THIS SESSION, BUT IN FACT THE SCHOOL ISN'T OPEN.

IT'S NOT?

NO.

IT'S SEPTEMBER, HARVEST TIME. THE CHILDREN ARE IN THE FIELDS.

I'D NOTICED THAT THEY DO HAVE CALLUSED HANDS.

THEY MANAGE, AFGHAN STYLE, TO LEARN A THING OR TWO, BUT ON THE WHOLE THEY'RE REALLY JUST LITTLE WORKERS OR LITTLE FIGHTERS.

AND THE AWFUL PART IS THAT, MORE AND MORE, THEIR ONLY ROLE MODELS ARE TEENAGERS WHO DON'T KNOW ANYTHING OTHER THAN FIGHTING, AND BRAG ABOUT IT. NOTHING ELSE IS AVAILABLE.

THERE'S NO ONE TO EXPLAIN TO THEM THAT KNOWING THINGS IS BETTER THAN HACKING EACH OTHER TO PIECES.

AND WHAT'S IT LIKE IN KABUL?

IN KABUL, THERE'S THE SECULAR COMMUNIST SCHOOL, BUT PURSUING HIGHER EDUCATION IS OUT OF THE QUESTION, ALSO BECAUSE OF THE WAR. THE BOYS GET DRAFTED INTO THE COMMUNIST ARMY, UNLESS THEY DESERT AND JOIN THE RESISTANCE, OR LEAVE THE COUNTRY ALTOGETHER.

NOT TOO CHEERFUL, IS IT?

NO. IT'S NOT CHEERFUL. I DON'T KNOW HOW LONG THIS WAR WILL LAST, BUT THE LONGER IT LASTS AND THE LONGER IT UPROOTS, MOWS DOWN, AND MUTILATES KIDS—THE HARDER IT'LL BE TO GET OUT OF IT.

A MOTHER SHOWS US HER BLIND DAUGHTER, WHO SEEMS TO HAVE A DROP OF GLUE IN EACH EYE.

AS WE LEAVE DARAIM, I FEEL I'VE CAUGHT A GLIMPSE OF A POSSIBLE AFGHAN PARADISE: A PRETTY TOWN, TASTY CAKES, A SENSIBLE COMMANDER, A SCHOOL, FARM WORK. A WORLD WHERE WORRYING OVER THE EYES OF A YOUNG BLIND GIRL AND THE BALLS OF A LITTLE BOY IS THE WORST PEOPLE HAVE TO CONTEND WITH.

MY FEELING OF BEING IN THE GARDEN OF EDEN GROWS STRONGER AS WE REACH A VALLEY, NEAR FEYZABAD, THAT IS LIKE ONE GIANT PEACH ORCHARD.

SOME VILLAGERS OFFER US PEACHES AND I GORGE MYSELF ON THEM, FEELING A FRENZIED NEED FOR VITAMINS. I EAT AT LEAST THIRTY OF THEM. THEY'RE DELICIOUS.

THE CONSEQUENCES DON'T TAKE LONG TO SHOW UP. IN THE NEXT VALLEY I HAVE A MASSIVE CASE OF THE RUNS. ROBERT'S COMMENT:

AFTER THE VALLEY OF PEACHES, THE VALLEY OF JAM.

AS THE SUN SETS, WE CROSS A WIDE RIVER ON A RAFT.

ONE LAST MARCH LEADS US TO OUR GOAL, YAFTAL, WHERE WE ARE GREETED, AT THE EDGE OF THE VILLAGE, BY COMMANDER BASSIR KHAN.
THE BEST PICTURES OF BASSIR KHAN ARE LOW-ANGLE SHOTS.
HE IS A POWERFUL FIGURE, RATHER FRIENDLY AND EXTREMELY WILY.

NAJMUDIN RETURNS TO HIS USUAL PLACE, TO THE LEFT OF HIS CHIEF. HE REPORTS ON HIS MISSION.

NEED I MENTION OUR RELIEF AT HAVING ARRIVED? YET YAFTAL IS NO HAVEN. FARAWAY EXPLOSIONS REMIND US OF THE FIGHTING GOING ON AND OF THE NEED FOR THE TEAM'S WORK. BUT NEVER MIND. ALL I CAN SEE, FOR THE TIME BEING, IS THAT THE FORCED MARCH IS OVER. IT LASTED A MONTH.

RÉGIS FISHES A COPY OF DOUBLE PAGE, A FRENCH MAGAZINE, OUT OF HIS SADDLEBAGS. IT CONTAINS SOME SPECTACULAR LARGE-SIZED COLOR PICTURES OF A BUZKASHI GAME, TAKEN BY SABRINA AND ROLAND MICHAUD.
THAT'S HIS PRESENT FOR BASSIR. HAPPY AND FLATTERED, THE LOCAL LORD SHOWS IT TO HIS MEN.

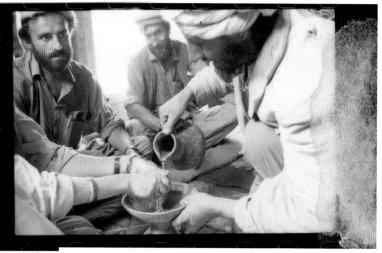

AFTER HAVING WASHED OUR HANDS, WE ARE TREATED TO A FEAST. THERE ARE WONDERFUL BREADS—PLAIN, BRIOCHE-LIKE, DECORATED, WALNUT-FILLED. VEGETABLE DUMPLINGS. AMAZING YOGURTS. MAGNIFICENT FRUIT, WHICH I'M CAREFUL TO ENJOY IN MODERATION. (BY THE WAY, IN AFGHANISTAN, THE GRAPES ARE SEEDLESS.)

WE STUFF OUR FACES. BASSIR TOO. IN THIS COUNTRY OF LEAN MEN, I FIND IT EASIER TO UNDERSTAND WHERE HIS PAUNCH COMES FROM.

BASSIR'S PERSONAL GUARD IS COMPOSED OF VERY YOUNG MEN WHO SHOW OFF THEIR WEAPONS. THAT'S WHAT THEY'RE MOST PROUD OF, HAVING A GUN AND GOING TO WAR.
I TURN MYSELF INTO A COURT PHOTOGRAPHER. HERE ARE BASSIR'S HORSE GROOM AND HIS BODYGUARD.

I'VE BEEN HOODWINKED. WE HAVE INDEED REACHED THE VALLEY OF YAFTAL, BUT WE'RE AT THE WRONG END OF IT. TWO MORE DAYS OF WALKING ARE NEEDED TO GET TO ZARAGANDARA, WHERE WE ARE GOING TO LIVE AND WORK.

AROUND THE HOUSES SOME AMPLE COW PATTIES HAVE BEEN PUT OUT TO DRY, AND WILL PROVIDE HEATING FUEL DURING THE COMING WINTER. WE START OUR HIKE IN GORGEOUS WEATHER. WE WALK THROUGH THE VALLEY. EVERYTHING SEEMS SIMPLE.

EVEN THOUGH THE GOING HAS BEEN TOUGH, BUT ALSO BECAUSE OF IT, I'M ALREADY FEELING A GREAT LOVE OF AFGHANISTAN, A GENUINE ATTACHMENT. A DAY LIKE TODAY ADDS TO THAT SENSATION. IT'S GLORIOUS.

ZARAGANDARA IS ON A MOUNTAINSIDE. HERE THE BOOMS OF WAR SOUND CLOSER.

HOW 'BOUT A LITTLE SPRINT TO THE FINISH LINE FOR THE LAST STAGE?

YOU GET A HEAD START, I'LL CATCH UP.

IF YOU WANT TO SNAP SOME PICTURES OF THE HOSPITAL BEFORE WE GET SET UP, NOW'S THE TIME.

WHERE IS THE HOSPITAL?

HERE.

YOU'RE REALLY GOING TO WORK IN THIS DUMP?

WHAT WERE YOU EXPECTING? THE MAYO CLINIC?

NO, BUT THIS IS SOME-THING ELSE! A GRUBBY, WINDSWEPT PORCH...

WE'LL GET A BETTER VIEW OF THE LAND-SCAPE.

THERE, WITH MY STETHOSCOPE HANGING FROM THE COAT RACK, IT'LL LOOK MUCH MORE LIKE A HOSPITAL.

YES, THAT'S IT! THAT'S WHAT WAS MISSING!

THE COMMUTE BETWEEN THE HOSPITAL AND THE HOUSE WILL BE MANAGE-ABLE. WE'LL BE LIVING JUST UP THE HILL, IN THIS FIVE-STAR HOTEL. IT'S PRETTY SPARTAN, BUT WE ARE SPARTANS.

101

THIS IS THE BED WHERE ALL SEVEN OF US WILL BE SLEEPING, LINED UP IN ROWS. IN AFGHANISTAN, FATIGUE GENERALLY MAKES UP FOR THE LACK OF COMFORT AND YOU SLEEP WELL.

AFTER HAVING PUT DOWN OUR BAGS, WE HEAD BACK DOWN TO SET UP THE HOSPITAL. THE SORT OF LAUNDRY ROOM AT THE END OF THE PORCH WILL BE THE INFIRMARY. WE LINE UP INSTRUMENTS AND MEDICINES ON THE SHELVES.

THE PORCH WILL BE THE CONSULTATION ROOM AND OPERATING THEATER. THE COURTYARD WILL SERVE AS A WAITING ROOM.

HEY, LOOK, GUYS!

I'VE FOUND THE TRUSTY OLD TABLE FROM PREVIOUS MISSIONS.

MSF: LA OÙ LES AUTRES NE VONT PAS
LE DOCTEUR A TOUJOURS RAISON
MIEUX VAUT ÊTRE RICHE ET EN BONNE SANTÉ QUE PAUVRE ET MALADE

MSF: GOING WHERE OTHERS WON'T GO / THE DOCTOR IS ALWAYS RIGHT / BETTER RICH AND HEALTHY THAN POOR AND SICK

THE FIRST NIGHT PASSES. IN THE MORNING A FAMILY BRINGS US CHORCHOY FOR BREAKFAST.

SINCE THE DAY BEFORE, WORD OF MOUTH HAS SPREAD THE NEWS OF THE HOSPITAL OPENING. THE WAITING ROOM IS FULL. AN AFGHAN MAN, WHO LEARNED RUDIMENTS OF MEDICINE DURING PREVIOUS MSF MISSIONS, IS IN CHARGE OF SORTING PATIENTS ACCORDING TO HOW SEVERE THEIR CONDITION IS. MAHMAD, AS ALWAYS, IS INTERPRETING.

مرا درمان کنید. یہ من وارد ببین.

HE'S MAKING A HELL OF A RACKET! WHAT DOES HE WANT?

HE'S SAYING HE'S SICK AND NEEDS TO BE TREATED. HE SAID BEFORE HE WAS ALWAYS THE FIRST TO REACH THE TOP OF MOUNTAIN PASSES BUT NOW HE ONLY COMES IN SECOND OR THIRD.

YES, BUT HOW OLD IS HE?

THE FIRST REAL PATIENT HAS NOTHING TO DO WITH THE WAR. IT'S A LITTLE BOY WHO HAS BADLY BURNED HIS FOOT BY FALLING INTO A BREAD OVEN. THIS IS A COMMON TYPE OF HOUSEHOLD ACCIDENT IN AFGHANISTAN. HIS FATHER AND SISTER ARE WITH HIM.

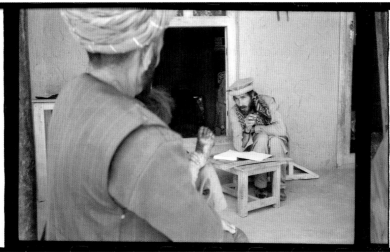

WHILE RÉGIS PREPARES THE ANESTHETIC FOR THE BOY, ROBERT EXAMINES HIS SISTER. HE HAS TO MANAGE THROUGH HER CLOTHING BECAUSE, AS FOR ALL WOMEN, LITTLE GIRLS CANNOT BE UNCLOTHED IN FRONT OF THE DOCTOR.

RÉGIS, ASSISTED BY EVELYNE, A NURSE, AND THE FATHER, GIVES THE BOY AN INJECTION IN THE BUTTOCKS. IF THESE PICTURES HAD SOUND, IT WOULD BE IN THE HIGH NOTES.

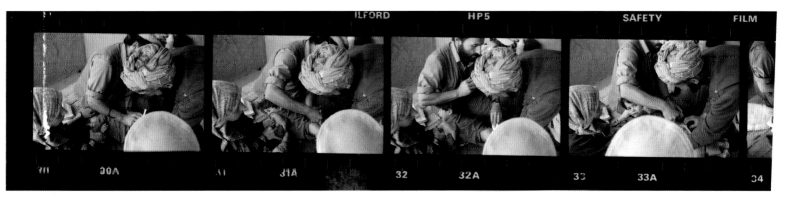

THEY CAREFULLY MONITOR THE BOY'S INCREASING DROWSINESS. ONCE HE'S ASLEEP, ROBERT GETS TO WORK.

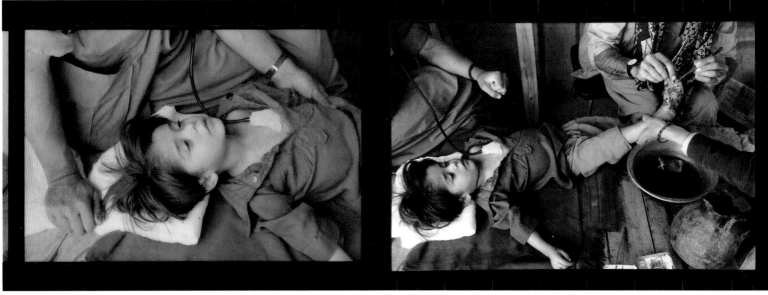

ALL GOES WELL. HE IS SENT TO THE ICU, MEANING THE COURTYARD, UNDER THE TREES.

RÉGIS DOESN'T STOP WATCHING OVER HIM UNTIL HE WAKES UP, AT WHICH TIME HE IS BROUGHT BACK ONTO THE PORCH.

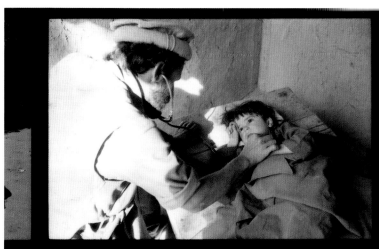 

THEN HE IS GIVEN THE YOGURT OF VICTORY. HE'LL HAVE TO RETURN TOMORROW FOR FOLLOW-UP CARE.

¡4   14A   15   15A   16   16A

WITH HIS FOOT REPAIRED, THE LITTLE BOY WOULD DO WELL TO KEEP IT AWAY FROM THE LANDMINES THAT THE COUNTRY IS LITTERED WITH.

18   18A   19   19A   20   20A

105

EVELYNE WAS THE ONE ASSISTING ROBERT AND RÉGIS WITH THE OPERATION. I'D SAY THAT EVELYNE IS THE BRAVEST AMONG US, BECAUSE SHE'S ABSOLUTELY NOT CUT OUT FOR THE FEATS SHE IS ACCOMPLISHING. SHE'S A NORMAL WOMAN AND NOT A PARTICULARLY ATHLETIC PERSON. EVERYTHING SHE ACHIEVES IS THE RESULT OF SHEER WILLPOWER AND DETERMINATION.

RÉGIS OFTEN TELLS HER:

EVELYNE, YOU'RE A SAINT.

YES, RÉGIS.

THE TWO CHARACTERS THAT SHOW UP NEXT ARE OUR FIRST WAR WOUNDED.

IF I UNDERSTAND CORRECTLY, THE ONE ON THE RIGHT, WITH THE BIG BANDAGE, HAD HIS TEMPLE NICKED BY A BULLET FROM AN AK-47. EACH IMPACT OF THESE BULLETS CAUSES THEM TO CHANGE COURSE. THAT'S WHY THEY CAUSE SO MUCH DAMAGE IN THE BODIES THEY HIT: THEY RICOCHET INSIDE. HE WAS LUCKY, IN A MANNER OF SPEAKING.

AFTER HAVING HIT HIS TEMPLE, THE BULLET WENT THROUGH HIS SHOULDER ABOVE THE LUNG AND WENT ON TO LODGE ITSELF, AT A MUCH SLOWER SPEED, IN THE CHEST OF HIS BUDDY, WHO FELL AND GOT HIMSELF A NICE BRUISE. IT CRACKS THEM UP. AFGHANS OFTEN LAUGH ABOUT SUCH THINGS.

THE OPERATING TABLE, INSTRUMENTS, AND SURGICAL SUPPLIES ARE PREPARED, AND THE TEAM SETS THE PATIENT DOWN. JOHN WILL BE IN CHARGE. I'M STRUCK BY A DETAIL: THE DEPTH OF THE WOUND. I HAD NO IDEA THAT IN THAT AREA OF THE TEMPLE THERE WAS SUCH A THICKNESS OF FLESH ABOVE THE CRANIAL BONE.

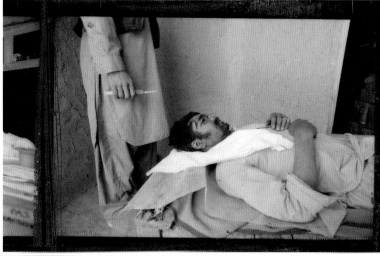
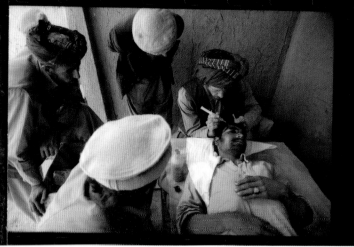

REGIS PROVIDES A RUNNING COMMENTARY ON THE OPERATION FOR THE BENEFIT OF A FEW AFGHAN TRAINEES WHO WANT TO BE ABLE TO PERFORM IT WHEN THE MSF PEOPLE ARE NO LONGER THERE. AND SOME BABAS LOOK ON WITH SYMPATHY.

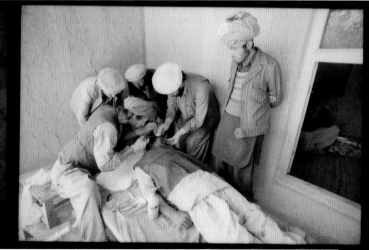

THAT EVENING WE PICK UP RADIO FRANCE INTERNATIONALE. GET SOME NEWS FROM THE WORLD. ONLY ONE STORY STRIKES ME: JACQUES-HENRI LARTIGUE IS DEAD.

SHIT!

IF I WERE ASKED TO NAME MY FAVORITE PHOTOGRAPHER, I WOULDN'T SAY LARTIGUE. BUT I LIKE HIM.

I FEEL THE NEED TO LOOK AT SOME PICTURES. IN MY BAG I HAVE A BOOK FROM A FRENCH PAPERBACK COLLECTION ON PHOTOGRAPHERS. IT'S THE ONE ON JOSEF KOUDELKA.

REACHING FOR IT, I PULL OUT ANOTHER BOOK.

STEVENSON!

I'D COMPLETELY FORGOTTEN ABOUT STEVENSON. VERY NAUGHTY OF ME, BUT I HAVE SOME EXCUSES. I SCAN THE FIRST LINES. THEY BRING ME BACK TO GERMSHESHMA, BEFORE OUR DEPARTURE. A CENTURY AGO, IT SEEMS.

I FEEL PRETTY SURE I'LL BE TOTALLY INCAPABLE OF READING THIS LITTLE BOOK BY THE END OF THE TRIP. MY MIND IS ELSEWHERE. BUT I'M HAPPY TO HAVE IT WITH ME, TO GIVE IT SOME FRESH MOUNTAIN AIR.

WE GO TO SLEEP AT SEVEN O'CLOCK.

BRODODOM

A RUMBLING AND A JOLT WAKE US UP. OR, RATHER, IT'S REALLY MAHMAD WHO WAKES US. HE CATAPULTS HIMSELF OUT OF THE HOUSE.

EVERYBODY OUT, QUICK! EARTHQUAKE! GET OUT!

TREMORS ARE VERY BRIEF, BUT THAT ISN'T THE IMPRESSION YOU GET. THEY FEEL LIKE THEY LAST A LONG TIME. TONIGHT, THERE'S ONLY ONE. NO DAMAGE. WE WAIT A BIT, THEN CRAWL BACK INTO OUR SLEEPING BAGS.

THE NEXT DAY THERE'S A CROWD IN THE WAITING ROOM. OUR AFGHAN RECEPTIONIST IS DOING HIS JOB OF SORTING AND CLASSIFYING PATIENTS.

TOWARD THE END OF THE DAY A MUJ' SHOWS UP. HE TALKS AT LENGTH WITH THE TEAM. EVIDENTLY HE HAS COME TO GET THE DOCTORS AND WANTS THEM TO FOLLOW HIM.

JULIETTE AND ROBERT FALL INTO STEP BEHIND HIM AND I TAG ALONG.

WHERE ARE WE GOING?

WE HAVE NO IDEA.

WE'RE SUPPOSEDLY GOING TO SEE A GUY WITH A HEAD WOUND, IN A VILLAGE THAT'S A HALF-HOUR'S WALK FROM HERE.

YOU HAVE TO WATCH OUT FOR AFGHAN HALF HOURS. FOR THEM, EVERYTHING IS ALWAYS "NAZDIK," NOT FAR.

SO THE VILLAGE COULD BE THIRTY MILES FROM HERE.

AND THE GUY WOUNDED IN THE KNEE.

TWO HOURS LATER, AS NIGHT FALLS, WE ENTER THE VILLAGE. THE WOUNDED MUJ' IS LYING IN THE MOSQUE. A FEW FARMERS ARE WATCHING OVER HIM.

AN INITIAL EXAMINATION SHOWS A HOLE IN THE RIGHT EYE. WE SPEND THE NIGHT BY HIS SIDE. IN THE MORNING, HE IS TAKEN OUTSIDE TO BETTER ASSESS HIS CONDITION AND ASK HIM QUESTIONS.

SO?

HIS EYE IS LOST. THE EYEBALL WAS PUNCTURED.

HOW'D IT HAPPEN?

HE DID IT TO HIMSELF. HE WAS RUNNING DURING A FIREFIGHT, WEAPON IN HAND, AND HE FELL HEAD FIRST ONTO THE BARREL OF HIS RIFLE.

GEEZ!

WE HAVE TO OPERATE TO TAKE OUT WHAT'S LEFT OF THE EYEBALL DEEP IN THE SOCKET.

CAN HE BE MOVED?

YES, OF COURSE. THE GUYS FROM THE VILLAGE WILL BRING HIM OVER TO US IN ZARAGANDARA IN THE COURSE OF THE DAY.

HE INSISTED THAT WE NOTIFY HIS FATHER, WHO'S IN ANOTHER VILLAGE.

AND WHAT DID HE SAY ABOUT HIS PUNCTURED EYE?

THAT IT WAS THE WILL OF ALLAH.

THAT'S AFGHAN FATALISM FOR YOU. EVERYTHING HAPPENS BY THE WILL OF GOD, SO WHATEVER HAPPENS TO YOU HAD TO HAPPEN.

POOR GUY! BLINDING HIMSELF WITH THE BARREL OF HIS OWN RIFLE!

I'VE SEEN EVEN BETTER, YOU KNOW.

IN THE LAST MISSION, I SAW A GUY COME IN WITH A HOLE WHERE HIS NOSE SHOULD'VE BEEN, A HOLE UNDER THE CHIN, AND A HOLE IN EACH HAND. ALL THAT DONE WITH ONE BULLET.

HANG ON—SAY THAT AGAIN, I DIDN'T GET IT.

ONE HOLE HERE, ONE HOLE THERE.

YES.

AND ONE HOLE IN EACH HAND. ALL WITH ONE BULLET. WHAT DO YOU THINK HAPPENED?

NO IDEA.

WELL, WHAT HAPPENED IS THAT THE GUY WAS SITTING LIKE THIS, WITH HIS CHIN AND BOTH HANDS RESTING ON THE MUZZLE OF HIS RIFLE. THERE WAS A BULLET IN THE BARREL.

AND HIS THREE-YEAR-OLD KID, WHO WAS PLAYING AT HIS FEET, PULLED THE TRIGGER.

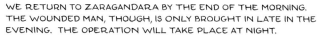

WE RETURN TO ZARAGANDARA BY THE END OF THE MORNING. THE WOUNDED MAN, THOUGH, IS ONLY BROUGHT IN LATE IN THE EVENING. THE OPERATION WILL TAKE PLACE AT NIGHT.

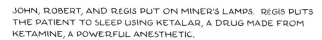

JOHN, ROBERT, AND RÉGIS PUT ON MINER'S LAMPS. RÉGIS PUTS THE PATIENT TO SLEEP USING KETALAR, A DRUG MADE FROM KETAMINE, A POWERFUL ANESTHETIC.

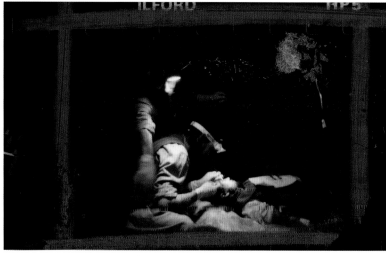

IN THE MIDDLE OF THE OPERATION, THE FATHER SHOWS UP. HE'S UTTERLY FRANTIC, AS YOU'D IMAGINE. MAHMAD REASSURES HIM, AND HE'S OFFERED SOMETHING TO EAT AND DRINK AND GIVEN A SEAT IN THE CORNER OF THE PORCH, WITH INSTRUCTIONS NOT TO MOVE.

SUDDENLY, A VISION OF HORROR: THE PATIENT'S LEFT EYE, THE GOOD ONE, OPENS AND STARTS LOOKING IN ALL DIRECTIONS.

IS HE WAKING UP?

111

NO, DON'T WORRY, THAT'S AN EFFECT OF THE ANESTHETIC. KETAMINE CAUSES A DEEP SLEEP, BUT IT DOESN'T PARALYZE MUSCLES AND IT ALLOWS SOME REFLEX MOTIONS.

HE REALLY SEEMS TO BE WATCHING US.

NO, HE CAN'T SEE A THING.

ON THE OTHER HAND, WITH HIS EYE OPEN LIKE THAT IT COULD DRY OUT AND CAUSE CORNEAL DAMAGE. THAT'S WHY I'M REGULARLY GIVING HIM SALINE SOLUTION.

IT TAKES ME A WHILE BEFORE I CAN HANDLE SEEING THIS EYE MOVE AROUND WHILE JOHN, UNFAZED, CONTINUES TO EMPTY OUT THE SOCKET NEXT TO IT.

THE OPERATION IS COMPLETED. THE PATIENT'S WOUND IS DRESSED, AND HIS HEAD WRAPPED IN A BANDAGE AGAIN. IN THE MORNING HE EMERGES. HE IS *ZOOF*, AS THE AFGHANS SAY, GROGGY.

THE FIRST PERSON HE SEES IS HIS FATHER, WHO HAS NOT LEFT HIS BEDSIDE FOR A MINUTE. IN A SLURRED VOICE, THE MUJ' ASKS RÉGIS, "DID YOU GIVE MY FATHER SOME TEA?"

112

AND THE SECOND THING HE ASKS FOR, WHEN HE HAS AWAKENED A BIT MORE, IS TO HAVE HIS RIFLE BROUGHT TO HIM. HE WANTS TO CHECK THAT HE CAN AIM WITH HIS LEFT EYE.

HE UTTERS A THIRD AND FINAL SENTENCE AS HE GETS UP: "I'LL HAVE A HARD TIME FINDING A WIFE AND GETTING MARRIED." THAT'S IT. LATER, WHILE CONVALESCING IN THE ZARAGANDARA MOSQUE, HE PROUDLY INVITES ME TO DO A PORTRAIT OF HIM.

THE MOSQUE IS USED AS AN ANNEX TO THE HOSPITAL FOR RECOVERING PATIENTS OR THOSE AWAITING TREATMENT. IT COULDN'T BE MORE BASIC: A DOOR, A CENTRAL WOODEN PILLAR, A FEW RECESSES IN THE WALLS, SOME CALLIGRAPHIES, AND STRAW AND CARPETS ON THE FLOOR. IT SERVES AS THE VILLAGE HALL.

A LITTLE BOY ARRIVES. HE LIFTS UP THE SLEEVE OF HIS SWEATER. A BULLET HAS GONE THROUGH HIS FOREARM.

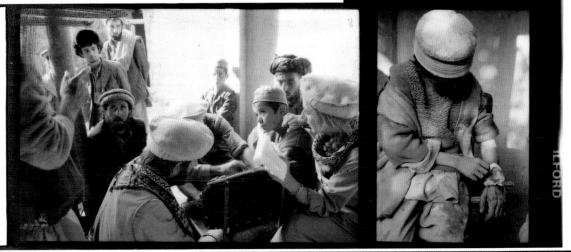

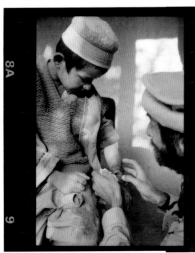

I'M IMPRESSED THAT HE'S NOT CRYING.

MANY OF THE CHILDREN HERE DON'T CRY. THEY WHIMPER WHEN THEY'RE IN PAIN, BUT THAT'S ALL. THEY TOUGHEN UP VERY EARLY.

EACH DAY BRINGS ITS SHARE OF WAR WOUNDED, BUT A GOOD PART OF THE WORK REMAINS DAY-TO-DAY HEALTH CARE— ILLNESSES, BIRTHS, HOUSEHOLD ACCIDENTS.

ONE DAY I FIND ROBERT AND RÉGIS ABSORBED IN LOOKING AT AN OBJECT THAT I HARDLY RECOGNIZE BECAUSE ITS PRESENCE SEEMS SO INCONGRUOUS.

WHAT ARE YOU LOOKING AT?

WHAT DOES IT LOOK LIKE? AN X-RAY.

BUT WHERE DID IT COME FROM?

FROM FEYZABAD. IT'S THE RUSSIANS THAT SENT IT TO US.

I CAN'T BELIEVE MY EARS.

YOU'RE IN TOUCH WITH THE RUSSIANS?

IT CAN HAPPEN.

WHEN WE GET SOMEONE WHO NEEDS AN X-RAY, OR SOME TREATMENT WE CAN'T PROVIDE, WE SEND HIM TO THE FEYZABAD HOSPITAL, ON A DONKEY, ACCOMPANIED BY AN OLD MAN. I WRITE A LETTER IN ENGLISH FOR THE RUSSIAN DOCTOR: "DEAR COLLEAGUE, I AM SENDING YOU THIS PATIENT," AND SO ON.

IN FEYZABAD, THEY DO THE X-RAY AND THE OLD MAN BRINGS IT BACK TO ME, OFTEN WITH A RESPONSE FROM THE RUSSIAN DOCTOR. HERE, HAVE A LOOK.

UNBELIEVABLE.

BUT DON'T YOU RISK GETTING DISCOVERED?

INCH' ALLAH! UP TO NOW WE HAVEN'T HAD ANY PROBLEMS!

LATER ON.

YOU KNOW, WAR IS ALWAYS MORE COMPLICATED THAN WE THINK. YOU MIGHT GO SEE A COMMANDER LIKE BASSIR AND FIND HIM IN THE MIDDLE OF A TALK WITH TEN RUSSIAN OFFICERS, DRINKING CUPS OF CHORCHOY.

REALLY?

IT'S NOT THAT HE'S SELLING OUT TO THE ENEMY, IT'S NOT THE "PEACE OF THE BRAVE," IT'S A KIND OF SPORADIC NEGOTIATION— "YOU LET MY CONVOY GO THROUGH, OR I'LL BOMB YOUR ROAD."

SO IN FACT, IT'S NOT ALL-OUT WAR ALL THE TIME.

THAT'S IT. THERE ARE TIMES WHEN NOBODY TALKS TO ANYBODY ELSE, GUNS ARE BLAZING ALL OVER THE PLACE, THEN IT COOLS DOWN AND THEY START DEALING WITH EACH OTHER AGAIN: "C'MON, DON'T BE A PAIN, LET ME GO THROUGH THIS TIME."

I IMAGINE IT'S LIKE THAT IN ALL WARS.

IT'S A BIT LIKE THE FRENCH NATIONAL ASSEMBLY. WE GET THE IMPRESSION THEY'RE ALWAYS AT EACH OTHER'S THROATS, BUT I'M SURE AT THE BREAK YOU'LL HAVE A COMMUNIST GOING FOR A DRINK WITH A CONSERVATIVE AND THEY'LL HAVE PLENTY TO TALK ABOUT.

YEAH, OF COURSE.

AND EARLIER YOU SAID YOU'D SEND A PATIENT TO FEYZABAD WITH AN OLD MAN. WHY AN OLD MAN?

AH, BECAUSE THOSE BABAS ARE REALLY CONVENIENT.

FIRST OF ALL, THEY HAVE INEXHAUSTIBLE STAMINA. SECOND, THE GOVERNMENT ARMY NO LONGER CONSCRIPTS THEM. AND THIRD, NOBODY SUSPECTS THEM OF BEING PART OF THE RESISTANCE. THEY'RE THE ONES WE SEND TO RUN ALL THE ERRANDS IN TOWN.

YOU HAND OVER THE SHOPPING LIST AND THE MONEY TO THE VILLAGE OLD-TIMERS, THEY ENTER FEYZABAD UNDER THE RUSSIANS' NOSES, AND TWO DAYS LATER THEY COME BACK WITH THE SUGAR, CAKES, TEA, AND CANDY.

WE EVEN PACK THEM FULL OF SECRET MESSAGES. YOU KNOW HOW THEY AVOID DETECTION DURING BODY SEARCHES?

UM... NO.

THE MESSAGES ARE WRITTEN ON CLOTH AND SEWN INSIDE THE CLOTHING. UNLIKE PAPER, WHICH CRINKLES, YOU CAN'T DETECT CLOTH IN A PAT-DOWN SEARCH.

PRETTY SMART.

THIS IS ONE SUCH SECRET MESSAGE. BEING ABLE TO READ IT WOULDN'T DO ME MUCH GOOD; IT'S CODED. MAHMAD TRANSLATED IT FOR ME AND ALL IT TALKS ABOUT IS CROPS AND IRRIGATION.

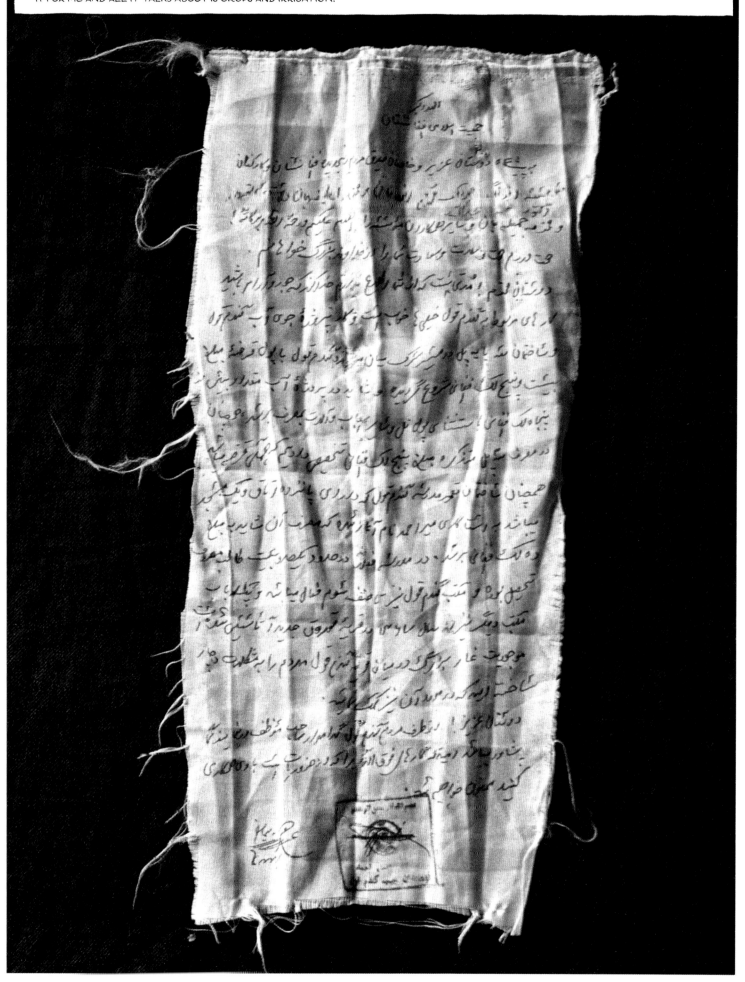

A HIKE MORE THAN THREE HOURS LONG BRINGS US—JULIETTE, RÉGIS, ME, AND A FEW LOCALS—TO PALANDARA.

THAT'S THE FUTURE HOSPITAL WHERE THE LOCAL TEAMS WE'RE CURRENTLY TRAINING WILL WORK, AND WHERE THE NEXT MSF MISSIONS WILL JOIN THEM.

ON THE WAY BACK WE STOP FOR A MOMENT. RÉGIS AND I ARE SITTING SIDE BY SIDE, CHATTING. WE SEE THIS ROCK IN FRONT OF US.

YOU KNOW, THAT ROCK, THERE...

YEAH?

I'VE BEEN WATCHING IT FOR A WHILE.

ME TOO.

DOESN'T IT REMIND YOU OF SOMETHING?

AH, YES.

WHAT?

A SUCHARD ROCHER.

THAT'S WILD! WE HAD EXACTLY THE SAME THOUGHT AT THE SAME TIME!

IT'S ALL THERE: THE MILK CHOCOLATE, THE HAZELNUT CHIPS... WE SHOULD OPEN IT UP TO SEE IF THE PRALINE'S INSIDE.

YOU KNOW WHAT? IF IT WERE A REAL ONE, THAT SIZE, I'D EAT IT IN NO TIME.

IT'S TRUE THAT THAT'S KIND OF MISSING AROUND HERE.

WE EXPOUND FOR HOURS ON OUR SUCHARD CHOCOLATE ROCHER AND HAVE A GOOD LAUGH.

THE NEXT DAY, THE MUJ'
BRING IN AMRULLAH ON A
STRETCHER.
AMRULLAH, 16, HAD THE
LOWER PART OF HIS FACE
TORN OFF BY SHRAPNEL
FROM AN ARTILLERY SHELL.

HE'S IN A HALF-COMA
AND IS BETTER OFF THAT
WAY. HIS WOUND IS
HORRIFYING. EVERYONE
IS PETRIFIED AT THE
SIGHT OF IT, EXCEPT
THE DOCTORS, WHO
IMMEDIATELY START
TREATING HIM.

AMRULLAH IS
TRANSFERRED FROM
THE STRETCHER TO THE
"OPERATING ROOM," ON
THE TERRACE.

DO THE DOCTORS BELIEVE
THAT THEY CAN REPAIR
SUCH A DISASTER? THEY
CERTAINLY INSPIRE THAT
BELIEF IN US. AGAINST ALL
ODDS, DESPITE THE DUST,
THE LACK OF SPACE, THE
BARREN CONDITIONS, WE
PLACE OUR TRUST IN THEM.

119

ILFORD
HP5
SAFETY
FILM

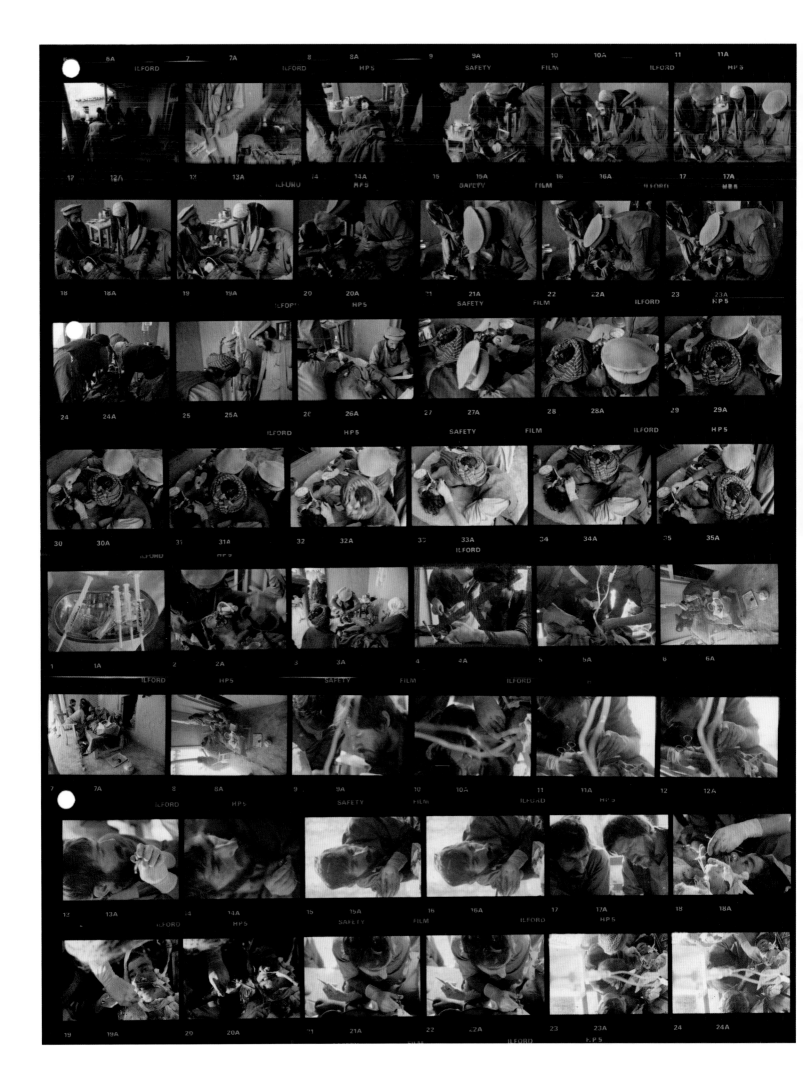

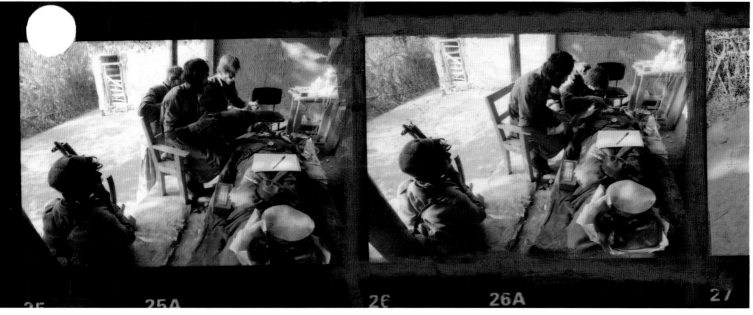

THE OPERATION CONTINUES LATE INTO THE NIGHT. I PHOTOGRAPH IT AT LENGTH, DOING MY BEST TO MAKE MY PRESENCE INCONSPICUOUS. WITHOUT THE DOCTORS' INTERVENTION, AMRULLAH MIGHT HAVE BEEN DEAD BY NOW. BUT HE ISN'T. HE IS RESTING.

I GO TO DO THE SAME. OUR ROOM SEEMS LARGER THAN USUAL, BECAUSE RÉGIS AND EVELYNE ARE WATCHING OVER AMRULLAH. EVERY DAY, I FEEL LIKE TELLING THEM HOW MUCH I ADMIRE THEM. I KNEW THEY'D JUST LAUGH AT ME FOR SAYING IT, BUT WHAT THEY'RE DOING IS PRETTY DAMN IMPRESSIVE.

SO, HAVING MADE SURE EVERYONE IS ASLEEP AND NOBODY CAN HEAR ME, I SAY OUT LOUD:

BRAVO.

AND FALL ASLEEP.

WHEN I LOOK UP FROM
THE OPERATING TABLE,
THIS IS WHAT I SEE.

THIS MAGNIFICENT AND
UNCHANGING LANDSCAPE
DOESN'T GIVE A DAMN
ABOUT WAR.

WHEN I LOOK UP FROM
THE OPERATING TABLE,
THIS IS WHAT I SEE.

THIS MAGNIFICENT AND
UNCHANGING LANDSCAPE
DOESN'T GIVE A DAMN
ABOUT WAR.

BACK TO WORK. THIS MAN CAME TO BRING US HIS LEFT FOOT.

HE WAS OPERATED ON IN THE LAST MISSION, BUT HE REFUSED TO HAVE HIS FOOT AMPUTATED. SO, PREDICTABLY ENOUGH, IT ROTTED THROUGH SO BADLY THAT HE TORE IT OFF HIMSELF YESTERDAY.

AND NOW HE'S BACK, SAYING, "CAN'T YOU PUT IT BACK FOR ME?"

I CAN'T BELIEVE IT.

RÉGIS GIVES AN UMPTEENTH PRACTICAL SEMINAR, WITH THE INDISPENSABLE MAHMAD TRANSLATING. IN SUCH CIRCUMSTANCES, YOU HAVE TO MAKE SURE YOU'RE UNDERSTOOD PERFECTLY.

THEN HE ANESTHETIZES HIS PATIENT AND JOHN PERFORMS AN AMPUTATION HIGHER UP, SO HE CAN CLEAN OUT THE WOUND.

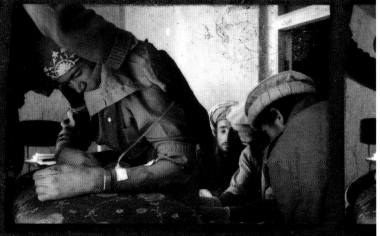

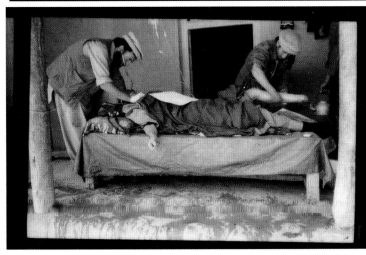

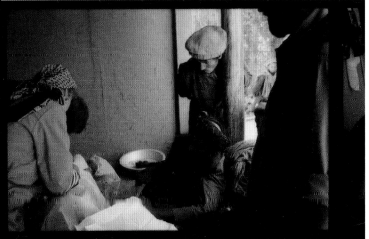

RÉGIS AND I LIKE TO TALK ABOUT OUR JOBS AND WE'RE CURIOUS ABOUT ONE ANOTHER. HE QUIZZES ME ABOUT PHOTOGRAPHY, AND I FIRE QUESTIONS ABOUT MEDICINE AT HIM.

YOU ANESTHETIZED ONLY THE LOWER BODY ON THAT GUY WITH THE ROTTED FOOT?

YES, I DID WHAT'S CALLED A SPINAL ANESTHESIA.

IT INVOLVES INSERTING A SMALL NEEDLE BETWEEN TWO LUMBAR VERTEBRAE TO INJECT THE ANESTHETIC INTO THE NERVE ROOTS OF THE SPINAL CORD. THAT WAY WE GET A SENSORY BLOCK, MEANING THAT WE NEUTRALIZE THE PAIN.

YOU SAW HOW WE SAT THE GUY DOWN AND GOT HIM TO BEND HIS BACK WITH HIS CHIN TO HIS CHEST? THAT WAY THE SPINE RELAXES, THE INTERVERTEBRAL SPACE OPENS AND WE CAN DO THE INJECTION.

ISN'T THAT THE SHOT THEY GIVE TO WOMEN DURING LABOR?

NO, FOR WOMEN IN LABOR WE USE EPIDURAL ANALGESIA. SAME PRINCIPLE, BUT MORE SOPHISTICATED. IT ALLOWS YOU TO PLACE A CATHETER, REINJECT ANESTHETIC DURING THE COURSE OF THE PROCEDURE, AND SO ON. WE CAN'T DO THAT HERE BECAUSE WE DON'T HAVE THE HIGHLY SANITARY CONDITIONS THAT IT REQUIRES.

THAT'S WHY I FIND WHAT YOU GUYS ARE DOING MIND-BOGGLING. I'VE SEEN OPERATING ROOMS BEFORE, IN FRANCE, WITH STATE-OF-THE-ART EQUIPMENT, WHOLE TEAMS OF PEOPLE, AN ULTRA-CLEAN ENVIRONMENT, THE WORKS. AND SEEING YOU HERE, IT'S SUCH A DIFFERENT WORLD!

IT'S THE SAME WORLD, THOUGH.

THE BASIS OF MEDICINE, WHETHER HERE OR IN FRANCE, IS ALWAYS THE SAME: IT'S CLINICAL OBSERVATION, THE STUDY OF SYMPTOMS. IT'S THE SCIENCE OF READING SIGNS. AND YOU WON'T FIND A BETTER SCHOOL FOR THAT THAN PRACTICING MEDICINE IN A SANITARY WASTELAND, LIKE WHAT WE DO HERE.

OPERATING IS NOT THAT COMPLICATED, YOU KNOW? AFGHAN PEASANTS CAN LEARN THAT. WHAT'S COMPLICATED IS KNOWING WHAT TO OPERATE ON, IT'S DIAGNOSIS.

I REALLY LIKE TECHNOLOGY. THANK GOD FOR CT SCANS AND SUPPLEMENTARY TESTS. BUT WHEN YOU DON'T HAVE THEM, YOU HAVE TO LEARN TO DO WITHOUT. AND THEN YOU RE-LEARN HOW TO PAY ATTENTION, HOW TO LISTEN TO A BODY, HOW TO INTERPRET A COLD SWEAT OR A TOENAIL THAT'S TURNING BLUE. YOU RE-LEARN THE ESSENCE OF THE JOB.

AT THE HOSPITAL OF SAINTE-FOY-LA-GRANDE, WHERE I USED TO WORK, I CAME INTO CONTACT WITH SOME EXCELLENT DOCTORS WHO HELPED PREPARE ME FOR THIS. JO DUBICQ WAS ONE OF THEM. HE WAS ONE OF THOSE DOCTORS WHO DON'T LET THEIR TEAM CARVE OUT A COMFORTABLE NICHE FOR THEMSELVES. HE CHALLENGED PEOPLE'S SKILLS, THEIR INTELLIGENCE, THEIR CURIOSITY.

I ALSO WORKED WITH A TRUE GENERAL SURGEON, SOMETHING THAT'S HARDER AND HARDER TO FIND NOWADAYS. HIS NAME WAS GUY LASSALLE. WELL, THIS GUY LASSALLE MADE ME PARTICIPATE IN WHAT HE WAS DOING, HE EXPLAINED THINGS TO ME, ADVISED ME. HE'S SOMEONE WHO'D DO AN AMAZING JOB HERE. YOU HAVE NO IDEA HOW MANY TIMES A DAY I THINK ABOUT HIM AS I'M CARRYING OUT A PROCEDURE.

I CAN ALSO TELL YOU ABOUT A LEADING AUTHORITY IN HIS FIELD, PROFESSOR CHEVAIS, WHO WAS A PIONEER OF EMERGENCY MEDICINE IN BORDEAUX. HE'S DEAD NOW, UNFORTUNATELY.

SHORTLY BEFORE HIS DEATH, HE WAS VERY ILL, BUT HE'D STILL COME TO THE HOSPITAL UNOFFICIALLY, PUT ON HIS SCRUBS, AND DO THE ROUNDS OF PATIENTS.

ONE DAY, I WAS LOOKING AFTER MY PATIENTS, AND WE'D JUST HAD WHAT WE CALL THE GRAND MASS—KNOW WHAT THAT IS?

NO.

IT'S WHEN THE HEAD DOCTOR AND HIS RESIDENTS DO THE ROUNDS AND THE BIG BOSS COMMENTS ON EACH PATIENT.

SO, ANYWAY, THEY'D JUST COME THROUGH, AND I SAW CHEVAIS COME INTO THE ROOM. HE LEANED OVER ONE PATIENT AND CALLED ME OVER. HE ASKED ME, "DID THEY SAY SOMETHING ABOUT THIS PATIENT'S FEVER?" I ANSWERED, "NO." THE GUY HAD A FEVER OF ABOUT 101.3°F.

SO CHEVAIS SAID TO ME, "WATCH AND LISTEN." HE REMOVED THE PATIENT'S SHEET—WE WERE ALONE WITH HIM—AND SAID, "FIRST, YOU GET AN OVERVIEW OF THE PATIENT. NEXT, WE EXAMINE HIM FROM HEAD TO TOE."

AND THAT'S WHAT HE DID. IN A FEW MINUTES OF OBSERVATION, HE FOUND TEN POSSIBLE CAUSES FOR THE FEVER: A BLOCKAGE IN A PROBE, A BADLY PLACED CATHETER CAUSING AN INFLAMMATION, ETC.

HE SPENT AN HOUR WITH ME EXPLAINING ALL THAT. CAN YOU BELIEVE IT? IT'S ENGRAVED IN MY MEMORY.

YOU KNOW, I ONLY HAVE ONE MEDICAL TEXTBOOK WITH ME HERE. I NEVER OPEN IT, BECAUSE I KNOW IT BY HEART, BUT I CARRY IT AROUND EVERYWHERE—IT'S THE NOTEBOOK I FILLED WHILE STUDYING WITH THOSE PEOPLE.

WHAT ABOUT THE GROUP YOU GUYS HAVE RIGHT NOW? IT SEEMS PRETTY GOOD.

YES, IT'S EXCEPTIONAL. WE OWE IT TO JULIETTE. SHE GATHERED US TOGETHER AND BROUGHT US HERE.

YOU'VE HEARD THE EXPRESSION, "I'D GO TO THE ENDS OF THE WORLD WITH THEM"? WELL, HERE WE ARE. WE'RE ALL DOING THINGS THAT WE WEREN'T TRAINED FOR. SOONER OR LATER WE ALL HAVE TO SHOULDER SOME HEAVY RESPONSIBILITIES. THAT'S WHAT BINDS US TOGETHER.

AND THE TRAINING YOU'RE GIVING THE AFGHANS, IT WORKS?

YES, IT WORKS. THEY HAVE TO BE ABLE TO MANAGE WHEN WE'RE NOT HERE, AND SOME OF THEM MANAGE VERY WELL.

WE DON'T TEACH THEM HOW TO DO COMPLEX OPERATIONS, MIND YOU. WE TEACH THEM, AS MUCH AS POSSIBLE, TO SAVE LIVES WITH THE RESOURCES THEY HAVE.

AND WHAT HAPPENS IF YOU'RE THE ONES WHO HAVE A PROBLEM?

TWO POSSIBILITIES: IF IT'S SOMETHING LIKE HAY FEVER, WE'LL HANDLE IT OURSELVES; IF IT'S SOMETHING SERIOUS, IT'S AGREED WITH THE MUJ' THAT THEY'LL HAND US OVER TO THE RUSSIANS.

THE DAYS PASS AND ALONG COME THE WOUNDED...

FOLLOWED BY MORE WOUNDED, AND MORE, AND STILL MORE WOUNDED.

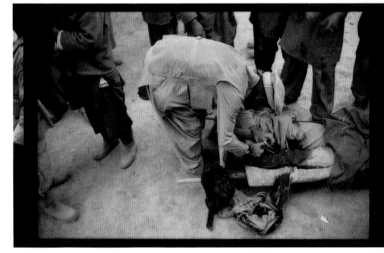

I WATCH ROBERT TREAT A MAN WITH A BULLET WOUND.

THAT MAN HAS WHAT YOU'D USUALLY REFER TO AS A "MINOR WOUND." IT'S USEFUL TO WITNESS WHAT A PERSON WITH A MINOR WOUND HAS TO GO THROUGH.

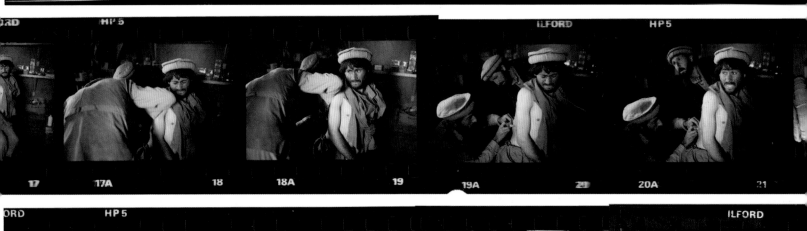

THAT'S A SCENE I'VE SEEN
A HUNDRED TIMES AT
THE MOVIES: THE HERO
TAKES A SWIG OF WHISKY,
BITES DOWN ON A PIECE
OF WOOD, AND AAARGH!
THEY EXTRACT THE
BULLET WITH PLIERS IN
ONE SHARP TUG, THEN
THE GUY WIPES THE
SWEAT FROM HIS BROW
AND IS FINE. THE TRUTH
IS THAT THE WHOLE
THING IS EXCRUCIATINGLY
PAINFUL.

ON THE DAWN OF SEPTEMBER 23RD, WE HEAR A MASSIVE BOMBING CLOSE BY.

SIX HOURS LATER, WE ENTER PÜSTÜK, GUIDED BY THE EMISSARIES WHO CAME TO GET US. THE WOUNDED HAVE BEEN SEPARATED FROM THE DEAD AND COLLECTED INTO A PART OF THE VILLAGE THAT HAS BEEN SPARED BY THE BOMBS.

THIS LITTLE GIRL HAD HER HAND BURNED.

JOHN FILLS A TEAPOT WITH AN ANTISEPTIC SOLUTION AND THE CHILD DIPS HER HAND IN IT. THEN SHE IS TREATED.

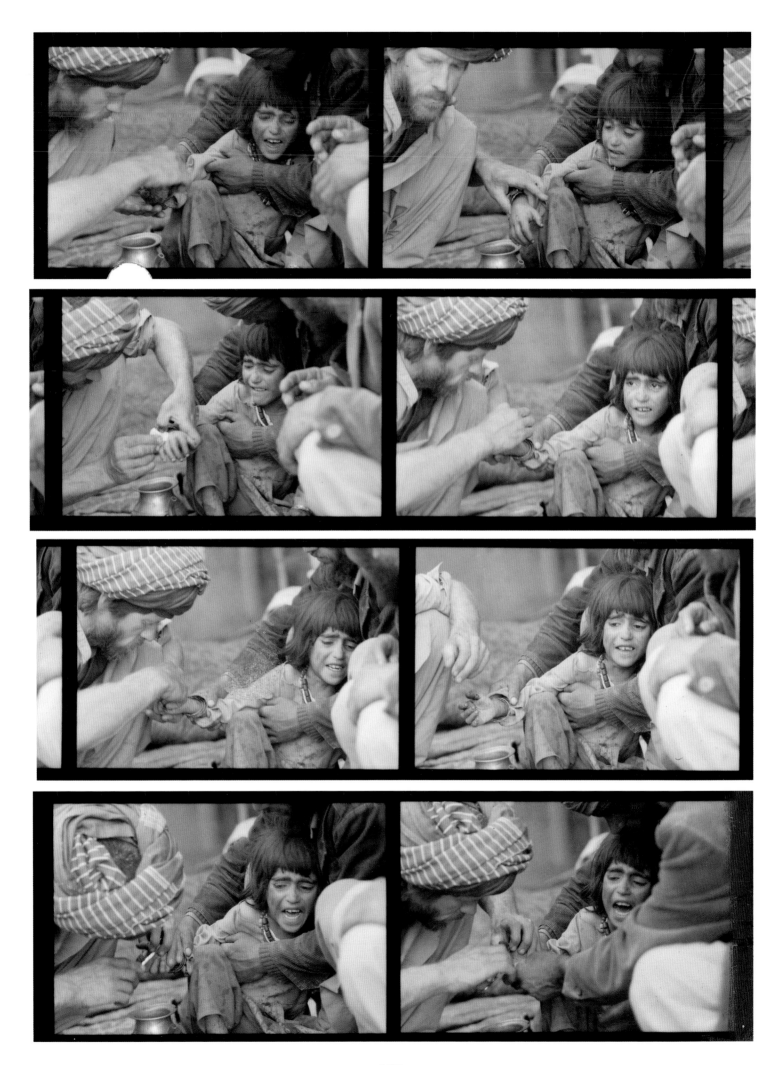

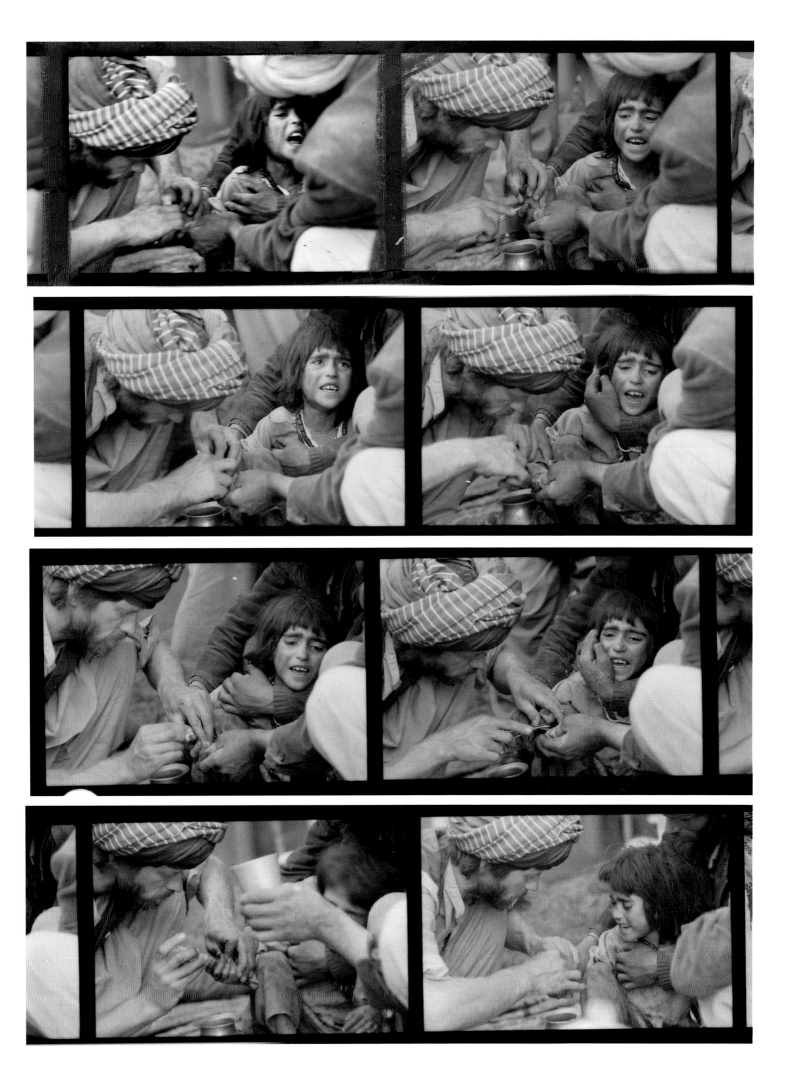

OTHER WOUNDED PEOPLE HAVE BEEN LAID DOWN IN A LARGE, DARK ROOM WITH ONE SKYLIGHT. IT'S THE VILLAGE BAKERY. IT'S FULL OF PEOPLE AND WHISPERS. JOHN, JULIETTE, AND I MAKE OUR WAY THROUGH.

SEVERAL WOMEN ARE THERE, SOME OF THEM WITH THEIR FACES UNCOVERED.

ASK THEM IF I CAN TAKE PICTURES.

I'M ALLOWED TO DO SO.

IN A CORNER, A WOMAN WITH A WHITE HEADSCARF IS WATCHING OVER TWO OF HER CHILDREN, A TEENAGE GIRL AND A BABY, BOTH BLOODIED. THE LITTLE BOY IS MAYBE TWO OR THREE. HE HARDLY MOVES BUT FROM TIME TO TIME LETS OUT A LITTLE WAIL OF "AOH."

"AOH."

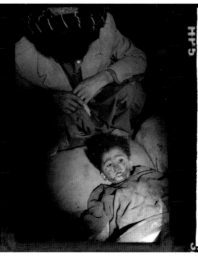

"AOH."

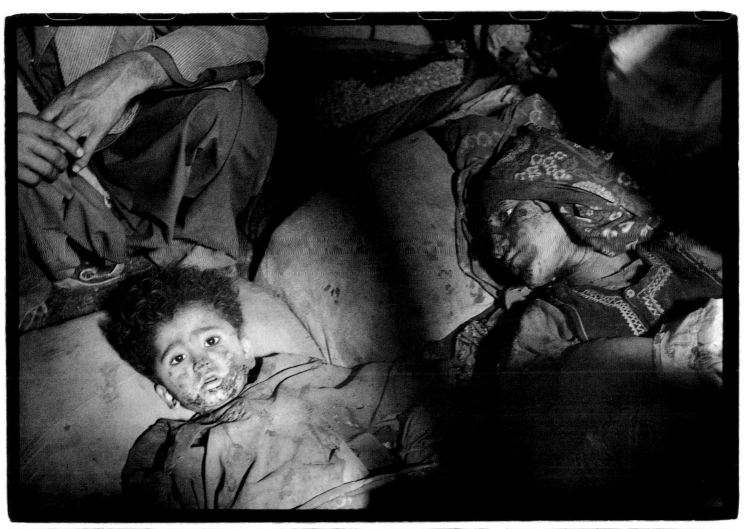

I PUT IN A NEW ROLL OF FILM.

JOHN COMES OUT OF THE BAKERY, IN STEP WITH A VILLAGER.

WHAT DOES HE WANT?

HE WANTS ME TO SEE HIS DAUGHTER. SHE HASN'T GOTTEN UP SINCE THE BOMBING.

INVITED BY THE FATHER, JOHN AND I ENTER A HOUSE.

IT'S TOO DARK TO TAKE PICTURES. IN ANY CASE, I DON'T FEEL LIKE IT. I SIT DOWN ON THE FLOOR.

THE LITTLE GIRL IS LYING IN THE CENTER OF THE ROOM. JOHN WHISPERS SOME SOOTHING WORDS AND STARTS EXAMINING HER.

THERE'S NO APPARENT WOUND. NO BLOOD, NO TEARS. JOHN HANDLES HER CAREFULLY.

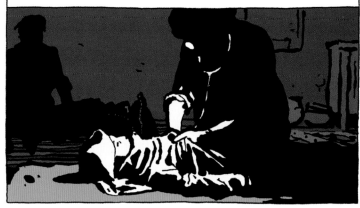

HE TRIES TO PICK HER UP.

SHE FALLS.

HE TRIES AGAIN.

SHE FALLS AGAIN.

STILL TALKING TO HER, HE CAREFULLY SHIFTS HER ONTO HER BELLY.

HE CAREFULLY PUSHES ASIDE HER CLOTHING AND SCRUTINIZES HER BACK.

COME AND SEE.

HERE.

THAT LITTLE DOT, THERE?

IT'S NOT A DOT, IT'S A HOLE.

A FRAGMENT OF SHRAPNEL GOT IN THERE AND CUT THE SPINAL CORD.

THAT MEANS SHE'LL NEVER WALK AGAIN.

AGHAST, I STARE AT THAT TINY DOT. THE PROJECTILE MUST HAVE BEEN NO BIGGER THAN A GRAIN OF RICE.

I THROW MYSELF BACK AND SIT DOWN WHERE I'D BEEN BEFORE.

I CRY SILENTLY, TO AVOID DISTURBING JOHN.

THEN I WALK OUT AGAIN.

OUTSIDE, I HEAR SOMEONE CALLING ME.

AHMADJAN!
AHMADJAN!

A PROCESSION IS JUST LEAVING THE BAKERY. THE MOTHER, THE WOMAN WITH THE WHITE HEADSCARF, IS CARRYING HER BABY IN HER ARMS. SHE IS THE ONE SHOUTING.

AHMADJAN!

HE DIED?

YES.

AHMADJAN. THAT WAS THE LITTLE BOY'S NAME.

HE MUST'VE HAD INTERNAL BLEEDING.

WHAT DID HIS CRIES MEAN? "AOH! AOH!"

THAT HE WAS THIRSTY.

JULIETTE FILMED THE CHILD'S DEATH.

THE MOTHER SAID TO ME, "FILM IT, JAMILA. PEOPLE HAVE TO KNOW."

THAT SENTENCE JOLTS ME OUT OF THE STATE I'VE BEEN IN FOR THE PAST HALF-HOUR, UNABLE TO TAKE PICTURES.

I HURRY BACK UP TO THE HOUSE OF THE LITTLE PARALYZED GIRL, TO RECORD HER BEING TAKEN TOWARD OUR CLINIC.

136

THEN ON HORSEBACK, ON A DONKEY'S BACK, ON A MAN'S BACK, OR CARRIED ON STRETCHERS, THE WOUNDED START OUT ON THE LONG AND ARDUOUS ROAD UPHILL TO ZARAGANDARA.

WE GET BACK. THE TEAM
DEALS WITH THE INFLUX
OF WOUNDED. WHILE
THE MOST SERIOUSLY
INJURED ARE TREATED
BEHIND BLANKETS, THE
OTHERS WAIT.

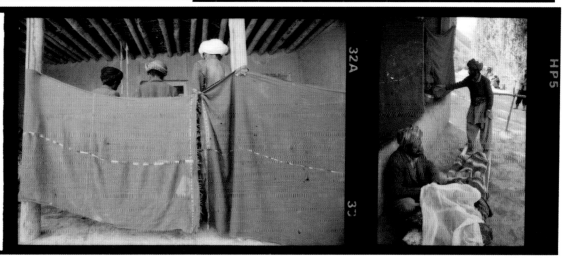

THE BROTHER OF A GUY WITH A WOUNDED KNEE RAISES A RUCKUS. HE DEMANDS THAT THE LOCAL BONESETTER TAKE CARE OF HIS BROTHER. RÉGIS IS ABSOLUTELY OPPOSED TO IT.

THAT'S COMPLETELY MORONIC!

THIS GUY DOESN'T HAVE A BONE OUT OF JOINT, HE HAS AN OPEN WOUND. IF HE TRIES TO RE-SET THE KNEE HE'S GOING TO DESTROY IT!

THE BONESETTER ARRIVES. RÉGIS BARS HIS WAY.

THE BROTHER INSISTS. THINGS TURN NASTY.

IN THE END RÉGIS IS FORCED TO LET THE BONESETTER GO OVER TO THE PATIENT.

AND IN NO TIME FLAT, THE BONESETTER HAS CAUSED IRREPARABLE DAMAGE.

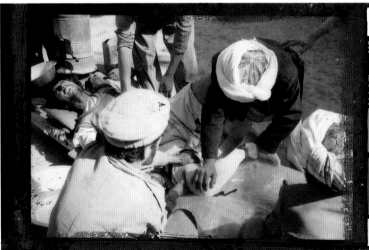

THE POOR GUY'S KNEE HAS LITERALLY EXPLODED.

PERFECT! I HOPE YOU'RE PROUD OF YOURSELVES!

THERE ARE SOME THINGS THEY KNOW HOW TO DO AND OTHERS NOT AT ALL. I HAVE THE SAME KIND OF FIGHTS WITH THE LOCAL MIDWIVES, THE MATRONS. THEY MAKE HORRIFIC BLUNDERS SOMETIMES.

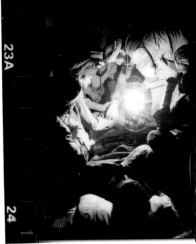

NIGHT HAS LONG SINCE FALLEN, BUT THE TREATMENTS CONTINUE.

JOHN, WHO HASN'T STOPPED BENDING OVER PATIENTS, HAS A TERRIBLY SORE BACK.

AS IF THERE HADN'T BEEN ENOUGH, ONE MORE PATIENT IS BROUGHT TO US. UNCHARACTERISTICALLY, THE MUJ' BRINGING HIM ARE GUFFAWING.

WHAT'S SO FUNNY IS THAT THE GUY HAS A BULLET IN THE ASS. AND IF HE CAUGHT A BULLET IN THE ASS, THAT MEANS HE WAS TURNING HIS BACK TO THE ENEMY, THE COWARD! THAT CRACKS UP THE AFGHANS.

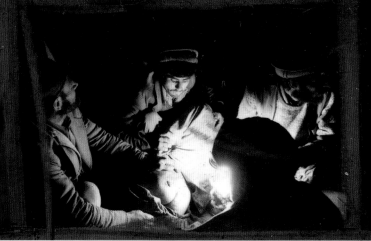

THE WOUND IS VERY DEEP. ROBERT INSERTS GAUZE WICKS TO PROBE AND DISINFECT IT. A MORE DETAILED EXAMINATION WILL HAVE TO WAIT UNTIL A SHORT WHILE LATER, WHEN THERE'LL BE DAYLIGHT AND WE'LL HAVE SLEPT A BIT.

SLEEPING A BIT. THAT'S WHAT'S IN STORE FOR RÉGIS, WHOSE ALARM RINGS EVERY TWO HOURS SO THAT HE CAN CHECK UP ON AMRULLAH AND THE OTHER WOUNDED, TREAT THEM, FEED THEM, AND WATCH OVER THEM.

IN THE MORNING, THE MUJ' WITH THE PIERCED POSTERIOR IS THOROUGHLY EXAMINED. IT TURNS OUT THAT THE HOLE IN HIS BUTTOCK WAS AN EXIT WOUND. THE BULLET ENTERED THROUGH HIS GROIN—SO, FROM THE FRONT—WITHOUT TOUCHING ANY VITAL ORGAN. HE WAS SLANDERED AND IS NOW REDEEMED.

THE DAY'S EMERGENCIES ADD TO THOSE OF PREVIOUS DAYS. THE COURTYARD AND THE MOSQUE ARE CONSTANTLY FULL.

AND THE OLDER CUSTOMERS AREN'T FORGOTTEN. THE STITCHES HAVE TO COME OFF THE EYELID OF THE MAN WHOSE EYE HAS BEEN ENUCLEATED; THE SCAR ON THE MUJ' WITH THE NICKED TEMPLE NEEDS TO BE CHECKED; AND SO ON AND ON. IT'S ENDLESS.

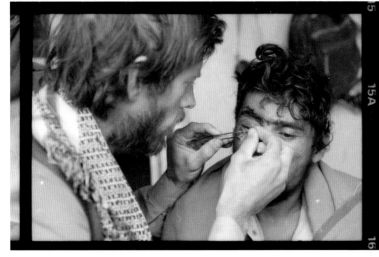

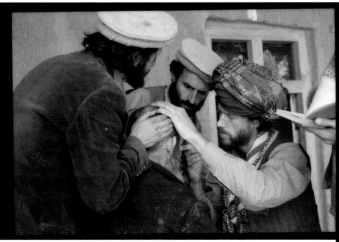

THE PEOPLE'S GRATITUDE IS TOUCHING. THEY ARE CONSTANTLY SEEING TO THE WELL-BEING AND COMPENSATION OF THE TEAM. WE ARE GIVEN WALNUTS, NECKLACES OF ALMONDS AND PISTACHIOS, DRIED APPLES AND APRICOTS, WATERMELONS, MELONS, EMBROIDERED HANDKERCHIEFS.

AT MY LAST MISSION HERE, I WAS EVEN OFFERED A BIG BRICK OF OPIUM!

BESIDES THE BREAKFAST CHORCHOY, WHICH IS SERVED TO US AT HOME EVERY MORNING, WE ARE REGULARLY INVITED BY ONE VILLAGER OR ANOTHER TO SHARE IN A MEAL. THIS OLD GENTLEMAN, FOR EXAMPLE, HAS US OVER FOR LUNCH.

JULIETTE IS INVITED TO SPEND THE NIGHT IN A NEIGHBORING VILLAGE, WITH A YOUNG COUPLE SHE MET HERE FOUR YEARS EARLIER. WHEN SHE RETURNS, SHE TELLS ME ABOUT IT.

THEY REALLY MARRIED FOR LOVE.

IT'S THE WOMAN WHO CHOSE THE MAN. ALL THE GUYS IN THE VILLAGE WERE PLAYING A BIG BUZKASHI GAME. THE WOMEN WERE WATCHING FROM THE ROOFTOPS. FOR HER, IT WAS LOVE AT FIRST SIGHT.

SHE MANAGED TO LET HIM KNOW. SO HE STARTED LOOKING OUT FOR HER WHEN SHE'D GO DOWN TO THE RIVER. SHE'S REALLY THE ONE WHO DID THE SEDUCING.

HOW IS THAT DONE AROUND HERE?

WELL, YOU WIGGLE A BIT, YOU SHOW YOUR ANKLES, YOU MOVE YOUR SHAWLS ASIDE—PRETENDING THAT IT'S TO AVOID GETTING THEM WET, BUT CASTING A FEW GLANCES AT THE SAME TIME. THAT KIND OF THING.

I SEE. THAT'S GOOD.

I MET THEM SHORTLY AFTERWARDS, WHEN THEY WERE NEWLYWEDS. IT WAS A JOY TO SHARE THEIR HOUSE, BECAUSE THEY WERE REALLY IN LOVE. ALL DAY LONG, HE'D KISS HER IN THE NECK, HE'D CUDDLE HER IN CORNERS, HE'D TICKLE HER WHILE SHE WAS MAKING BREAD. THEY LAUGHED ALL THE TIME.

AND NOW, I SHOW UP FOUR YEARS LATER AND WHAT DO I SEE? A SECOND WIFE!

FOR A COUPLE THAT WAS SO CLOSE AND SHARED SO MUCH, THAT SURPRISED ME. I ASKED HER, "HOW COME YOUR HUSBAND TOOK A SECOND WIFE?" DO YOU KNOW WHAT SHE ANSWERED?

NO.

SHE SAID: "I'M THE ONE WHO FOUND HER FOR HIM."

"YOU SEE, MY HUSBAND'S A RICH MAN, HE HAS A LOT OF GOATS AND HE'S AWAY A LOT WHEN THEY TAKE THE ANIMALS TO THE HIGH PASTURES—SO I REALLY NEEDED SOMEONE ELSE."

HAHAHA!

THAT'S FUNNY, BECAUSE IT'S NOT AT ALL THE IDEA WE GET BACK HOME CONCERNING MARRIED LIFE IN AFGHANISTAN.

BUT THOSE IDEAS WE GET ARE ALL WRONG!

ALL WE EVER SEE IS THE SAME POOR HELPLESS WOMAN UNDER HER CHADRI.

HONESTLY, HAVE YOU SEEN A LOT OF CHADRI SINCE WE GOT HERE? BESIDES THE ONES WE PUT ON TO CROSS THE BORDER?

NO, NOT MANY.

FIRST OF ALL, THE CHADRI IS ESSENTIALLY AN URBAN PHE-NOMENON. IN A SMALL VILLAGE, EVERYONE'S RELATED, SO YOU DON'T NEED TO COVER YOURSELF. PLUS A CHADRI'S EXPENSIVE. EVEN IF SHE WANTED ONE, A PEASANT WOMAN COULDN'T AFFORD IT.

THEN YOU HAVE TO UNDERSTAND THAT THE CHADRI IS SOMETHING PRETTY RECENT. IT'S ONLY ABOUT A CENTURY OLD. BEFORE THAT, A LOT OF WOMEN IN THE CITIES WOULD NEVER SET FOOT OUTSIDE THEIR HOUSE, NOT IN A LIFETIME.

SERIOUSLY?

YEAH, SERIOUSLY. IN A BIG CITY, A WOMAN IS BOUND TO BUMP INTO STRANGERS. THAT'S WHY THE INTRODUCTION OF THE CHADRI GAVE THEM GREATER AUTONOMY AND FREEDOM. AT LAST THEY WERE ABLE TO LEAVE THEIR HOMES.

IN ANY CASE, PEOPLE MAKE IT INTO AN EXAGGERATED AND IDIOTIC SYMBOL. THE REAL PRIORITIES FOR WOMEN ARE ACCESS TO HEALTH CARE, TO EDUCATION, TO WORK, AND TO THE LEGAL SYSTEM. NOT CLOTHES.

LET ME TELL YOU A FUNNY STORY. WHEN I WAS A TEENAGER IN KABUL, MY BEST FRIEND WAS AN AFGHAN GIRL FROM AN ARISTOCRATIC FAMILY THAT WAS REALLY WESTERNIZED. NO WAY WOULD YOU FIND A *CHADRI* IN THEIR HOME.

BUT SHE'D BOUGHT A *CHADRI* HERSELF SO SHE COULD GO MEET HER BOYFRIEND WITHOUT ANYONE FINDING OUT.

AT THE MOMENT, IT'S A REAL TOOL OF RESISTANCE. A LOT OF WOMEN ARE CARRYING WEAPONS UNDER THEIR *CHADRI*. IN THE BIG CITIES, WOMEN ARE TAKING PART IN THE RESISTANCE, ACTIVELY AND FIERCELY.

WE DON'T HEAR ABOUT ALL THAT.

TO KNOW THINGS ABOUT AFGHAN WOMEN, YOU HAVE TO GO INTO THEIR HOUSES. THINGS ARE MUCH LESS FORMAL INSIDE THE HOUSES THAN OUTSIDE THEM.

I'M LUCKY TO BE ABLE TO GO EVERYWHERE. AS THE LEADER OF THE MISSION I'M ABLE TO GO AMONG THE MEN, AND AS A WOMAN I'M ABLE TO JOIN THE WOMEN. AND I CAN ASSURE YOU THAT OUR DEALINGS ARE PERFECTLY NATURAL AND SPONTANEOUS.

WHEN I COME INTO A VILLAGE, THE WOMEN HAVE BEEN TOLD THAT I'M COMING AND THEY PREPARE A MEAL FOR ME. THEY ALL WANT TO SEE JAMILA, THE FOREIGN WOMAN DRESSED AS A MAN. THE FIRST THING THEY DO, MOSTLY, IS TOUCH MY BREASTS TO MAKE SURE I'M REALLY A WOMAN. WE HAVE A GOOD LAUGH.

THEN WE SIT DOWN AND WE EAT. WE TALK ABOUT EVERYTHING, LIFE, CHILDREN, AND A LOT ABOUT POLITICS. WHAT I LEARN FROM THEM IS CRUCIAL, ESPECIALLY WHEN THEY ARE PART OF THE ENTOURAGE OF THE LOCAL LEADERS, BECAUSE THEY HAVE A VERY POWERFUL INFLUENCE ON THEM. THE AFGHAN WOMAN IS THE CUSTODIAN OF VALUES, THE MORAL REFERENCE POINT.

I'M MUCH MORE EFFECTIVE IN MY DEALINGS WITH THE MEN AS A RESULT OF HAVING MET THE WOMEN AND OBTAINED SOME INSIDE INFORMATION.

YES, I UNDERSTAND.

AND THEY'RE FUNNY. YOU SHOULD HEAR THEM GOSSIPING ABOUT THE MEN, YOU'D SPLIT YOUR SIDES LAUGHING.

I'M GOING TO GROW SOME BOOBS SO I CAN COME WITH YOU NEXT TIME.

WE'VE BEEN IN ZARAGANDARA FOR NEARLY A MONTH. WE'RE STARTING TO TALK ABOUT OUR DEPARTURE, WHICH HAS TO TAKE PLACE BEFORE THE FIRST SNOWFALL.

ROBERT AND EVELYNE ARE STAYING. THE TWO OF THEM ARE GOING TO RUN THE HOSPITAL TOGETHER, AND ANOTHER MISSION WILL TAKE OVER NEXT SUMMER.

SO, ROBERT, HOW DO YOU FEEL ABOUT SPENDING A YEAR HERE?

CLICK

"I FEEL GREAT."

"YOU KNOW, I'M GLAD TO BE HAVING THIS ADVENTURE AS A PART OF A TEAM, BUT ONCE YOU GUYS HAVE TAKEN OFF AND WE'RE STUCK HERE, TOTALLY LOST— I HAVE THE FEELING THAT THAT'S WHEN THINGS WILL REALLY BEGIN."

"I ALREADY STAYED OVER ONE WINTER IN THE PREVIOUS MISSION, WITH SYLVIE. THE CONDITIONS WERE THE SAME, EXCEPT THAT THE TRIP OVER WAS WAY WORSE THAN THIS TIME. FOR STARTERS, TWO MONTHS IN PRISON AT THE PESHAWAR FORT, BECAUSE WE'D GOTTEN NABBED AT THE BORDER."

"THEN A THREE-MONTH TRIP, INCLUDING BEING HELD PRISONER FOR TWO WEEKS BY A COMMANDER (DON'T EVER ASK ME TO SHAKE HANDS WITH THAT CREEP), RACKETEERED EVERY STEP OF THE WAY, ABANDONED BY OUR ESCORT TWO PASSES BEFORE OUR DESTINATION... NOTHING BUT JOY, BASICALLY."

"THAT WINTER I HAD THE BEGINNINGS OF APPENDICITIS. I WAS INCHES AWAY FROM TURNING MYSELF OVER TO THE RUSSIANS. I DIDN'T TAKE ANY PAINKILLERS, SO I COULD GAUGE MY LEVEL OF PAIN, AND I STUFFED MYSELF WITH ANTIBIOTICS. IT PASSED, EVENTUALLY."

"THERE WERE WOLVES. YOU COULDN'T GO OUT AT NIGHT TO TAKE A PISS BECAUSE OF THE WOLVES. IN THE MORNING YOU'D SEE THEIR PAWPRINTS IN THE SNOW, AROUND THE HOUSES. AT THE END OF THE WINTER, WE HAD NOTHING LEFT TO EAT. WE'D BOIL A FEW TREE LEAVES AND EAT THEM LIKE SPINACH."

SO WHAT MADE YOU COME BACK?—

"THE PEOPLE."

"I'LL TELL YOU A STORY, TO GIVE YOU AN IDEA OF THE GENEROSITY OF THESE PEOPLE. EVERY DAY, THEY'D BRING US BREAD. AS TIME WENT ON, THAT BREAD BECAME MORE AND MORE DISGUSTING. BY THE END, THERE WAS MORE SOIL THAN BREAD IN IT."

"ONE DAY WE TOLD THE BAKER, PRETTY TACTLESSLY, THAT WE DIDN'T WANT ANY MORE, THAT WE WERE GOING TO THROW IT OUT. HE LOOKED AT US A BIT SHEEPISHLY AND ASKED US NOT TO THROW IT OUT BUT TO GIVE IT BACK TO HIM."

"THAT AFTERNOON WE FOUND OUT THAT, FOR THE PREVIOUS MONTH, NOBODY IN THE AREA HAD BEEN EATING BREAD. ALL THE FAMILIES HAD SCRAPED THE BOTTOM OF THEIR WHEAT STORES SO THAT SYLVIE AND I COULD CONTINUE TO HAVE SOME."

SO, NATURALLY, ONCE YOU'VE LIVED THROUGH SOMETHING LIKE THAT, YOU COME BACK AND YOU DO IT AGAIN.

WELL, WELL! LOOK WHO'S HERE: NAJMUDIN.

HE KNOWS WE'RE LEAVING SOON. HE CAME TO INVITE US TO HIS VILLAGE FOR A MEAL IN OUR HONOR.

OH, THAT'S NICE. WHEN?

WHAT DO YOU MEAN, WHEN? YOU'VE GOT A BUSY SCHEDULE?

YUP, I'LL HAVE TO CHECK IF I'M AVAILABLE.

THE MEAL AT NAJMUDIN'S WILL BE IN FIVE DAYS. IN THE MEANTIME, THE MUJ' ORGANIZE A LITTLE TOURIST EXCURSION FOR US. WE HEAD OFF ON FOOT TO VISIT THE "SANGAR," THE ENTRENCHED POSITIONS OF THE RESISTANCE BUILT ON THE FRONT LINE AROUND FEYZABAD.

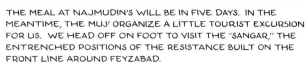

I MADE A DECISION ABOUT OUR RETURN TO PAKISTAN. WE WON'T BE GOING BACK EXACTLY THE WAY WE CAME.

OH, YEAH?

WHAT ROUTE ARE YOU PLAN-NING TO TAKE?

WE'LL BE GOING THROUGH KESHEM VALLEY, FARTHER WEST. I WENT THERE LAST TIME AND I WANT TO MAKE A QUICK ASSESSMENT OF HOW THINGS ARE GOING OVER THERE.

HOW MUCH TIME WILL THAT ADD TO THE TRIP?

A WEEK.

A WEEK!

I FEEL AS IF THE WHOLE HIMALAYAN RANGE HAS BEEN DROPPED ON MY SHOULDERS.

I SUDDENLY REALIZE HOW FED UP I AM WITH BEING IN A GROUP, WITH ALWAYS TAGGING ALONG.

I DON'T WANT TO GO TO KESHEM. I WANT TO GO BACK TO FRANCE.

MY SUPPLY OF FILM IS DWINDLING, SO I'LL HAVE TO START RATIONING MYSELF—SOMETHING I HATE TO DO. THE WORST THING THAT COULD HAPPEN TO ME WOULD BE TO FIND MYSELF UNABLE TO TAKE PICTURES. THAT WOULD KILL OFF ANY REMAINING DESIRE TO BE HERE.

WE COME UP TO THE FAMOUS "SANGAR." IN THE DISTANCE YOU CAN MAKE OUT THE FEYZABAD AIRPORT, HELD BY THE SOVIET FORCES. RÉGIS TAKES PICTURES OF IT.

SINCE THAT WAS THE HIGHLIGHT OF OUR LITTLE WALK, WE EAT A FEW WATERMELONS AND HEAD BACK.

TELL ME SOMETHING, HOW LONG DOES IT TAKE ONE OF THOSE SMALL CARAVANS THAT HEAD BACK EMPTY TO PAKISTAN TO MAKE THE TRIP?

IT DEPENDS.

LESS TIME THAN ON THE WAY OVER HERE?

OH YEAH, MUCH LESS. IF ALL GOES WELL, IT TAKES ROUGHLY TWO WEEKS.

WHY DO YOU ASK?

JUST CURIOUS.

BY THE TIME WE GET BACK, I'VE MADE MY DECISION. JULIETTE CERTAINLY ISN'T GOING TO LIKE IT. TO AVOID SPOILING THE PARTY, I'M PLANNING TO TELL HER ONLY AFTER THE MEAL AT NAJMUDIN'S.

THE DAY OF THE MEAL COMES QUICKLY. AFTER A FEW HOURS' WALK, WE'RE HUGGING NAJMUDIN AND HIS COMPANIONS.

THEY'VE REALLY GONE TO TOWN ON THE MEAL. AT BASSIR KHAN'S, A MONTH AGO, WE SHARED THE SUMPTUOUS DAILY FARE OF A POWERFUL LEADER. BUT THERE'S NOTHING DAY-TO-DAY ABOUT THIS EVENT. IT'S A REAL COUNTRYSIDE BANQUET FOR A SPECIAL OCCASION, SOMETHING COUNTRY PEOPLE DON'T HAVE TOO OFTEN. AND NEITHER DO WE.

MAN, THIS IS SO DELICIOUS!

THIS TOO! HAVE YOU TRIED IT?

NAJMUDIN PRESIDES OVER THE MEAL.

WE CAN TELL HE IS HAPPY TO HAVE BROUGHT US TOGETHER AND SADDENED TO SEE US LEAVE.

WHEN THE TIME COMES TO HEAD BACK, THE HUGS ARE VERY MOVING. I HEAR THE EXPRESSIONS MAHMAD TAUGHT ME: MAY PEACE BE WITH YOU, MAY YOU STAY HEALTHY, MAY YOU STAY ALIVE. THEY SOUND PARTICULARLY APPROPRIATE.

I WALK ALONGSIDE JULIETTE FOR A LONG WHILE AND NEITHER OF US SPEAKS.

I WANT TO TELL YOU... NAJMUDIN AND I ARE NOW BROTHER AND SISTER BEFORE THE KORAN.

FROM NOW ON I'LL CALL HIM "MY BROTHER NAJMUDIN" AND HE'LL CALL ME "MY SISTER JAMILA."

DID YOU MINGLE YOUR BLOOD?

ALMOST. HE ASKED ME, "ARE WE GOING TO SEE EACH OTHER AGAIN?" I TOLD HIM THAT YES, I'D BE BACK AND THAT MY HEART BELONGS TO THIS COUNTRY.

SO HE TOOK OUT HIS POCKET KORAN, WRAPPED IN AN EMBROIDERED CLOTH, AND WE SWORE TO BE BROTHER AND SISTER TO EACH OTHER.

WHAT DOES THAT MEAN?

THERE'S A VERY STRONG FEELING BETWEEN US, YOU KNOW. BUT IT'S A FEELING THAT WE HAD TO CLARIFY TO OURSELVES AND TO OTHERS, TO MAKE IT VIABLE.

FOR ME, THE TASK I'VE TAKEN ON IS SUCH THAT I'LL NEVER BE ROMANTICALLY INVOLVED WITH AN AFGHAN. AND FOR HIS PART, HE'S MARRIED, HE'S A DEVOUT MUSLIM, AND HE'S A LEADER. IT'S VERY IMPORTANT THAT HE PROTECT HIS HONOR AND MINE.

BROTHER-AND-SISTER-HOOD BEFORE THE KORAN SETTLES EVERYTHING. WE CAN TOUCH EACH OTHER, SHAKE HANDS, OR HUG, WITHOUT SPARKING GOSSIP. IT'S OFFICIAL, IF YOU LIKE. I'VE REALLY BECOME HIS SISTER.

TOO BAD.

HAHAHA! THAT'S LIFE!

I'M FOND OF NAJMUDIN TOO.

WHO WOULDN'T BE? HE'S LOYAL, HE'S DEDICATED, HE'S A LEADER WHO DOESN'T HAND OFF THE MENIAL JOBS TO OTHERS, HE'S GENTLE, HE'S CONSTANT, HE NEVER SHOUTS, AND HE'D GET HIMSELF KILLED TO SAVE US.

HE TAKES AFTER HIS SISTER.

THANKS. I WISH.

I HAVE SOMETHING TO TELL YOU, TOO.

OKAY.

I WANT TO LEAVE NOW AND GO BACK TO PAKISTAN ALONE.

WHAT'S COME OVER YOU?

LISTEN, THE RETURN PATH THROUGH KESHEM IS JUST TOO LONG FOR ME. I TOTALLY UNDERSTAND THAT YOU NEED TO GO, BUT AS FAR AS I'M CONCERNED, THERE'S NO REASON WHY I SHOULD. I'VE COVERED THE MISSION. MY JOB IS HERE.

A MONTH IN PESHAWAR, PLUS A MONTH OF TRAVELING, PLUS A MONTH HERE: IT'S BEEN THREE MONTHS SINCE I LEFT FRANCE. I NEED TO GO HOME AND DEVELOP MY PICTURES.

YOU'LL GO HOME, BUT WITH US. IT'S TOO DANGEROUS TO DO IT ON YOUR OWN.

I CAN PERFECTLY WELL JOIN A SMALL CARAVAN LEAVING FROM YAFTAL. RÉGIS TOLD ME IT WOULDN'T TAKE MORE THAN TWO WEEKS.

SUPPOSING YOU DID THAT, HOW WOULD YOU MANAGE?

YOU DON'T SPEAK THE LANGUAGE. YOU'VE BEEN AMONG US THE WHOLE TIME.

EXACTLY. THAT'S WHAT I WANT—TO BE LEFT TO MY OWN DEVICES AND HAVE TO MANAGE.

I WAS TALKING TO ROBERT ABOUT HIS STAY OVER THE WINTER AND HE SAID SOMETHING THAT STRUCK ME. HE SAID, "IT'S WHEN YOU GUYS ARE GONE AND I'M ON MY OWN THAT THINGS WILL REALLY BEGIN."

THAT'S WHAT I WANT. I WANT TO BE ALONE IN THIS COUNTRY.

I CAN UNDERSTAND THAT, BUT PUT YOURSELF IN MY SHOES FOR A SECOND. IF I LET YOU GO AND SOMETHING HAPPENS TO YOU, I'LL BLAME MYSELF FOR THE REST OF MY LIFE.

IN THE FUTURE, YOU CAN COME BACK AS MUCH AS YOU LIKE, UNDER YOUR OWN RESPONSIBILITY. FOR NOW, YOU'RE UNDER MINE.

NO.

I'M NOT UNDER YOUR RESPONSIBILITY, JULIETTE. THE MEDICAL TEAM IS, BUT I'M NOT.

I'M A PHOTOGRAPHER. I ACCEPTED THIS ASSIGNMENT FREELY, I SAW IT THROUGH FREELY AND, NOW THAT IT'S ENDING, I'M GOING HOME FREELY.

OKAY.

WHAT YOU'RE SAYING ABOUT RESPONSIBILITY IS NOT STRICTLY TRUE. I'M THE ONE WHO CONVINCED YOU TO COME HERE AND WHO BROUGHT YOU HERE. THAT'S ENOUGH TO MAKE ME RESPONSIBLE FOR YOU AND YOU KNOW IT.

I DO EVERYTHING I CAN TO ENSURE THAT THE PEOPLE I SEND ON A MISSION COME BACK IN ONE PIECE. AT THE SAME TIME, MY ROLE ISN'T TO PREVENT THEM FROM LIVING THEIR LIVES AND TAKING RESPONSIBILITY FOR THEIR OWN CHOICES.

SO I'M HANDING BACK TO YOU THE RESPONSIBILITY THAT I HAVE OVER YOU. YOU'RE A BIG BOY. IF YOU WANT TO LEAVE, LEAVE.

I'LL TALK TO BASSIR AND ASK HIM TO PROVIDE YOU WITH AN ESCORT UP TO PAKISTAN. IT'LL TAKE AT LEAST THREE OR FOUR DAYS.

THANKS, JULIETTE.

I'LL LOOK BOTH WAYS BEFORE CROSSING THE STREET.

YOU BETTER.

155

SO THAT'S IT. BASSIR AGREES TO ORGANIZE A SMALL CARAVAN FOR ME. HE ALSO WANTS TO GIVE ME A GIFT. I CLIMB THE HILL TO THE TAILOR'S HOUSE.

THE GIFT IS AN OVERCOAT. MY MEASUREMENTS ARE DULY NOTED AND I'M PROMISED, FOR THREE DAYS LATER, A WOOLEN COAT WITH A BELT, BUTTONS AND A REEFER-STYLE COLLAR.

I'M IN A SUSPENDED STATE, JUST LIKE HOW I USED TO FEEL AS A KID IN THE LAST DAYS OF SCHOOL BEFORE THE SUMMER BREAK. I TAKE SOME PICTURES TO SAY GOOD-BYE TO ZARAGANDARA, BUT MY MIND IS ALREADY WANDERING IN THE MOUNTAINS.

JULIETTE GIVES ME A USEFUL LITTLE ENGLISH-PERSIAN DICTIONARY THAT I LEARN TO HANDLE AS QUICKLY AS MY CAMERAS.

IS THIS WATER BOILED? *IIN AAB JOSH-DAADA AST?*

NO, THIS WATER IS NOT BOILED. *NE, IIN AAB JOSH-DAADA NEST.*

IT'S SUPPLEMENTED WITH A SMALL MEDICAL GLOSSARY DRAFTED BY MSF FOR INTERVIEWING PATIENTS, UNDERSTANDING THEIR ANSWERS, AND PRESCRIBING TREATMENT.

I HOPE I WON'T NEED IT.

Are you ill?	: Mariz asti?
I am ill	: Mariz astam
Where does it hurt?	: Koudja dard mekona?
It hurts here	: Indja dard mekona
I have a headache	: Sar'm (= sar e man) dard mekona
My feet hurt	: Paah'm dard mekona (– my foot is hurting ma)
	[Wherever possible, plurals are expressed with a collective singular]
My heart hurts	: Qalb'm dard mekona
Do your kidneys hurt?	: Gorda dard mekona?
Do you have diarrhea?	: Pitch asti? (or: pitch shodi?)
Are you vomiting?	: Estefroq mekoni? (I'm vomiting: estefroq mekonam)
Are you coughing?	: Sulfa mekoni? (I'm coughing: sulfa mekonam)]

ON THE EVE OF MY DEPARTURE, I LISTEN DUTIFULLY TO THE LAST PIECES OF ADVICE.

WHEN YOU'RE ASKING FOR FOOD, DON'T SAY "NAN KHORDAN MEKHAAHAM," "I WANT TO EAT." THAT'S TOO DIRECT. INSTEAD SAY "NAN BOKHORAN."

NAN BORORAN.

THAT'S THE CONDITIONAL TENSE. IT'S MORE POLITE.

AND DO US A FAVOR, DON'T EAT ALL THE CHOCOLATE ROCHER THAT YOU PASS BY.

LEAVE SOME FOR YOUR BUDDIES WHO'LL BE COMING AFTER YOU.

AT LAST, IT'S THE MORNING OF THE MOMENTOUS DAY. A VILLAGER IS GOING TO ACCOMPANY ME TO YAFTAL-E-DAYAN. I SAY GOODBYE TO EVERYONE AND RÉGIS BORROWS MY CAMERA TO KEEP A RECORD OF MY GLORIOUS DEPARTURE.

THE PROBLEM IS THAT I'VE WOKEN UP WITH A BAD CASE OF DIARRHEA AND THE PAIN IS BECOMING UNBEARABLE.

I TURN TO RÉGIS AND SAY, "MY STOMACH IS KILLING ME. DO YOU HAVE SOMETHING I COULD TAKE?"

HE GETS ME SOMETHING CALLED BUSCOPAN AND I TAKE A PILL OF IT. I POSTPONE MY DEPARTURE AND WAIT, DOUBLED OVER WITH PAIN, FOR THE MEDICATION TO PRODUCE ITS EFFECT.

THE EFFECT ISN'T LONG IN COMING. I'M SUDDENLY OVERTAKEN BY A SENSATION OF EXTREME HEAT, I START SWELLING UP LIKE THE MICHELIN MAN AND MY BALLS ITCH UNBEARABLY. THE DIAGNOSIS IS AN ALLERGY TO SCOPOLAMINE, AN INGREDIENT IN BUSCOPAN.

RÉGIS RUSHES BACK TO THE PHARMACY, BRINGS BACK SOME PHENERGAN AND GIVES ME AN ABUNDANT SHOT OF IT IN THE BUTTOCK. MY SWELLING STOPS INSTANTLY.

AFTER THAT I SLEEP FORTY-EIGHT HOURS, NONSTOP.

THAT WAS WHAT YOU MIGHT CALL A FALSE START.

YOU WERE A BETTER MATCH FOR YOUR EGO BEFORE, BUT YOU LOOK BETTER THIS WAY.

WAS I REALLY THAT SWOLLEN?

YOU COULD'VE BEEN BREJNEV'S SON.

BY THE WAY, HOW'S THE GUT? WANT ANOTHER LITTLE HELPING OF BUSCOPAN, FOR THE ROAD?

I THINK I'LL PASS.

I VIEW THAT MISHAP AS A SMALL SETBACK. IT DOESN'T AFFECT MY DETERMINATION TO LEAVE.

MY HORSE IS SADDLED UP ONCE AGAIN. I DO THE ROUNDS OF FAREWELLS AND THIS TIME SET OFF FOR GOOD.

I FEEL A BIT WEAK AND CONVALESCENT, BUT I LIKE THE STATE OF MIND I'M IN. IN ALL MY LIFE, I'VE NEVER BEFORE MADE SUCH A LEAP INTO THE UNKNOWN.

AND, AS ROBERT WOULD SAY, WITH HIS HINT OF A SOUTHERN FRENCH ACCENT, I FEEL GREAT.

Part 3

THERE. MY FIRST EVENING ALONE.
A LITTLE VILLAGE, HIGH UP, NICE SCENERY. NO COMPLICATIONS.
I FEEL A RUSH OF HAPPINESS.
WE'VE DONE A GOOD DAY'S WALK.
I'M LEAN AS A BROOMSTICK BUT I FEEL GREAT.
THEORETICALLY, IN TWO WEEKS' TIME I'LL BE IN PAKISTAN, PHONING HOME.
I HAVE THE PLEASANT SENSATION OF BEING IN CONTROL OF MY TRIP.

OBVIOUSLY, MY GUIDE AND I DON'T TALK MUCH. WE EXCHANGE A FEW GESTURES, TWO OR THREE WORDS, TWO OR THREE SMILES.

OKAY. I'LL FOLLOW YOU.

BALEY.

WE SETTLE DOWN IN THE MOSQUE.

I LIKE MOSQUES. THEY'RE LIKE WHAT CHURCHES SHOULD BE, OR HAVE BEEN: PLACES THAT WELCOME TRAVELERS, HAVENS IN A NO-FRILLS WAY. INSIDE THEM, PEOPLE BEHAVE WELL, BUT WITHOUT FORMALITY.

YOU TAKE OFF YOUR SHOES, GRAB THE CORNER YOU WANT, PUT YOUR STUFF DOWN. YOU CAN EAT THERE, HAVE A CHAT WITH SOMEONE. YOU'LL SLEEP THERE. IT'S ALMOST A HOSTEL.

ON THE OTHER HAND, IT'S TRUE THAT WHEN YOU HAVE THE WOOD STOVE DRAWING AT FULL STRENGTH AND TWO HUNDRED GUYS SLEEPING SIDE BY SIDE IN AN AWFUL STENCH, WITHOUT A BREATH OF FRESH AIR, YOU'LL BE BETTER OFF SLEEPING OUTSIDE. EVEN IF IT MEANS GETTING WALKED ON BY A HORSE.

BUT HERE, IT LOOKS PRETTY QUIET. IT'S A SIMPLE SQUARE ROOM WITH BARE ADOBE WALLS. NOT EVEN A CARPET ON THE FLOOR, JUST STRAW. A HOUSE LIKE ANY OTHER.

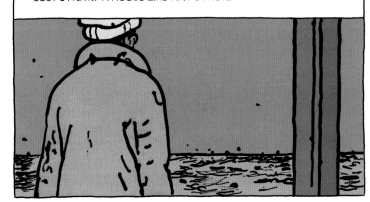

THE IMAM WELCOMES ME—AT LEAST, I THINK THAT'S WHAT HE SAYS.

OUTSIDE, THE SUN IS GOING DOWN. IT'S ABOUT 5 PM. THE IMAM GOES OUT TO MAKE THE CALL TO PRAYER.

169

THAT CALL IS ONE OF THE MOST MAJESTIC THINGS I'VE EVER EXPERIENCED. HE FACES THE MOUNTAINS, CUPS HIS HANDS AROUND HIS MOUTH, AND SINGS OUT THE CALL.

I HEARD IT FOR THE FIRST TIME IN DJIBOUTI FIVE YEARS AGO. I WAS STAYING IN AN APARTMENT ON A PLAZA. AT 4 A.M. THE MUEZZIN WOULD MAKE THE CALL TO PRAYER. AT FIRST IT WAS IRRITATING BECAUSE IT WOKE ME UP. THEN IT BECAME ONE OF MY FAVORITE MOMENTS IN THE DAY. NEVER COULD REMEMBER THE PHRASE THEY SING, THOUGH.

IN BIG CITIES LIKE CAIRO OR KHARTOUM THE CALL IS PRE-RECORDED WITH FANCY VOCAL EFFECTS. HERE IT'S RAUCOUS, BARE, AND IT BOUNCES OFF THE PEAKS, ON AND ON.

OVERCOME WITH EMOTION, I START WRITING A FEW WORDS TO DOMINIQUE, MY GIRLFRIEND. I DESCRIBE THIS MOMENT TO HER, THE DAY'S WALK, THE TWO ADOLESCENT MUJ' WE ENCOUNTERED, WHO POSED WITH THEIR WEAPONS.

LITTLE BY LITTLE THE FAITHFUL START TO ARRIVE.

I GO IN WITH THEM. THE MOSQUE IS FILLING UP.

THEY LOOK AT ME WITH CURIOSITY. USUALLY ANY TRAVELER THEY SEE WILL BE AN AFGHAN, WHO'LL PRAY WITH THEM. THIS EVENING, WORD GETS AROUND THAT THIS GUY IN THE CORNER, THERE, IS A FOREIGNER WHO WON'T BE PRAYING WITH THEM.

170

THE PRAYING BEGINS. WHAT I LIKE IS THAT THEY AREN'T ALL VERY DILIGENT. SOME OF THEM ARE CASTING LOOKS IN MY DIRECTION AND FALLING BEHIND THE OTHERS.

I DON'T DARE TAKE PICTURES.

AS SOON AS IT'S DONE, A FEW OF THEM COME OVER, SIT DOWN, AND START ASKING ME QUESTIONS.

THUMBING THROUGH MY LITTLE DICTIONARY AS FAST AS I CAN, I TRY TO INTRODUCE MYSELF AND FIGURE OUT WHAT THEY'RE ASKING ME.

AHMADJAN...
AKS GREFTAN...
UM...
FARASAWI...

I HEAR "MUSSULMAN? MUSSULMAN?" APPARENTLY, IT'S MY RELIGION THAT THEY'RE INTERESTED IN HEARING ABOUT FIRST.

ISAWI.

I'M ISAWI, CHRISTIAN.

ISAWI IS OKAY. IT PASSES MUSTER. I CERTAINLY CAN'T SAY THAT I'M NON-PRACTICING. THAT WOULD BE WORSE THAN A BLUNDER.

MOST OF THEM HAVE NEVER SEEN A FOREIGNER. THEY THINK THERE'S NO OTHER LANGUAGE THAN THEIR OWN AND FIGURE THAT THE REASON I DON'T UNDERSTAND THEM IS THAT I MUST BE DEAF. THEY REPEAT THEIR QUESTIONS, YELLING LOUDER AND LOUDER.

THERE'S NO HOSTILITY, THOUGH. I FEEL STUPID, AS YOU DO WHEN YOU DON'T UNDERSTAND A THING AND CAN'T SAY A WORD, BUT NOT AT ALL UNCOMFORTABLE.

KALISAA... UM... NAM...
NAMAAZ KHAANDAN.

I DO CAUSE AN AWKWARD MOMENT AT ONE POINT, BY SAYING THAT I'M NOT MARRIED AND DON'T HAVE KIDS. AT MY AGE, CLEARLY, THAT ISN'T THE DONE THING.

ازدواج نکرده؟

کلاسیک

HAHAHA!

PRETTY QUICKLY, HAVING SEEN THAT NOTHING MUCH CAN BE EXPECTED OF ME, THEY GET UP, POLITELY TAKE THEIR LEAVE, AND GO OUT.

زنده باشی

الله حافظ

ZENDABOSHEE, DJURBOSHEE.

I STAY ALONE WITH MY GUIDE. WE SPREAD OUT OUR THINGS. THE IMAM BRINGS TEA, MILK, AND BREAD.

WE DINE IN SILENCE. FOR DESSERT, WE HAVE KOLCHA, CAKES THAT ROBERT SLIPPED INTO MY BAG AS I WAS LEAVING.

BEFORE GOING TO SLEEP, I GO OUT TO TAKE A LEAK. MY GUIDE FOLLOWS ME.

UM... NO... *NEIH*. ME ALONE... TAKE A PEE... ALONE.

چی؟

WHEN YOU REALLY HAVE TO GO, THERE ARE BETTER THINGS TO DO THAN TO LOOK FOR THE VERB "TO PEE" IN AN ENGLISH-DARI DICTIONARY.

TO PEE? TO PISS?

ESPECIALLY WHEN IT'S NOT INCLUDED.

UM... I PSS... PSS... PSCHIIT.

LUCKILY, I HAVE A FLASH OF INSPIRATION.

AO GARM?

آب گرم؟

BALEY.

ALONE AT LAST.

172

AO GARM MEANS HOT WATER. THAT THOUGHT SAVED ME. WHILE HE GOES TO GET ME SOME I HAVE TIME TO MEDITATE ON THIS AFGHAN PARADOX: YOU CAN'T HAVE ONE MINUTE ALONE IN SUCH A SPARSELY POPULATED COUNTRY.

AFTERWARDS I CONTINUE TO WRITE IN MY NOTEBOOK, UNTIL I'M COMPLETELY EXHAUSTED.

THE NEXT MORNING, AFTER THE HOSPITABLE IMAM HAS TREATED US TO A TASTY BREAKFAST, MY GUIDE LOADS UP THE HORSE AND WE LEAVE FOR YAFTAL-E-PAYAN.

I'M LOOKING FORWARD TO THE NEXT FEW HOURS, FEELING OPTIMISTIC. THAT EVENING I'LL REACH BASSIR'S PLACE, HE'LL LAVISH ON ME ONE OF THOSE FEASTS THAT NO ONE DOES BETTER, HE'LL ASSIGN ME AN ESCORT, AND I'LL BE ON THE ROAD BY DAYBREAK, WITHOUT MISSING A BEAT.

IT'S NICE BEING ON YOUR OWN. BUT IT SURE CAN FEEL EMPTY.

I RECITE MY SMATTERING OF PERSIAN OUT LOUD. I IMAGINE MY BUDDIES ARE NEXT TO ME, AND I TALK TO THEM.

IN YAFTAL-E-PAYAN, BASSIR KHAN WELCOMES ME. HE POINTS TO A CORNER OF THE ROOM WHERE HE'S CONDUCTING HIS BUSINESS, INVITING ME TO SETTLE DOWN THERE.

I HAVE THE HONOR OF SHARING HIS EVENING YOGURT, BUT I NOTICE WITH DISAPPOINTMENT THAT HE MAKES NO REFERENCE TO MY ESCORT, NOR TO MY DEPARTURE THE NEXT MORNING.

AFTER THE MEAL, HIS BODYGUARD COMES TO SIT DOWN IN FRONT OF ME, ARMED WITH HIS HUGE RPK ASSAULT RIFLE.

HE LAYS IT DOWN NEXT TO HIM, GRABS IT BY THE BUTT...

174

AND VOILÀ.

HE PUTS IT DOWN BETWEEN US, AS IF TO SAY: YOUR TURN NOW.

THE OTHERS WATCH ME MOCKINGLY. AN IDEA CROSSES MY MIND

IT WORKS.

THAT GETS THE EVENING STARTED. I'M TREATED, LIKE YESTERDAY, TO A FULL PRESS CONFERENCE. THE PRIOR TRAINING HELPS AND I MANAGE BETTER, ESPECIALLY SINCE THE QUESTIONS ARE THE SAME ONES.

ISAWI.

I DON'T REPEAT THE GAFFE OF BEING A BACHELOR. THIS EVENING I'M MARRIED AND HAVE A FIVE-YEAR-OLD SON.

YAK BATCHA PANJ SAAL.

I HANDLE MY DICTIONARY PRETTY SMOOTHLY.
AS A RESULT, AT TIMES, THERE ARE THE MODEST BEGINNINGS OF A REAL CONVERSATION.
BUT IT'S A VICIOUS CIRCLE. THE MORE I ANSWER, THE MORE QUESTIONS SPRING UP.
THEY TAKE TURNS. THEIR CURIOSITY IS ENDLESS.
DOES A CHRISTIAN HAVE TO DO PRAYERS? HOW MANY TIMES A DAY?
I GIVE A SIMPLE ANSWER: A CHRISTIAN PRAYS ONCE A WEEK IN CHURCH
(LIKE THEY DO ON FRIDAY AT THE MOSQUE) BUT, WHEN TRAVELING WHERE THERE ARE NO CHURCHES,
HE ISN'T REQUIRED TO PRAY.
THAT CONFIRMS THAT BEING CHRISTIAN IS NOT AS GOOD AS BEING MUSLIM.
I GO WITH THE FLOW. THAT'S THE SMART THING TO DO.
THE GOAL HERE IS TO RETURN TO PAKISTAN, NOT TO STIR UP TROUBLE.
THE WORST THING TO SAY WOULD BE THAT I'M A NON-BELIEVER AND THAT NONE OF THIS MATTERS TO ME.
FOR EXAMPLE, EXPLAINING THAT I WAS BAPTIZED AS A CATHOLIC BUT THAT I DIDN'T HAVE MY CHILD
BAPTIZED WOULD MEAN BIG TROUBLE, WITH A BULLET IN THE HEAD AS THE LIKELY OUTCOME.

AT SEVEN THIRTY, THE EQUIVALENT OF WHAT WOULD BE WELL PAST MIDNIGHT IN FRANCE, THEY FINALLY LEAVE ME ALONE.

I DOZE OFF IN A CORNER OF THE LARGE ROOM, WHILE BASSIR, AT THE OTHER END, HAS HIS LEGS MASSAGED.

THE NEXT DAY BRINGS A LETDOWN: NO HORSE, AND NO ESCORT. I SPEND THE WHOLE MORNING TRYING TO ASK WHY NOT.

MAN KHAASTAM... ASP?

AS FAR AS I CAN MAKE OUT, THE ANSWERS ARE ALL THE SAME: DON'T WORRY, WE KNOW YOU WANT A HORSE, IT'S COMING, YOU'LL GET IT.

BUT NOTHING COMES. IN THE AFTERNOON, TO UNWIND MY NERVES, I WALK AROUND THE VILLAGE (WHICH I'M NOT ALLOWED TO LEAVE) AND TAKE SOME PICTURES.

I'M IN A FOUL MOOD. NAÏVELY, I HAD THOUGHT A HORSE WOULD BE WAITING FOR ME AND THAT ALL I'D HAVE TO DO WOULD BE TO PACK IT UP AND HEAD OFF. BUT THAT'S HOW IT WORKS WHEN YOU GO PICK UP A PARCEL SOMEWHERE IN PARIS.
THINGS DON'T WORK THAT WAY IN AFGHANISTAN.
TIME IS THE LEAST OF THEIR CONCERNS.

LITTLE BY LITTLE, THE PICTURES PRODUCE THEIR CALMING EFFECT AND I COOL DOWN.

I TRY TO SEE THE POSITIVE SIDE OF THINGS: AT LEAST I'M EATING LIKE A KING AND THE FOOD GIVES ME MY STRENGTH. ALL IN ALL, THIS IS DOING ME SOME GOOD.

I SPEND THE END OF THE DAY WITH BASSIR. HE RECEIVES VISITS FROM SOME MUJ', FROM FARMERS BRINGING HIM GRAPES, FROM EMISSARIES, CLERGYMEN, TRAVELERS FROM KABUL. HE IS PROUD TO SHOW ME ALL THOSE COMINGS AND GOINGS.

HE ALSO ENJOYS SHOWING OFF MY PRESENCE BY HIS SIDE, AS IF THE WEST HAD PUT A PHOTOGRAPHER AT HIS SERVICE.
I FEEL LIKE I'M STARTING TO PUT DOWN ROOTS.

178

SO MUCH SO THAT I START BUDDING LIKE A TREE. DURING THE NIGHT, A BOIL DRILLS INTO MY RIGHT ARM, JUST BELOW THE TRICEPS. IT UNNERVES ME.

IN THE MORNING, THERE'S NO MORE TALK OF A HORSE THAN THE DAY BEFORE.

ASP? PAKISTAN?

اسپ؟ پاکستان؟

ONCE AGAIN, I WANDER AIMLESSLY THROUGH THE VILLAGE.

I PASS A GROUP OF ARMED TEENAGERS. THEY WANT ME TO TAKE PICTURES OF THEM. SOME OF THEM ASK TO LOOK THROUGH THE VIEWFINDER OF MY CAMERA.

I FEEL UNCOMFORTABLE IN THE MIDST OF THOSE KIDS, WHO POINT THEIR GUNS AS IF THEY WERE TOYS.

THIS ONE IS HAVING FUN WITH THE BARREL OF A SMALL RUSSIAN AUTOMATIC PISTOL. I'VE SEEN THE MSF DOCTORS TREAT PEOPLE WHO WERE ACCIDENTALLY WOUNDED BY THAT SORT OF THING.

OF COURSE THERE HAS TO BE A SHOOTING CONTEST.

اون سنگو را آنجا می بینی؟

NO WAY OF DUCKING OUT.

ONE OF THEM SHOWS ME A SMALL BOULDER A GOOD DISTANCE AWAY, AND AIMS AT IT.

HE HITS IT.

RIGHT AFTER THAT, A SERIES OF DETONATIONS HACKS AT MY EARDRUMS. THE OTHER KIDS ARE CONCENTRATING THEIR FIRE ON THE POOR ROCK.

I WATCH THE ROCK EXPLODE AND JUMP IN A SHOWER OF DUST.

MY TURN.

AND THEN, BY SOME MIRACLE...

AS I'M RAISING THE GUN, A TERRIFIED GUY RUNS OUT SCREAMING FROM BEHIND THE ROCK, FOLLOWED BY A FEW GOATS.

A GOATHERD HAS BEEN THERE ALL ALONG AND WE HADN'T SEEN HIM. I TAKE ADVANTAGE OF THE DIVERSION TO GIVE THE WEAPON BACK AND SNEAK AWAY.

TACHAKOR.

THE GOATHERD, THE GOATS, AND I GET OFF LIGHTLY.

I WRITE, I READ. I REOPEN MY STEVENSON BOOK AND, ALTHOUGH I'M NOT MAKING ANY HEADWAY IN BADAKHSHAN, AT LEAST I'M ADVANCING THROUGH THE CEVENNES MOUNTAINS.

AND, FOLLOWING A NOW-ESTABLISHED RITUAL, I ATTEND BASSIR'S AUDIENCES AND ANSWER THE INVARIABLE EVENING QUESTIONS.

MAN ISAWI.

AT NIGHT, THE BOIL THAT'S THRIVING ON MY ARM CONTINUES TO DOG MY SLEEP.

THE THIRD DAY AT BASSIR'S FLOWS AT A SNAIL'S PACE. I NO LONGER ASK ANY QUESTIONS. I'M GETTING BOGGED DOWN.

AT THE END OF THE FOURTH DAY, JULIETTE AND JOHN, WHO ARE RETURNING TO PAKISTAN VIA ANOTHER ROUTE BUT HAVE THIS PORTION OF THE JOURNEY IN COMMON WITH MINE, ARRIVE IN YAFTAL-E-PAYAN. I'M AS RELIEVED AS THEY ARE SURPRISED.

DIDIER? WHAT THE HELL ARE YOU DOING HERE?

I HAVE NO IDEA. BASSIR'S HOLDING ME HERE. CAN'T SEEM TO GET MY HORSE AND MY ESCORT.

CAREFUL WITH MY ARM. I HAVE A BOIL.

181

JULIETTE ARRANGES IT FOR ME. AT LAST BASSIR APPOINTS ME AN ESCORT OF FOUR GUYS AND A GRAY HORSE. I'LL LEAVE THE NEXT MORNING.

HE WASN'T HOLDING YOU BACK ON PURPOSE, BUT HE HAS A STAFFING PROBLEM. IT'S LATE IN THE SEASON AND MOST CARAVANS HAVE GONE ALREADY. HE DOESN'T HAVE A LOT OF PEOPLE LEFT.

I'M INTRODUCED TO MY GUIDES, WHO LOOK NONE TOO IMPRESSIVE. STILL, ONE OF THEM HAS A FRIENDLY FACE. I ASK HIM WHAT HE DOES FOR A LIVING.

"TCHOPAN": SHEPHERD.

I RECOVER MY OPTIMISM, WHICH IS FORTUNATE, BECAUSE IT COMES IN HANDY RIGHT AWAY.

SO, SHOW ME THIS BOIL.

IT'S HERE.

YOU'RE GONNA OPEN IT?

YEAH.

WITH YOUR SWISS ARMY KNIFE?

YEAH.

BUT AREN'T YOU GOING TO STERILIZE IT?

IF YOU WISH.

JOHN WIPES THE KNIFE'S BLADE ON HIS SLEEVE.

THERE. STERILE ENOUGH FOR YOU?

UGH!

DON'T MOVE.

HE INCISES IT. I HAVE A GREAT TIME.

CAN'T PROMISE YOU ANYTHING, 'CAUSE THAT BUMP WASN'T VERY RIPE. BUT YOU SHOULD BE OKAY.

THANKS.

OVER DINNER, MAKING THE MOST OF MY EXPERIENCE OF THE PAST FEW DAYS, I ASK JULIETTE FOR SOME CLARIFICATION.

HOW DO YOU SAY, FOR EXAMPLE, "LEAVE ME ALONE, I WANT TO TAKE A LEAK"?

THE NEXT DAY, WHILE MY FOUR GUYS LOAD UP THE HORSE, BASSIR GATHERS HIS MEN TO SALUTE OUR DEPARTURE.

ONE OF THE MUJ' HANDS ME SOME HORSESHOES, WHICH I POCKET.

SO, FROM NOW ON WE WON'T BE THERE TO BAIL YOU OUT, YOU KNOW?

YEAH, BUT I'LL BE FINE, REALLY, THANKS.

FOR THE LAST TIME, ARE YOU REALLY SURE YOU WANT TO GO ALONE?

ABSOLUTELY SURE.

SO, SEE YOU IN PESHAWAR. AND WATCH OUT FOR LANDMINES. NEVER LEAVE THE PATH.

SEE YOU IN PESHAWAR. CAREFUL—MY BOIL.

SAY HI TO EVERYONE IN TESHKAN!

I WILL!

183

WE DON'T HAVE ANY WEAPONS. CARAVANS GOING TO PAKISTAN NEVER CARRY ANY. IT'S JUST AS WELL.

MY FOUR GUYS SEEM KIND OF STRANGE. THEY AMBLE CASUALLY ALONG. I WAS EXPECTING TO HAVE TO RUN AFTER THEM BUT I FIND MYSELF ALMOST WAITING FOR THEM.

THE KOKCHA RIVER COMES WITHIN VIEW. ON THE WAY OVER, WE TOOK A RAFT LATE AT NIGHT AND I WASN'T ABLE TO TAKE PICTURES BECAUSE IT WAS TOO DARK.

THE RIVER IS OVERLOOKED BY A ROAD USED BY SOVIET AND GOVERNMENTAL CONVOYS. THE CARAVANS OF MUJ' CROSSING IT POST LOOKOUTS EVERYWHERE, BUT YOU CAN'T DALLY. I LIKE THOSE MOMENTS WHEN EVERYBODY GETS BUSY. NOBODY PAYS ATTENTION TO ME.

THE PEOPLE COMING IN THE OPPOSITE DIRECTION ARE ARMED TO THE TEETH. THEY CARRY HEAVY ARTILLERY SHELLS. AS SOON AS THEY REACH LAND, THEY LOAD THEM BACK ONTO THEIR MULES, TWO OR THREE PER ANIMAL.

THE SOUND EFFECTS ARE PARTICULARLY RICH, WITH SCREAMS, WHINNYING, AND BRAYING REVERBERATING IN THE CANYON, THE SOUND OF WATER, ROCKS BANGING AGAINST EACH OTHER, THE SPLASHING OF HORSES THAT ARE SWIMMING ACROSS.

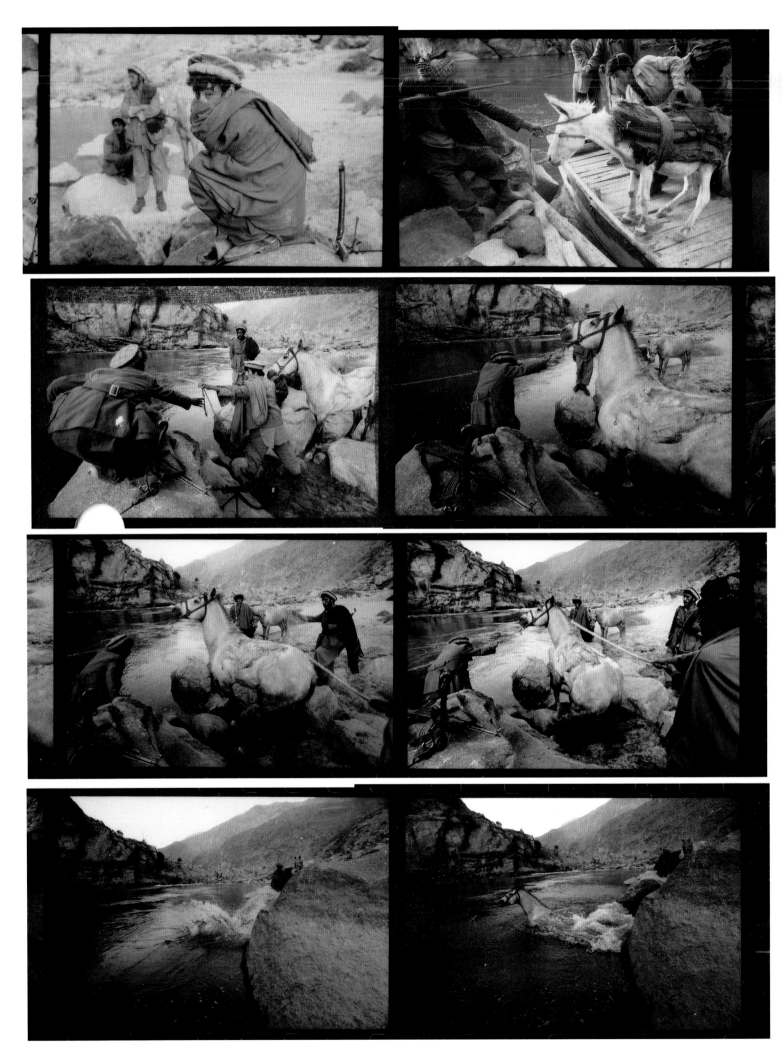

WE MAKE IT THROUGH. WE HAVE TO MAKE A STOP, AT A GOOD DISTANCE FROM THE ROAD, TO RUB DOWN THE HORSE AND TIE UP THE LOAD AGAIN.

THE MORE I OBSERVE MY ESCORT THE MORE CONVINCED I BECOME THAT THEY'RE INCREDIBLY LAZY.

AT LEAST THEY KNOW HOW TO LOAD UP THE PACKS ON THE HORSE, SOMETHING I'M COMPLETELY INCAPABLE OF DOING. I BARELY KNOW HOW TO MAKE MY BED. I GUESS THE PRINCIPLE'S THE SAME IN BOTH CASES—YOU HAVE TO TUCK THINGS IN PROPERLY IF YOU WANT THEM TO HOLD.

WHEN IT'S TIME TO HEAD OFF AGAIN, I'M THE ONE WHO HAS TO TELL THEM, "LET'S GO."

ARAKAT!

DARK THOUGHTS BREW IN MY HEAD.

WHO THE HELL ARE THESE GUYS?

THE DAY'S WALK ENDS AT A PACE I'M NOT ACCUSTOMED TO: A CRAWL. I DON'T SAY ANYTHING. IT'LL BE A LONG TRIP, I'LL HAVE PLENTY OF OPPORTUNITIES TO COMPLAIN.

DURING THAT NIGHT'S REST STOP, I FEED MY HORSE AND HE POSES FOR ME. AT THE VILLAGE, I BUY THE OATS THAT HE'LL CARRY AND EAT THE NEXT DAY.

188

DINNERTIME PROVIDES AN OPPORTUNITY TO CHAT WITH MY CLOWNS. AS BEFORE, TCHOPAN IS THE NICEST OF THE BUNCH. I GIVE THEM A DEMONSTRATION OF MY INCREASINGLY SKILLFUL DICTIONARY-THUMBING.

NONE OF THEM ARE MUJ'. WHY AM I NOT SURPRISED? THEY ARE JUST FOUR HILLBILLIES FROM YAFTAL, OF THE MOST BASIC SORT.

TCHOY GARM AST... NAN KHUB AST...

HA HA HA!

I EVEN PUSH MY LUCK AND TRY TO DESCRIBE TO THEM WHAT FRANCE AND PARIS ARE LIKE: STREETS, CARS, BUILDINGS, DEPARTMENT STORES.

I END UP DREAMING ABOUT IT THAT NIGHT. I FIND MYSELF BRINGING MY HORSE TO GRAZE ON THE LAWN OF THE INVALIDES PLAZA. THEN I LEAVE HIM THERE AND VERY APPROPRIATELY GO OFF TO LIE DOWN IN A REAL BED, WHERE MY DREAM TAKES AN EROTIC TURN.

PARIS... QARYA BISSIOR KALAAN...

THE NEXT DAY WE SET OFF FOR TESHKAN, HOME OF THE WAKIL, WHERE HALF THE MSF TEAM HAS STAYED.

189

MY SURGE OF SYMPATHY FOR MY FOUR GUYS HAS DEFLATED. THEY'RE ALWAYS BEHIND; IT'S A PAIN. I START BAWLING THEM OUT.

BIYA! ARAKAT KO!

AT NOON, WE STOP IN A *CHAYRANA* INN FOR LUNCH. THEY SULK VISIBLY AND START TALKING BEHIND MY BACK, EXCEPT TCHOPAN, WHO LOOKS EMBARRASSED.

AN HOUR LATER, THEY RUN OUT OF STEAM ON A FAIRLY STEEP SLOPE. THEY'RE HUNGRY AGAIN, THEY'RE TIRED, THEY WANT TO STOP YET ONCE MORE. ON TOP OF IT, I CAN TELL THEY HAVE NO IDEA WHERE WE ARE.

وایسیم

هستیم

I YELL AT THEM. NO WAY ARE WE GOING TO STOP. WE HAVE TO GET TO TESHKAN.

ZUD! ZUD! NO STOP! DAWAN DADAN!

I REALIZE AT THAT POINT THAT THE RETURN TRIP RESTS SQUARELY ON MY SHOULDERS. THERE'S NOTHING TO EXPECT FROM MY ESCORT. I WASN'T ASKING TO BE CARRIED IN A SEDAN CHAIR, JUST TO BE GUIDED AND ACCOMPANIED. INSTEAD I FIND MYSELF IN THE ABSURD POSITION OF GUIDING MY GUIDES.

I'M ON MY OWN.

190

IN TESHKAN, SITTING ON CARPETS, I'M REUNITED WITH SYLVIE, ODILE, TALL RONALD, AND THE WAKIL, WHO HAS ONE OF HIS ADJUTANTS BY HIS SIDE.

I HAVE A SIDE CONVERSATION WITH ODILE TO ASSESS THE SITUATION.

BASSIR GAVE ME A BUNCH OF USELESS CREEPS.

YOU POOR THING!

I CAN'T REALLY BLAME HIM, THOUGH. HE CAN'T AFFORD TO ASSIGN FOUR MUJ' TO A GUY WHO'S GOING BACK ALONE. HE'S KEEPING HIS MUJ' FOR THE WINTER OR SENDING THEM WITH MAJOR CARAVANS.

OKAY, BUT THERE'S A DIFFERENCE BETWEEN THAT AND GIVING ME DAWDLERS WHO DON'T EVEN KNOW THE WAY!

YOU KNOW THE WAY. IT'S THE WAY WE CAME OVER.

IN ANY CASE, I'M GOING TO SKETCH THINGS OUT FOR YOU. AND I'M ALSO GOING TO ASK SOME GUYS FROM HERE TO GIVE A GOOD BRIEFING TO YOUR ESCORT ABOUT THE ITINERARY FOR THE NEXT FEW DAYS. BECAUSE THERE'S THAT SOVIET GUARD POST IN SKAZAR THAT YOU HAVE TO WATCH OUT FOR.

A BIT LATER.

FROM TIME TO TIME, ABOUT ONCE A WEEK, I MAKE MYSELF AN IMAGINARY MEAL. I SUMMON UP A FEW FABULOUS DISHES AND SAVOR THEM, CHEWING SLOWLY.

DURING THE PREVIOUS MISSION, RÉGIS MADE ME A MAP OF THE WINES OF SOUTHWESTERN FRANCE. I KEPT IT AND I WASH DOWN MY MEAL WITH THE FINEST VINTAGES.

IT'S DELICIOUS.

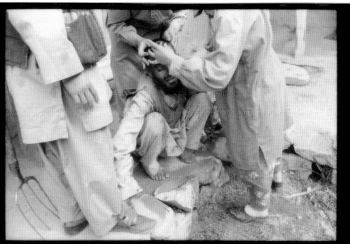

THE NEXT MORNING, THE WAKIL LINES UP ALL HIS MEN IN FRONT OF HIS BARRACKS CALLED A KOKHARGA, FOR A MARTIAL PICTURE.

ALL THAT COMMOTION FOR PICTURES THEY'LL NEVER SEE.

OKAY, SEE YOU, LATIFA. EAT AN IMAGINARY MEAL TO MY HEALTH.

I'LL DO IT TONIGHT. PIKE QUENELLES WITH A GLASS OF DRY WHITE WINE. AND SWEET FRITTERS FOR DESSERT.

WE LEAVE TESHKAN.

THIS GUY, WHO OVERTAKES US, CARVED HIS RIFLE OUT OF A TREE TRUNK.

SYLVIE'S RIGHT, I KNOW THE WAY. BESIDES, THERE'S ONLY ONE WAY TO GO: THE CARAVANS' ROUTE. AS LONG AS WE'RE MEETING SOME CARAVANS, WE'RE ON THE RIGHT PATH. THERE'S LITTLE CHANCE THAT I'LL GET LOST. THAT'S NOT WHAT I'M WORRIED ABOUT.

WHAT I WORRY ABOUT IS HAVING TO LEAD THIS TRIP, KNOWING WHEN TO SET OFF, WHEN TO STOP. CAREFULLY ASSESSING EACH STAGE, TO AVOID ENDING UP STUCK AT THE TOP OF A PASS, BLOCKED BY SNOW. GETTING THE TIMING RIGHT FOR GOING THROUGH THE PLACES THAT CAN GET BOMBED. BUYING THE RIGHT SUPPLIES.

ON THE WAY OVER, THE TEAM WAS PLANNING ALL THAT FOR ME. ALL I HAD TO WORRY ABOUT WERE MY CAMERAS AND MY FILM. I DIDN'T HAVE TO WORRY ABOUT SURVIVING. AND I EXPECTED MY ESCORT TO HANDLE THAT NOW. BUT NO, NOT A CHANCE. IT ALL BRINGS HOME HOW POWERLESS AND VULNERABLE I AM.

I'M STUCK HAVING TO WAIT FOR THOSE FOUR GOONS.

IT ISN'T THAT I DON'T LIKE THEM. I CAN PUT MYSELF IN THEIR SHOES: THEY EXPECTED TO SPEND THE WINTER IN THEIR VILLAGE, AND THERE THEY ARE, HAVING TO TAG ALONG UP AND DOWN MOUNTAINS WITH SOME FRENCHMAN—MIGHT AS WELL SAY A MARTIAN—WHO, ON TOP OF IT, IS YELLING AT THEM. I'D BE GRUMBLING, TOO.

I DON'T MEAN THEM ANY HARM, BUT THEY'RE GETTING ON MY NERVES. THEY'RE SOFTIES, AND THE ROAD AHEAD IS TOUGH. AT LEAST EIGHT PASSES TO CROSS, NONE LOWER THAN 11,000 FEET. A CASUAL STROLL WON'T CUT IT.

OUR SLOW PACE COULD'VE BEEN PLEASANT IF IT WEREN'T SO IRRITATING, SO ALARMING. PUMPED UP WITH RED BLOOD CELLS AS I AM, I FEEL PRACTICALLY NO FATIGUE. AND THE MOUNTAINS ARE AS BEAUTIFUL AS EVER. BUT I TRUNDLE ALONG WITH DOWNCAST EYES. I CONTINUE, ALMOST DESPITE MYSELF, TO SHOOT THE PICTURES OF A STORY I'VE ALREADY WRAPPED UP.

194

AT VILLAGE STOPS, OR WHEN WE PASS OTHER CARAVANS, THE BEHAVIOR OF MY GUYS BECOMES SUSPECT. THEY TALK TO THE AFGHANS WE MEET, POINTING AT ME WITH EXPRESSIONS OF SARCASM OR HOSTILITY. I START WONDERING IF THEY HAVE SOMETHING UP THEIR SLEEVES.

I SEE TCHOPAN AS A POTENTIAL ALLY IN CASE OF TROUBLE. HE ISN'T AS DECEITFUL AS THE OTHERS. I TRY TO PRESERVE A BOND OF TRUST WITH HIM.

I FIGURE HE WOULDN'T BETRAY ME. BUT I DOUBT HE'D HAVE THE STRENGTH OF CHARACTER TO PREVENT HIS BUDDIES FROM DOING SO.

THE FIRST SIGNIFICANT PASS IS THE ARASH PASS. WE START OUT WITH A TRAFFIC JAM. THE FLOCK STRETCHES ON ENDLESSLY. THE DUST WE'RE BREATHING IS FILLED WITH THE SOUR SMELL OF THE SHEEP. I DON'T EVEN REGISTER THE SMELL OF HORSES ANYMORE: IT HAS BECOME MY OWN.

196

AFTER THAT FLOCK I PRESS AHEAD A BIT. I'VE DECIDED TO CLIMB AT A STEADY CLIP, AND LET THE OTHERS FIND A WAY TO KEEP UP.

OF COURSE, AT THAT RATE, I QUICKLY LEAVE THEM BEHIND. I FIND MYSELF ALONE, TAKING ON A SLOPE THAT SEEMS MORE LIKE AN ENDLESS PILE OF CRUSHED STONES THAN A MOUNTAIN.

A FIGURE APPEARS.

A GUY WEARING A WHITE TURBAN. HE DOESN'T HAVE THE LOOK OF A MOUNTAIN-DWELLER, MORE LIKE A KIND OF SCHOLAR.

HE GETS STRAIGHT DOWN TO BUSINESS: "WHAT RELIGION ARE YOU?"

IT'S A QUESTION I'M STARTING TO GET USED TO. PANTING, I ANSWER:

ISAWI.

HE SPEAKS TO ME AS TO A CHILD, WITH A LOT OF GESTURES.

ISAWI, THAT'S KHUB, THAT'S GOOD. MUSLIM IS BISSIOR KHUB, MUCH BETTER. HE'LL GO TO HEAVEN AND I WON'T.

BUT I'D BETTER NOT BE YAHUD. YAHUD IS KHALOP, REALLY BAD. HE SAYS THAT WITH A FURROWED BROW.

AND WITH THAT, HE JUST WALKS OFF.

THE WHOLE THING LASTS EXACTLY THIRTY SECONDS.

JUST TO BE SURE, I CHECK IN MY DICTIONARY THAT I'VE UNDERSTOOD CORRECTLY: YAHUD DOES MEAN JEWISH.

WHAT DOES A GUY LIKE HIM THINK A JEW IS? WHATEVER HE KNOWS WAS PICKED UP FROM A DOCTRINE THAT, IN TURN, HE'S SPREADING ALONG THE HIGH ROADS. HOW MANY TRAVELING SALESMEN LIKE HIM ARE THERE IN AFGHANISTAN?

I REFLECT FOR A MOMENT ON THE BATTLE OF RELIGIONS AS I WATCH MY FEET TRUDGING ALONG OVER THE STONES.

THE ISSUE TAKES ON THE APPEARANCE OF THE MOUNTAIN I'M CLIMBING: ARID, CRUSHING, ENDURING.

IN THE END, WHAT DEPRESSES ME IS THAT THIS GUY DIDN'T GIVE A SHIT ABOUT WHAT I WAS DOING THERE OR WHERE I WAS GOING.

AT THE SUMMIT, I WALK IN THE CLOUDS, SHIVERING IN THE COLD FOG. COMING BACK DOWN, I COME ACROSS THE SUN AGAIN, AS IF HE WERE LIVING ON A LOWER FLOOR.

I SIT DOWN, SHELTERED FROM THE WIND, TO LET THE FOUR GUYS CATCH UP WITH ME. I'M IN A BETTER MOOD. I CLEARED THE PASS. I FEEL LIKE TAKING OUT MY NOTEBOOK AND DOING SOME WRITING.

I REALIZE THAT I HAVE TO GO EASY ON THOSE GUYS. WE'RE A KIND OF BROTHERHOOD. EVEN IF THEY GET ON MY NERVES, I HAVE TO SMOOTH MY ROUGH EDGES, LIKE IN A FAMILY. LIKE IT OR NOT, WE'RE GOING TO BE LIVING TOGETHER FOR A GOOD TEN DAYS.

I START NOTICING THE BEAUTY OF MY SURROUNDINGS AGAIN, AS IF MY CAPACITY TO BE MOVED WERE THAWING IN THE HEAT.

ANOTHER MAN WITH FUNKY GLASSES.

THE FOUR BOZOS ARRIVE. THEY TAKE A BREAK THAT I DON'T BEGRUDGE THEM. AT LAST, WE HEAD OFF AGAIN.

BARELY FORTY MINUTES LATER, AS BAD LUCK WOULD HAVE IT, WE COME ACROSS A STOPPED CARAVAN, WHOSE PEOPLE ARE PRAYING. THE OPPORTUNITY IS JUST TOO GOOD FOR MY RASCALS, AND THEY RUSH OVER TO KNEEL DOWN TOO.

INSTEAD OF CHAMPING AT THE BIT, I TAKE ADVANTAGE OF THE OPEN AIR TO BREAK ONE OF MY LONG-STANDING ▓▓▓▓▓ ▓▓▓ ▓▓▓▓▓ PRAYER FROM EVERY ANGLE.

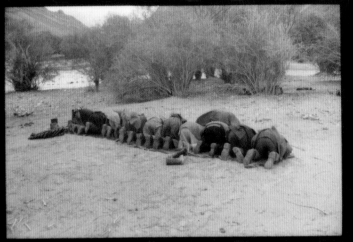

LEAVING AS SOON AS THE PRAYER WAS OVER WOULD'VE BEEN TOO EASY. MUCH BETTER TO SPEND AN ENDLESS AMOUNT OF TIME TAKING GROUP PHOTOS, WHICH PROVIDE OPPORTUNITIES FOR DELIGHTFUL JOKES, LIKE PUTTING AN AFGHAN CAP, THE PAKOL, ON MY HORSE.

THAT'S HOW IT ALWAYS GOES WITH THEM. I TRY TO BE UNDERSTANDING, BUT I JUST CAN'T HELP IT, THEY GRATE ON MY NERVES.

AT THE NEXT STOP, TCHOPAN INSISTS ON TAKING A PICTURE OF ME. I MIME TWO OR THREE INSTRUCTIONS AND LET HIM HAVE A GO. WE'LL SEE WHAT COMES OF IT.

JOHN'S OPERATION MIGHT NOT HAVE KILLED ME, BUT IT HASN'T KILLED THE BOIL ON MY ARM EITHER. IT ISN'T LOOKING GOOD. I CHANGE MY BANDAGE.

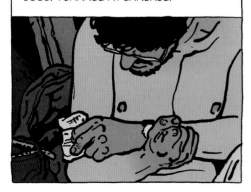

SWEAT AND FRICTION HAVE CORRODED THE SHEATH ON THE TEMPLES OF MY GLASSES. THE METAL IS CHAFING MY EARS AND CAUSING AN INFECTION. I TRY TO FIX UP A PROTECTIVE LAYER USING GAUZE.

MY GUMS ARE INFLAMED, TOO. EVEN THOUGH I'M NOT REALLY FEELING THE EXHAUSTION, I'M STARTING TO SHOW SIGNS OF WEAR PHYSICALLY.

201

THE NEXT DAY, WE LOAD UP THE HORSE AND LEAVE IN THE EARLY MORNING.

WE APPROACH MAIDAN, THE LAPIS LAZULI MINE. TWO SHEPHERDS ARE LEADING THEIR FLOCK ACROSS A RIVER. I COVER THE EVENT.

THE DOG COMES LAST. AFGHAN DOGS—AND I DON'T MEAN AFGHAN HOUNDS, JUST THE MUTTS WE PASS ON THE ROAD—DON'T HAVE A LOFTY PLACE IN THE SOCIAL ORDER. I MUST SAY, THEY'RE VERY UGLY AND OFTEN UNFRIENDLY.

WE'RE ON THE RIGHT TRACK. I'M BACK ON THE NARROW, DIZZYING PATHS WHERE I LOST MY CAMERA'S SUN COVER. I STILL HAVEN'T GOTTEN OVER IT AND I CATCH MYSELF LOOKING FOR IT OUT OF THE CORNER OF MY EYE.

THE NIGHT AHEAD OF US WILL BE A NIGHT OF MARCHING, BECAUSE WE'RE APPROACHING THE SOVIET POSITION OF SKAZAR. MY GUYS KNOW THAT AND ARE UNEASY.

ANXIETY HAS A MIRACULOUS EFFECT AND, FOR THE FIRST TIME, I SEE THEM TAKE AN INITIATIVE. THEY NEGOTIATE OUR JOINING ANOTHER CARAVAN.

WE GET THROUGH WITHOUT INCIDENT, RUSHING FORWARD AS FAST AS THE MOONLIGHT ALLOWS.

THE EFFORT TAXES THEM. DESPITE A GENEROUS BREAK IN THE MORNING, THEY DALLY MORE THAN EVER. OUR EXCHANGES GROW HEATED IN THE AFTERNOON.

I'M ON EDGE. I'M AWARE THAT THE NEXT DAY, AFTER THE REST STOP IN ANJOMAN, THE REAL HARDSHIP WILL BEGIN. WE'LL HAVE TO GET THROUGH THE KALOTAC PASS, THE FAMOUS FORK BETWEEN BADAKHSHAN AND PANJSHIR, ONE OF THE TOUGHEST OF THE ENTIRE TRIP. THERE COULD BE BOMBING, THERE COULD BE SNOW, AND IT'S EASY TO GET LOST, LIKE THAT DONKEY MINDER WE FOUND AGAINST ALL ODDS, ON THE WAY OVER.

I WALK ANGRILY, IN A LEADEN MOOD, AND I DON'T TAKE ANY PICTURES.

AFTER WE GET TO ANJOMAN, I REALIZE MY HORSE HAS LOST A HORSESHOE.

THAT'S BAD NEWS. I'VE OFTEN SEEN HORSES LOSE THEIR SHOES. I KNOW YOU HAVE TO SHOE THEM AS QUICKLY AS POSSIBLE TO PREVENT THEIR GETTING INJURED.

LUCKILY, I HAVE THE HORSESHOES THAT THE MUJ' FROM YAFTAL-E-PAYAN GAVE ME. I TRY TO HAND ONE TO MY GUYS.

ASP... NAAL JAANESHIN SHODAN.

JAANESHIN SHODAN.

ابن كار را بلد نيستيم

بلد نيستيم

NAAL JAANESHIN SHODAN!

قدرت بكين!

HA HA!

HAHAHA!

I FLY INTO A RAGE.

WHAT THE FUCK IS YOUR PROBLEM?!

I'LL SHOE THE GODDAMN HORSE MYSELF! *PEDER NALAT!*

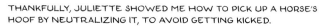

THANKFULLY, JULIETTE SHOWED ME HOW TO PICK UP A HORSE'S HOOF BY NEUTRALIZING IT, TO AVOID GETTING KICKED.

GIVE ME.

I NEED NAILS. SOME NAILS. BAM! BAM!

AH, THANKS. *TACHAKOR.*

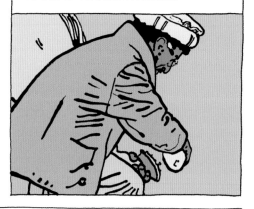

I PLANT MY NAILS AS BEST I CAN, IN THE HOLES LEFT BY THE PREVIOUS ONES. I'M AFRAID OF HURTING MY HORSE.

THERE. I'VE TRIED MY HAND AT WHILE-YOU-WAIT RESOLING. MY HORSE HASN'T BUDGED. I HOPE IT'LL HOLD.

I GRAB MY STUFF AND RUSH INTO THE MOSQUE WITHOUT SAYING A WORD.

I DON'T SHARE THE MEAL OF MY ESCORT.

THEY FALL ASLEEP. I DON'T. I'VE COME DOWN WITH A BUG.

I SPEND THE NIGHT OUTSIDE PATHETICALLY EMPTYING MYSELF OUT.

BY MORNING I'M DRAINED AND FROZEN. I HAVEN'T HAD EVEN A MINUTE OF SLEEP.

WE STILL SET OFF. WE HAVE TO REACH A HUT ON THE SIDE OF A LAKE. WE'LL GET THERE BY NOON AND WILL STAY THERE UNTIL THE EVENING, BEFORE CROSSING THE KALOTAC PASS BY NIGHT.

FOR THE FIRST TIME IN OUR TRIP, I BRING UP THE REAR. MY EYES ARE BURNING, MY BELLY IS A PAINFUL JUMBLE, AND MY LEGS WOBBLE.

TO AVOID THINKING OF ANYTHING, I START COUNTING MY STEPS.

AT LAST, WE REACH THE LAKE. I'M EXHAUSTED.

I SAY TO THE FOUR: "I'M NOT FEELING WELL. I NEED TO REST. WE AREN'T LEAVING TONIGHT, WE'LL GO TOMORROW MORNING."

THEY HAVE A BRIEF CONSULTATION. I CAN TELL THEY'RE FREAKING OUT.

ONE OF THEM EXPLAINS TO ME WITH MUCH GESTICULATION THAT, BY DAY, PLANES BOMB THE PASS—BOOM BOOM. WE ABSOLUTELY HAVE TO GO BY NIGHT.

PLANES? WHAT PLANES? THERE ARE NO PLANES.

TAYAARA NIST.

ON THE WAY OVER, WE CROSSED THE PASS AT THE END OF THE AFTERNOON. THERE'S NO REASON WHY WE CAN'T CROSS IT TOMORROW AT DAWN.

KALOTAC KOTAL... FARDAA WAQT...

BUT UNTIL THEN I HAVE TO SLEEP, OKAY? SICK. NEED TO GET STRENGTH BACK.

MAN KHAAB KARDAN...

HE STARTS UP AGAIN: BY DAY, THE PLANES BOMB THE PASS—BOOM BOOM, WE HAVE TO CROSS BY NIGHT.

I CUT THE DISCUSSION SHORT. WE'LL DO AS I SAID AND NOT OTHERWISE.

BAASH! MAN ENTEZAAR KASHIDAN.

I MUDDLE THROUGH THE AFTERNOON IN THE HUT. I DRINK WATER BUT CAN'T SWALLOW ANY SOLID FOOD. MY STOMACH STILL FEELS LIKE IT CAN'T HOLD ANYTHING.

NIGHT FALLS. WE STAY PUT.

IN A HALF-DAZED STATE, I WATCH THE STONES IN THE WALL DARKEN.

208

THE BASTARDS. THEY'RE GONE.

THEY LEFT ME THE HORSE, MY BAGGAGE, AND SOME BREAD, WHICH I EAT. I SLEPT WELL AND I FEEL BETTER.

I DON'T HAVE MUCH CHOICE. I SURE DON'T WANT TO GO BACK. I COULD STAY HERE, BUT FOR WHAT? WAIT FOR ANOTHER CARAVAN TO COME THROUGH? THERE'S NO GUARANTEE THAT THERE'LL BE ONE GOING WHERE I'M HEADED, EITHER TODAY OR IN THE NEXT DAYS.

NO, THE ONLY THING TO DO IS TO KEEP GOING.

I CURSE MYSELF FOR NEVER HAVING LEARNED TO SADDLE THIS HORSE PROPERLY.

I REMOVE HIS NIGHT BLANKET, PUT ON HIS PACKSADDLE. NONE OF THE MOTIONS COME NATURALLY.

THEN I LOAD HIM UP.

THERE ARE ROPES EVERYWHERE. I CROSS THEM, TANGLE THEM UP, TIE THEM TOGETHER WITHOUT MUCH LOGIC. I TRY AS BEST I CAN TO IMITATE WHAT I'VE SEEN.

IT SEEMS TO HOLD UP. I SLIP THE BRIDLE ON HIM.

HE'S DOCILE.

SHALL WE GO?

210

THE ASCENT BEGINS IN THE EARLY MORNING. MY WATCH SHOWS 5:10 AM. THE WEATHER IS GRAY, THE ROCKS ARE SLIPPERY. IT'S DRIZZLING. TO AVOID GIVING IN TO ANXIETY, I CAST MY MIND AROUND FOR REASONS TO BE GLAD. DON'T REALLY FIND ANY.

EACH STEP THE HORSE TAKES CAUSES MY POORLY TIED BAGGAGE TO SWAY, AND LOOSENS THE ROPES.

IT'S BARELY A QUARTER TO SIX WHEN I HAVE TO COMPLETELY UNLOAD AND RELOAD THE HORSE.

I START OVER AGAIN TWENTY MINUTES LATER.

I START OVER AGAIN FORTY-FIVE MINUTES LATER.

I START OVER AGAIN TWENTY MINUTES LATER.

I START OVER AGAIN THIRTY MINUTES LATER.

AND AGAIN.

AND AGAIN.

AND AGAIN.

AND AGAIN. WITHOUT EVER GETTING THE KNACK OF IT AND GETTING IT TO HOLD IN PLACE.

I PASS A CARAVAN THAT I TRY TO INTEREST IN MY PREDICAMENT. THEY GREET ME POLITELY BUT DON'T STOP.

SAME THING A FEW HUNDRED YARDS FARTHER UP.

IT'S NOW 3 PM, NEARLY NIGHTFALL. I'M FAR FROM THE SUMMIT, AND I'M STARTING TO GET SERIOUSLY WORRIED.

I'M EXHAUSTED, AND FRUSTRATED BY THE RELOADING. MY HORSE IS PANTING, TOO. HE HAS SORES. I WON'T BE ABLE TO CROSS THE PASS BEFORE NIGHTFALL. IT'S TAKEN ME TEN HOURS TO GET TO THIS POINT—THERE'S NO POINT TRYING TO TURN AROUND TO GO BACK DOWN.

FOR THE UMPTEENTH TIME, I UNLOAD AND RELOAD MY STUFF.

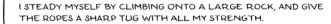

I STEADY MYSELF BY CLIMBING ONTO A LARGE ROCK, AND GIVE THE ROPES A SHARP TUG WITH ALL MY STRENGTH.

AH!

212

FUCK.

MY LEG IS BUSTED, I'M SURE—CAUGHT BETWEEN THE HORSE AND THE BIG ROCK.

HE GETS UP. MY LEG HURTS LIKE HELL.

IT HURTS, BUT THE BONE IS INTACT— JUST A BIG BRUISE. I MASSAGE MY CALF.

THE FALL CAUSED THE BAGGAGE TO SLIP YET AGAIN.

I ADJUST IT ONCE MORE AND WE HEAD OFF.

IT'S THE LAST STAGE OF THE CLIMB UP THE KALOTAC. WE'RE OVER 16,000 FEET HIGH. IT STARTS SNOWING.

THE AIR IS THIN. THE HORSE PAUSES EVERY THREE STEPS TO CATCH ITS BREATH. WE CAN'T GO ANY FARTHER.

SUDDENLY, IN FRONT OF ME, A CARAVAN APPEARS OUT OF THE CURTAIN OF SNOW.

THE LEAD MEN PASS ME BY WITHOUT SLOWING DOWN. I HAVE TO STOP ONE OF THEM.

I THROW MYSELF IN THEIR MIDST.

ASALAAMALEIKUM!

AND THERE, AMAZED, I RECOGNIZE THE WAKIL'S SON.

THE SON OF THE WAKIL OF TESHKAN, WHOM JULIETTE INTRODUCED ME TO AT THE HORSE MARKET IN PESHAWAR.

BAASH! MAN... FARASAWI! UM... TABIB JAMILA... WAKIL RAFIQ!

آنکه وانوکا اس کنلدہت

COMON VA TA FAM?

WHAT?

اینی چها رمکن؟   COMON VA TA FAM?

MA FEMME?

OF COURSE! "COMMENT VA TA FEMME?" HOW'S YOUR WIFE. MY WIFE'S FINE, SHE'S GREAT.

KHUB, KHUB.

I TRY TO DESCRIBE THE STATE I AM IN. ALONE. ABANDONED. EXHAUSTED HORSE. LOAD MESSED UP. ALL THAT USING MY TINY DICTIONARY, AS THE WIND TURNS THE PAGES AND SNOWFLAKES WET THEM.

MAN TANHAA... KHASTA...

HE ANSWERS QUICKLY, JABBERING IN HIS LANGUAGE.

من ، رفتن پین بالا ول من ، نرستادن کنی باین کہ

HE CAN'T STOP. HE HAS TO GO DOWN, BUT ONCE AT THE BOTTOM HE'LL SEND FOR HELP. SOMEONE WILL COME.

AT LEAST, THAT'S WHAT I UNDERSTAND. HE'S ALREADY MOVING AWAY.

THE THOUGHT CROSSES MY MIND THAT I SHOULD FOLLOW HIM. BUT I DON'T MOVE.

THE ONLY THOUGHT I HAVE ROOM FOR IN MY MIND IS GETTING BACK TO PAKISTAN.

I'M PRACTICALLY AT THE TOP OF THE PASS. AND I REMEMBER VERY CLEARLY THAT ON THE OTHER SIDE, A LITTLE WAY DOWN, THERE'S A FOREST WHERE WE SLEPT ON THE WAY OVER. IN THAT FOREST THERE'LL DEFINITELY BE ENCAMPMENTS, CAMPFIRES.

THE EVENING LIGHT IS PALLID BECAUSE OF THE SNOW. BIG CLOUDS PASS AROUND US. WE RESUME OUR CLIMB.

THE HORSE'S SLOW PACE AT LEAST HAS THE BENEFIT OF STABILIZING THE PACKS. I RECOVER A BIT OF MY OPTIMISM. MEETING THAT GUY LIFTED MY SPIRITS. HE'S YOUNG, BUT HE'S A COMMANDER. HE SAID HE'D SEND SOMEBODY, AND HE WILL.

HAHAHA!

AND THERE WAS THAT MOMENT OF "COMMENT VA TA FEMME?" I KNOW WHERE THAT CAME FROM. IT WAS RÉGIS AND ROBERT WHO TAUGHT HIM THAT: "IF YOU MEET A FRENCHMAN, YOU NEED ONLY ONE GREETING: COMMENT VA TA FEMME?"

COMON VA TA FAM? HAHA!

BUDDIES WHO MANAGE TO MAKE YOU LAUGH IN THEIR ABSENCE—AND AT THAT ALTITUDE—SURE DESERVE SOME CREDIT.

THE SUMMIT. WE'VE BEEN PURSUING IT FOR SIXTEEN HOURS.

WE EMBARK ON THE DESCENT. MY KNEES ARE ACHING. SUDDENLY, FEAR GRIPS ME: A PANIC, A DESPERATE NEED TO BE ELSEWHERE.

COME ON, LET'S GO!

COME ON!

WE CAN'T STOP.

RRRRAC TSS TSSS!

MOVE IT!

MOVE, DAMN IT!

MOVE!

YAH!

YAH! YAH!

MOVE IT!

COME ON, LET'S GO!

YAH!

SOMEBODY HELP!
YAH!
YAH! YAH!
YAH!
YAH!
PLEASE HELP!
YAH!
YAH...
OH, MY GOD.
WHAT AM I DOING?
I'M BEATING MY HORSE.

PULL YOURSELF TOGETHER.

SUDDENLY I'M NOT AFRAID ANYMORE. IT PASSED.

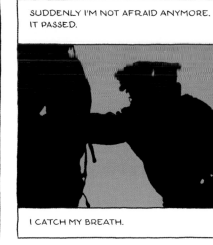

I CATCH MY BREATH.

THIS HORSE WON'T GO ANY FARTHER.

I START UNLOADING HIM METHODICALLY.

WE'RE ON A VERY NARROW PATH, STEEPLY INCLINED AND FULL OF ROCKS. IT STOPPED SNOWING.

ONCE THE HORSE IS FULLY UNLOADED, I COVER HIM.

AND, THEN, WITHOUT WAITING, I FEED HIM. NEVER MIND THE ADVICE I'VE BEEN GIVEN.

I UNFURL MY SLEEPING BAG ACROSS THE PATH.

THE HORSE HAS FINISHED EATING. I TIE HIM TO A ROCK.

I HAVE TWO SURVIVAL BLANKETS, STILL UNUSED. I ROLL MYSELF IN THEM.

I TUCK MYSELF INTO THE BAG.

THERE.

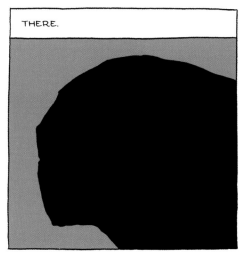

218

I STAY ON THE PATH BECAUSE OF MINES. RUSSIAN PLANES DUMP ANTIPERSONNEL MINES, WHICH ARM UPON HITTING THE GROUND. THEY LOOK LIKE LARGE BUTTERFLIES. STRATEGIC PLACES LIKE THIS PASS ARE FILLED WITH THEM. CARAVANS DO THEIR BEST TO CLEAR THE PATH BY EXPLODING THE MINES THEY SPOT. BUT YOU CAN'T STRAY FROM THE PATH. THERE ARE BOUND TO BE SOME MINES JUST A FEW YARDS AWAY.

IT GETS LIGHTER OR DARKER AS CLOUDS PASS BY OVERHEAD. I'M HUNGRY AND THIRSTY. I HAVEN'T EATEN ANYTHING ALL DAY, OBSESSED AS I WAS WITH THE WALK. MY CANTEEN IS EMPTY. I FISH SOME DRIED FRUITS OUT OF THE BOTTOMS OF MY POCKETS. THAT'S ALL I HAVE. THEY MAKE ME EVEN THIRSTIER.

I PACK SNOW INTO MY CANTEEN AND PUT IT INSIDE MY SLEEPING BAG. WITHIN FIFTEEN MINUTES, I'LL HAVE WATER.

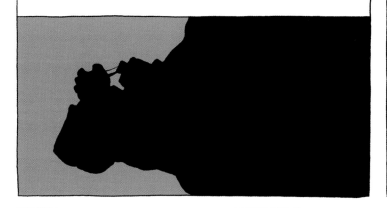

I'M DUMBSTRUCK BY MY EPISODE OF INSANITY. I CAN STILL FEEL THE IMPACT OF MY FISTS ON THE HORSE'S NECK. HE HASN'T BUDGED. A HORSE'S NECK IS REALLY TOUGH, REALLY MUSCULAR.

IN ALL MY LIFE I'VE NEVER FELT SUCH FEAR. IT LEFT ME AS SUDDENLY AS IT HAD COME, BUT IN THE MEANTIME I COMPLETELY LOST MY MIND. I HAVE NO IDEA HOW LONG IT LASTED.

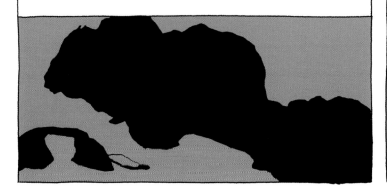

I CAN'T STOP THINKING ABOUT THE LOOK ON THE FACE OF THE GUY WHO GOT LOST IN THE SAME PLACE ON THE TRIP OVER AND CAUGHT UP WITH US IN ANJOMAN—THE EXPRESSION OF TERROR ON HIS FACE AND, ESPECIALLY, WHAT THE AFGHANS HAD BEEN SAYING BEFORE HE WAS RECOVERED: "HE'S DONE FOR. YOU CAN'T SURVIVE ALONE UP THERE FOR A WHOLE NIGHT."

I TAKE OUT ONE OF MY CAMERAS. I CHOOSE A 20MM LENS, A VERY WIDE ANGLE, AND SHOOT FROM THE GROUND.

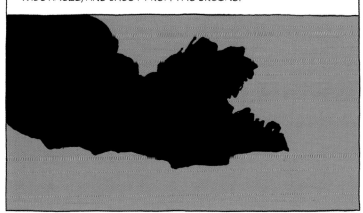

TO LET PEOPLE KNOW WHERE I DIED.

CLICK

THE SNOW MUST'VE MELTED BY NOW.

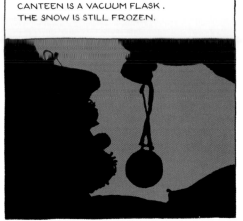

DAMN IT. I'D FORGOTTEN THAT MY CANTEEN IS A VACUUM FLASK. THE SNOW IS STILL FROZEN.

I PUT SOME IN MY MOUTH, BUT IT'S NOT THE SAME. DOESN'T QUENCH YOUR THIRST.

I HEAR THE HORSE SLIP ON THE ROCKS. HE'S TRYING TO FIND A SECURE FOOTING. WHAT A FOOL I WAS TO LIE DOWN UNDER HIM. IF HE FALLS, HE'LL CRUSH ME.

TOO BAD. I DON'T HAVE THE STRENGTH TO MOVE.

I RUMMAGE FOR MY NOTEBOOK, A PENCIL, AND MY FOREHEAD LAMP. I WRITE:
"OCTOBER 17, 1986.
DOMINIQUE, THIS IS WHERE MY JOURNEY ENDS.
MY ESCORT DUMPED ME AT THE FOOT OF THE KALOTAC PASS.
I'M STUCK AT THE SUMMIT, ALONE.
I CAN'T SEE HOW I'M GOING TO MAKE IT OUT OF HERE.
MY HORSE WON'T MOVE ANY MORE.
IT'S FREEZING.
I'M IN MY SLEEPING BAG AND I'M WAITING.
I HOPE THAT THIS NOTEBOOK AND MY PICTURES WILL REACH YOU.
I'M THINKING OF MY MOM—TELL HER—
AND OF YOU."

224

I WRITE DOMINIQUE'S ADDRESS IN BIG LETTERS IN THE FLYLEAF. I PACK UP THE NOTEBOOK AND SHOVE MY FREEZING HANDS INTO MY ARMPITS.

IT STARTS SNOWING AGAIN.

SEVERAL TIMES THE HORSE SKIDDING JOLTS ME ABRUPTLY OUT OF MY DROWSINESS.

EACH TIME, I TUCK MY HEAD IN, MY HEART POUNDING. NOTHING HAPPENS.

MY HEART RATE SLOWS. I GROW DROWSY AGAIN AND DOZE.

UNTIL THE HORSE SKIDS AGAIN.

STILL, I DON'T COME OUT OF THE SLEEPING BAG. THE COLD WOULD CLOBBER ME.

MY MIND HAD BEEN SET ON THE IDEA OF GOING HOME. NOW I ONLY HAVE THE THOUGHT OF DYING.

A GROUP COMES THROUGH, HALF TRAMPLING ME.

DOESN'T EVEN STOP.

THEN ANOTHER.

SAME THING.

KHUB ASTIN? ARE YOU OKAY?

NEI.

NOT GREAT, NO.

225

A CARAVAN.
A WOLF-FACED MAN, WHO SEEMS TO BE THE LEADER.
I COME OUT OF MY SLEEPING BAG, INTO THE FROSTY DAWN.
I TRY TO CONTROL MY SHAKING TO TAKE A PICTURE.

HE SAYS "COME" AND MOTIONS THAT I SHOULD GATHER MY THINGS.

I MAKE CLEAR TO HIM THAT I DON'T KNOW HOW TO LOAD UP MY HORSE. HE ANSWERS IN CRUDE ENGLISH THAT HE'LL TAKE CARE OF IT AND TAKE ME WITH HIM. BUT FIRST I HAVE TO PAY.

MONEY.

HOW MUCH WOULD HE CHARGE?

HOW MUCH?

TWENTY THOUSAND.

20,000 AFGHANI.

I HAVE MONEY ON ME—QUITE A BIT, IN FACT. ABOUT 300 DOLLARS AND 250,000 AFGHANI, IN THICK WADS. I CAN'T MANAGE TO TAKE OUT THE 20,000 WITHOUT HIS SEEING THE REST. IT'S EMBARRASSING.

INCH ALLAH. DON'T HAVE MUCH CHOICE.

THERE.

THEY LOAD UP MY HORSE, WHO SETS OFF AGAIN WITH A TAP.

AND OFF WE GO.

WE HEAD DOWN. I FOLLOW THEM, FEELING STIFF, SORE, DIZZY.

LAST NIGHT, I THOUGHT I WAS TWO HOURS' WALK AWAY FROM THE FOREST. WE WALK FOR NEARLY FIVE HOURS BEFORE REACHING IT. AND THOSE AREN'T FIVE HOURS AT THE PACE OF MY FORMER ESCORT. I'VE FOUND SOME REAL MUJ', AND THEY EAT UP THE MILES.

I BARELY RECOGNIZE THE FOREST I'D SEEN ON THE WAY OVER. OBVIOUSLY, AUTUMN HAS TAKEN ITS TOLL.

AT LAST, WE TAKE A BREAK.

THEY START A FIRE, MAKE TEA, AND PASS AROUND A THICK, SWEET CAKE.

IN A MIXTURE OF PERSIAN, ENGLISH, AND SIGN LANGUAGE I EXPLAIN TO THE WOLF WHO I AM AND WHAT I'M DOING THERE: THE MSF MISSION, THE PHOTOS, THE RETURN ALONE, BASSIR'S GUYS ABANDONING ME. THE WOLF LISTENS.

AFTER I'VE FINISHED, THE WOLF TELLS ME I'M LUCKY HE PICKED ME UP, BECAUSE THE KALOTAC PASS IS CRAWLING WITH WOLVES. REAL ONES.

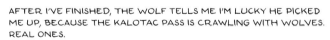

WOLVES UP THERE.

WE WALK WITHOUT A MOMENT'S REST UNTIL THE EVENING STOP. I INSTANTLY SLEEP LIKE A STONE.

GETTING UP IS TOUGH, AT ONE AM. I FEEL AWFUL, LIKE I'VE BARELY SLEPT. WHERE WILL I FIND THE STRENGTH TO KEEP UP WITH THEM?

EVEN AS I ASK MYSELF THE QUESTION, I'M ALREADY ON MY WAY.

I HAVE TO SHAKE OFF A HUGE RELUCTANCE TO TAKE PICTURES. BUNDLES OF INTERESTING SCENES AND PANORAMAS SLIDE BY UNCAPTURED. I CAN'T CONVINCE MYSELF TO SHOOT THEM.

I MANAGE TO WITH THAT CRIPPLED BABA. IT'S A KIND OF SELF-PORTRAIT. THAT'S HOW I FEEL.

IN THE EVENING I REDISCOVER THE FEELING OF HAVING NO PRIVACY. WHEN I OPEN A BAG THEY'LL COME SEE WHAT'S INSIDE. IF I TAKE MY CASE OF TOILETRIES WITH ME TO WASH UP AT THE RIVER, TWO OR THREE GUYS WILL FOLLOW ME.

I CAN'T STAND IT ANY MORE.

CAN'T YOU GIVE ME A SINGLE FUCKING BREAK?

I LOOK FORWARD TO ONLY ONE MOMENT: WHEN I CAN SLIP INTO MY SLEEPING BAG.

AS NIGHT FALLS IT RUBS AWAY MY SURROUNDINGS. THE HALO OF MY FOREHEAD LAMP CREATES A LITTLE INTANGIBLE HOUSE.

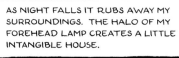

I WRITE FOR A SHORT WHILE, THEN CURL UP.

THIS UGLY, DIRTY, UNCOMFORTABLE CORNER BECOMES MY HOME, AND I FEEL MY ONLY MOMENT OF WELL-BEING OF THE DAY.

HUH?

ONE AM. WE HIT THE ROAD AGAIN.

THE DAWN REVEALS TO MY EYES WHAT MY LEGS HAVE ALREADY OBSERVED: THE PRESENCE OF THE POJOL PASS, WHICH WE'VE ALREADY STARTED CLIMBING.

I'M STRUGGLING. THE HORSE TOO.

SHORTLY BEFORE THE SUMMIT, WE PASS AN ARMED CARAVAN.

A BIT LATER, AT THE TOP, MY GROUP STOPS. SINCE I'M BRINGING UP THE REAR, I THINK THEY'RE WAITING FOR ME. BUT THAT ISN'T IT.

THE WOLF COMES TOWARD ME AND SAYS:

MORE MONEY.

AH, THE SON OF A BITCH. GOOD TIMING.

I'D BEEN EXPECTING IT AND HAD PUT A CERTAIN AMOUNT IN A POCKET, TO AVOID HAVING TO TAKE OUT EVERYTHING I HAVE. FIVE THOUSAND TWO HUNDRED AFGHANIS. I HAND THEM OVER.

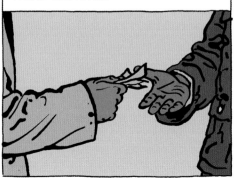

I'M STARTING TO WONDER HOW THESE GUYS ARE PLANNING TO FINISH ME OFF.

A FEW HUNDRED YARDS LATER, MY HORSE COLLAPSES.

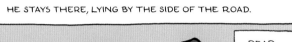

HE STAYS THERE, LYING BY THE SIDE OF THE ROAD.

DEAD.

NO WAY. I CAN'T ACCEPT THAT.

NO. NOT DEAD. LOOK: ALIVE.

DEAD.

THE WOLF IS RIGHT. HE'S DYING.

I WANT TO END HIS AGONY, BUT I'M IN A CARAVAN GOING FROM AFGHANISTAN TO PAKISTAN. WITHOUT FIREARMS.

THE WOLF AND THE OTHERS ARE ALREADY UNTYING MY THREE LARGE BAGS.

THEY SET THEM DOWN AT THEIR FEET AND THE WOLF SAYS:

MORE MONEY.

231

I BLOW MY TOP.

BASTARDS!

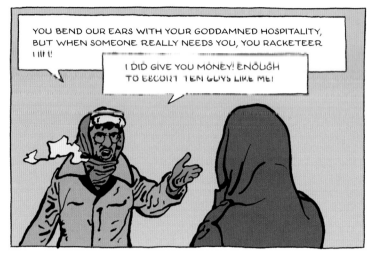

YOU BEND OUR EARS WITH YOUR GODDAMNED HOSPITALITY, BUT WHEN SOMEONE REALLY NEEDS YOU, YOU RACKETEER THEM!

I DID GIVE YOU MONEY! ENOUGH TO ESCORT TEN GUYS LIKE ME!

I AIN'T GIVING NO MORE! SO YOU CAN JUST LEAVE ME HERE!

YOU GIVE MORE MONEY.

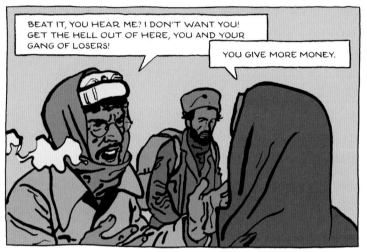

BEAT IT, YOU HEAR ME? I DON'T WANT YOU! GET THE HELL OUT OF HERE, YOU AND YOUR GANG OF LOSERS!

YOU GIVE MORE MONEY.

YOU GIVE MORE MONEY.

I FORK OVER ANOTHER FIVE THOUSAND.

THE GUYS TAKE UP THE BAGS WHILE I SWALLOW MY ANGER.

THEY MAKE ME SICK. I MAKE MYSELF SICK. I LEAVE MY DYING HORSE AND WE HEAD OFF.

OFTEN, AT THE BACK OF CARAVANS YOU CAN SEE A SHEEP TROTTING ALONG.
IT'S BEEN BOUGHT AT THE PREVIOUS REST STOP AND WILL BE SACRIFICED AT THE NEXT BIVOUAC.
I HAVE A FEELING THAT I'M THAT SHEEP.
PARANOIA COMES OVER ME IN WAVES.
I TELL MYSELF, YOU'RE IN A TRAP.
YOUR LIFE DEPENDS ON GUYS WHO WANT TO TAKE IT FROM YOU.
YOU'RE RUNNING TO CATCH UP WITH YOUR EXECUTIONERS.
AND WHAT CAN YOU DO ABOUT IT? NOTHING.
I'M SURE THEY'RE WEARING ME OUT DELIBERATELY.
THOSE BRUTAL AWAKENINGS IN THE MIDDLE OF THE NIGHT,
THOSE UNBEARABLE MARCHES UNTIL 7:00 IN THE EVENING ARE GOING TO MAKE ME KEEL OVER.
ONCE I'VE KEELED OVER, ALL THEY'LL HAVE TO DO IS PICK UP MY MONEY AND LET ME DIE IN A CORNER.
UNLESS THEY KILL ME BEFORE THAT.

THIS EVENING, THERE'S NONE OF THE FLEETING HAPPINESS I EXPERIENCED LAST NIGHT AS I SLIPPED INTO MY SLEEPING BAG. TOO MUCH ANGUISH.

I'M AFRAID THEY'RE GOING TO BUMP ME OFF DURING MY SLEEP. I'M IN SUCH A NERVOUS STATE THAT I CAN'T SLEEP. I WRITE.

AS I WRITE, I'M ALERT TO EVERY SOUND. I WRITE SO THAT MY MURDERERS WILL SEE I'M BUSY AND POSTPONE MY KILLING. I WRITE TO CONFIRM IN WRITING THAT I'M GOING INSANE.

MY HANDWRITING IS TERRIBLE. IT STRIKES ME, BECAUSE I USUALLY WRITE NEATLY. NOW, IT'S FAT AND FORMLESS, LURCHING FORWARD.

ONE AM. WE'RE OFF AGAIN.

WE GO THROUGH KANTIWA. IN THE AFTERNOON, THEY PUT MY BAGS DOWN.

MORE MONEY.

FIVE THOUSAND AFGHANIS.

I PAY FOR EVERYONE'S DINNER. ANOTHER SLEEPLESS NIGHT SPENT EXPECTING TO HAVE MY HEAD SMASHED IN WITH A ROCK.

THE NEXT DAY IT'S PORUNS.

YOU GIVE MONEY.

EIGHT THOUSAND AFGHANIS.

234

IT'S OCTOBER 22, AND AT THE END OF THE DAY WE REACH A *CHAYRANA* THAT'S RUN BY A GIANT.

IT'S THE FIRST TIME SINCE I'VE GROWN TO MY ADULT HEIGHT THAT I'VE MET A MAN SO TALL THAT I ONLY REACH THE HEIGHT OF HIS WAIST.

THE MAN TERRIFIES ME. HE'S AN OGRE. HE HAS A FEW SHEEP, WHICH LOOK LIKE TOY POODLES AROUND HIM.

THE OTHERS SEE HOW SCARED I AM. THEY WANT ME TO TAKE A PICTURE OF THE OGRE. BUT FIRST THE WOLF TAKES ONE OF ME.

AND THEN NIGHT FALLS AND THERE I AM, LIKE A CHILD, SLEEPING BETWEEN THE WOLF AND THE OGRE.

BUT THAT'S PUTTING IT TOO MILDLY. A CHILD WOULD LISTEN TO HIS FEAR AND FLEE. NO, I'M DEFINITELY A SHEEP. I STAY THERE, STUCK IN A STUPOR, WAITING TO HAVE MY THROAT SLIT.

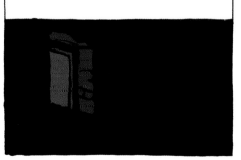

AND WHEN A HAND FALLS ON MY SHOULDER, I UNDERSTAND THE MOMENT HAS COME.

235

ONE AM. WE SAY GOOD-BYE TO THE OGRE AND LEAVE.

SEEING THE SUN AGAIN AFTER THAT TERRIFYING NIGHT FILLS ME WITH A KIND OF GRATITUDE. I EXPRESS IT BY SHOOTING PICTURES OF THE WOLF AND HIS MEN DURING A PRAYER BREAK BY THE SIDE OF A STREAM.

THEN WE TAKE ON THE PAPROK PASS.

I'VE TALKED A LOT ABOUT RELIGION OVER THE PAST DAYS, DISPLAYING A FAITH THAT IN FACT I DON'T HAVE MUCH OF.

BUT I HAVE TO ADMIT THAT, ASCENDING THIS PASS, I PRAY WITH THE DEEPEST FERVOR THAT I'LL MAKE IT TO THE TOP.

AND ONCE I'VE REACHED THE TOP OF CALVARY, NEXT COMES THE CRUCIFIXION.

MONEY.

I DON'T EVEN YELL ANY MORE. NOT ENOUGH AIR IN MY LUNGS. HOW MUCH DO YOU WANT?

THIRTY THOUSAND.

THIRTY THOUSAND.

GOLLY. THIRTY THOUSAND. GO FOR THIRTY THOUSAND.

TWENTY... TWENTY-FIVE...

MY NEST EGG IS VANISHING AT AN ALARMING SPEED.

I DON'T REMEMBER WHO SAID, "GOING UP IS TIRING, GOING DOWN IS PAINFUL." BUT IT'S TRUE.

ON THE OTHER SIDE OF THE PAPROK PASS, WE STOP IN A CHAYRANA THAT'S PACKED WITH TRAVELERS.

I WATCH THE FACES.

FOR GOD'S SAKE!

THAT GUY, OVER THERE, WAS ONE OF THE MEN FROM MY FIRST ESCORT. ONE OF THOSE WHO CUT AND RAN.

HE SAW ME TOO. HE SLIPPED AWAY THROUGH THE CROWD.

THIS GUY—ONE OF THOSE WHO LEFT ME ON KALOTAC KOTAL.

THERE I AM, REPORTING THOSE WHO ABANDONED ME TO THOSE WHO ARE RACKETEERING ME. PRETTY STUPID.

I WALK AROUND THE *CHAYRANA* AND ITS SURROUNDINGS, LOOKING FOR HIM. HE'S VANISHED.

IT WAS HIM, I COULD SWEAR.

FARTHER ON, I DROP ANOTHER EIGHT THOUSAND AFGHANIS.

GO AHEAD, GUYS, LAUGH, YOU HAVE PLENTY TO BE PROUD OF.

WE REACH A VILLAGE THAT I RECOGNIZE: BARG-E-MATAL.

I REMEMBER THAT THE LOCAL CHIEF IS THE CHUBBY, BEARDED DRUG DEALER WHO WAS JULIETTE'S POINT MAN IN THE NEIGHBORHOOD. I EVEN RECALL HIS NAME.

AIDER SHAH.

PLEASE, LET HIM BE THERE! I'M FEVERISH WITH HOPE AND ANGUISH WHILE I WAIT FOR HIM. I NERVOUSLY BONE UP ON MY DICTIONARY'S PHRASES TO FIGURE OUT WHAT TO SAY TO HIM.

PAISA... DOZDI KARDAN...

THERE HE IS. HE OPENS HIS ARMS AND DROWNS ME IN HIS HUGE BEARD.

خوش آمدین

HE RECOGNIZES ME. HE KNOWS I WAS PART OF JAMILA'S CREW. AS BEST I CAN, I TELL HIM THAT I'M ON MY WAY TO PAKISTAN, THAT I'M SICK, THAT THE MEN WHO ARE WITH ME ARE NOT GOOD PEOPLE AND THEY'VE TAKEN MY MONEY.

HIS REACTION IS INSTANT: HE FIRES MY ESCORT, MAKING SURE THEY RETURN MY LUGGAGE TO ME, THEN HE INTRODUCES ME TO HIS NEPHEW AND GIVES HIM INSTRUCTIONS.

THE NEPHEW LEADS ME TO A WOODEN HOUSE, ON THE EDGE OF A STREAM.

IN THAT HOUSE, A ROOM.

I COLLAPSE ONTO THE BED.

I FALL ASLEEP.

WHEN I WAKE UP, THE NEPHEW BRINGS ME A MEAL.

A KIND OF RAVIOLI WITH VEGETABLES, IN A RED SAUCE WITH AN EGG YOLK ON TOP. AND SOME TEA.

I FALL BACK ASLEEP WITH THOSE FLAVORS IN MY MOUTH.

I GO THROUGH THE SAME SEQUENCE SEVERAL TIMES: WAKING UP, EATING, SLEEPING, WAKING UP, EATING, SLEEPING...

UNTIL I EMERGE FROM THE FOG FOR GOOD AND REALIZE THAT I'VE SLEPT FOR A GOOD FORTY HOURS.

IT'S OCTOBER 25TH, AROUND NOON. A COOL AND SUNNY DAY.

240

AIDER SHAH HAS SAVED MY HIDE.
IN ONE MINUTE, WITH AUTHORITY AND GENEROSITY HE HAS PULLED ME OUT OF
A THREE-WEEK-LONG NIGHTMARE.
I TELL HIM HOW GRATEFUL I AM.
HERE IS A TRULY KIND GUY—A STRONG AND PATERNAL FIGURE.
ON THE WAY OVER, I HAD BEEN ON MY GUARD WHILE CROSSING NURISTAN,
BECAUSE OF THE BAD RAP THE PEOPLE FROM BADAKHSHAN GIVE THE NURISTANI.
AND HERE IT IS THAT IN NURISTAN I AM HOUSED,
FED, PROTECTED, PUT BACK ON MY FEET.
PRACTICALLY ADOPTED.
TRUTH BE TOLD, THEY ARE PRETTY CRAFTY.
WHAT I EAT DURING MY STAY IN BARG-E-MATAL IS NOTHING LIKE
THE FOUL GRUB SERVED IN THEIR *CHAYRANAS*.
I DEVELOP A PASSION FOR THEIR RAVIOLI-LIKE THINGIES.

AIDER SHAH TELLS ME THAT
A YOUNG AMERICAN WOMAN
IS STAYING IN BARG-E-MATAL.
A DOCTOR, IF I UNDERSTAND
CORRECTLY. SHE KNOWS
ABOUT ME. I CAN GO SEE
HER, IN THAT HOUSE,
OVER THERE.

241

FINALLY, YOU'RE UP!

WOW.

SHE'S REALLY PRETTY. SHE GREETS ME WARMLY AND CHEERFULLY, THEN ASKS ME WHERE I'M FROM.

FRANCE.

REALLY! MY HUSBAND IS FRENCH!

SHE'S MARRIED TO A FRENCH JOURNALIST, WHO IS COVERING A STORY IN THE INTERIOR OF THE COUNTRY. THIS IS THEIR RENDEZVOUS POINT. SHE'S WAITING FOR HIM AND TREATING THE LOCAL PEOPLE IN THE MEANTIME. IN THE PAST, SHE WORKED FOR UNICEF.

SUDDENLY, MY MEMORY NUDGES ME. I ASK HER WHERE IN FRANCE HER HUSBAND IS FROM.

ALSACE.

SHE'S THE WIFE OF THE MAN FROM ALSACE I MET AT THE AMERICAN CLUB IN PESHAWAR—THE *"MALGRÉ NOUS."* HE HAD SHOWN ME HER PICTURE. I RECOGNIZE HER NOW.

I MET YOUR HUSBAND IN PESHAWAR LAST SUMMER.

WE ARE FLOORED BY THE COINCIDENCE. TO CELEBRATE, SHE OPENS A POT OF JAM.

WHAT AN INDESCRIBABLE PLEASURE, TO BE ABLE TO CHAT WITH AN ATTRACTIVE YOUNG WOMAN WHILE EATING SOME JAM.

DID YOU MAKE IT?

HAHA! NO, MONSIEUR!

THANKFULLY, SHE ISN'T A MISSIONARY, SO I DON'T GET LECTURED ON JESUS AND WHATNOT. I CAN FINALLY SAY THREE WORDS WITHOUT EXPLAINING THAT I'M ISAWI, MARRIED, AND A FATHER.

AND WHAT'S EVEN MORE OF A RELIEF IS THAT I CAN UNDERSTAND EVERYTHING AND TALK WITHOUT STUMBLING ON EVERY WORD.

WE DISCUSS HER HUSBAND'S INCREDIBLE LIFE—HIS WORK ON CHILD SOLDIERS, ECHOING HIS OWN ADOLESCENCE. SHE'S WORRIED ABOUT HIM, BECAUSE HE SHOULD ALREADY HAVE BEEN BACK SEVERAL DAYS AGO.

I LEAVE HER TO HER CONSULTATION.

AIDER SHAH AND HIS NEPHEW TAKE OUT THEIR BEST HORSES AND TREAT ME TO A PARADE WORTHY OF A MILITARY ACADEMY.

242

THE NEXT DAY I SAY GOOD-BYE TO THE AMERICAN DOCTOR WITH THE JAM.

SAY HELLO TO YOUR HUSBAND FOR ME.

I SURELY WILL.

I RENT A HORSE AND A GUIDE FROM AIDER SHAH. FIVE THOUSAND AFGHANIS.

WE HUG, FRIENDS FOR LIFE.

FOR THE FIRST TIME MY ROUTE STRAYS FROM THE ONE WE TOOK ON THE WAY OVER. INSTEAD OF HEADING FOR THE DEWANA BABA, WE'RE GOING TO CROSS THE BUM BORET PASS, WHICH IS ON A STRAIGHTER PATH TOWARD THE PAKISTANI BORDER AND CHITRAL.

243

THE LAST PASS OF THE TRIP. I CAN'T BELIEVE. MY LEGS. THEY'RE CLIMBING UP EFFORTLESSLY.

WE REACH A HUT WHERE WE SPEND THE NIGHT. A CARAVAN IS THERE, MADE UP OF BOTH MEN AND YOUNG BOYS.

THE NEXT MORNING, MY GUIDE AND I GO DOWN THE OPPOSITE SIDE OF THE PASS. WE PAUSE AT THE ENTRANCE TO A VALLEY.

IT'S THE KALASH VALLEY, ONE OF THE ENTRY POINTS INTO PAKISTAN. IF I WALK STRAIGHT IN THAT DIRECTION, I'LL REACH THE VILLAGE OF BUM BORET.

THERE'S A ROAD DOWN BELOW. ALL I'LL HAVE TO DO IS HITCH A RIDE TO CHITRAL.

MY GUIDE TAKES MY BAGS OFF THE HORSE AND I LOAD THEM UP. WE HUG AND GO OUR SEPARATE WAYS.

I LEAVE AFGHANISTAN AND ENTER PAKISTAN.

I'M CARRYING HEAVY BAGS, BUT I'M IN GOOD SHAPE. IN ANY CASE, THE ROAD ISN'T SUPPOSED BE TOO LONG.

I'VE READ SOME THINGS ABOUT THE KALASH PEOPLE. THEY'RE A VERY EXOTIC GROUP WITHIN PAKISTAN. THIS PLACE WAS A TOURIST DESTINATION BEFORE THE WAR.
I READ THAT THERE WERE FLOWERS EVERYWHERE: IN THE VALLEY, ON WOMEN'S DRESSES, AT THE BALCONIES OF THE WOODEN HOUSES.
A BIT LIKE BAVARIA.

THREE HOURS LATER, I COME INTO BUM BORET.

I FIND A KIND OF BACKPACKERS' LODGE. THE ONLY AVAILABLE ACCOMMODATION.

THE GUY RUNNING THE PLACE OFFERS ME A ROOM ON THE SECOND FLOOR, WITH A TABLE, A CHAIR, A BED. IT ISN'T EXACTLY LUXURIOUS, BUT AT LEAST IT'S FURNISHED.

I EAT, DRINK, REST. AS NIGHT FALLS, THERE'S A KNOCK AT MY DOOR.

A COP. I IMMEDIATELY UNDERSTAND THAT I'VE BEEN SOLD OUT.

WHO ARE YOU? WHAT ARE YOU DOING HERE?

I AM A

YOU CROSSED THE BORDER ILLEGALLY.

HE STARTS RUMMAGING THROUGH MY THINGS.

YOU TRAFFICKER.

NO. I AM NOT.

YES YOU ARE. I KNOW

HE SEARCHES FOR MONEY BUT DOESN'T FIND IT. WHICH MAKES SENSE, BECAUSE I HAVE IT ON ME.

WHERE IS YOUR MONEY?

I DON'T HAVE ANY.

YOU GIVE MONEY. YOU PAY TAX.

NO. I DON'T.

THEN YOU ARE PRISONER. YOU GIVE ME YOUR KEY.

CLICK-CLACK. HE LOCKS ME IN.

THE ANGER I FEEL TOWARD THIS GUY KEEPS ME FROM FEELING DEPRESSED. I TRY TO CALM DOWN AND THINK THINGS THROUGH.

I DECIDE I'M BEING STUPID. I DO HAVE SOME MONEY. BETTER TO GIVE HIM A BIT AND GET OUT OF THERE RIGHT AWAY. I'M TOO CLOSE TO MY GOAL TO LET MYSELF GET LOCKED UP LIKE AN IDIOT.

FIRST I HIDE MY DOLLARS. I QUICKLY TAKE OUT THE FILM FROM MY THREE CAMERAS AND REPLACE IT WITH THE BILLS, TIGHTLY ROLLED UP.

THEN I TAKE OUT TWO THOUSAND AFGHANIS AND A FEW HUNDRED RUPEES.

BOM BOM

246

YES?

I CHANGED MY MIND. I PAY.

I HAND OVER THE AFGHANI BILLS.

ANY RUPEES?

PLUS FIVE HUNDRED RUPEES.

OKAY, YOU GIVE MORE.

THAT'S ALL I HAVE.

YOU GIVE A CAMERA.

NO.

YOU GIVE THE SLEEPING BAG.

NO.

I GAVE MONEY. NOW LET ME GO.

YOU GIVE MORE.

I WON'T.

THEN YOU ARE PRISONER.

CLICK-CLACK. BACK TO SQUARE ONE.

THAT GUY ISN'T CONTENT WITH A BAKSHEESH. HE WANTS EVERYTHING. OBVIOUSLY, THE LAST THING TO DO IS GIVE HIM ANY MORE.

WHAT DO YOU WANT?
TO PISS.
NOW DON'T WE LOOK SMART, THE TWO OF US.
YOU GIVE MONEY.
VA TE FAIRE FOUTRE.
I HAVE A NICE VIEW OF THE MOUNTAINS. I MAKE THE MOST OF IT THROUGHOUT THE FOLLOWING DAY, OCTOBER 28TH.
AT LEAST HE HASN'T DECIDED TO STARVE ME. I GET TWO DECENT MEALS. GIVEN THE AMOUNT OF EXERCISE I'M GETTING, THERE'S NO NEED FOR MORE.
THAT EVENING, HE CONDUCTS ANOTHER SEARCH. HE NEGLECTS TO OPEN MY CAMERAS.
THERE'S SOMETHING STRANGE ABOUT HIS ATTITUDE. HE COULD POINT HIS GUN TO MY HEAD AND EXTORT WHATEVER HE WANTS THROUGH THREATS OR BEATINGS, OR EVEN BUMP ME OFF IN A CORNER, BUT NO. HE ONLY HOLDS ME PRISONER, WHICH SHOWS A CERTAIN WORK ETHIC.
IT COULD ALSO LAST A LONG TIME.

WHAT DO YOU WANT?

TO PISS.

I'M NOT TRYING TO GET ON YOUR NERVES, BUDDY. I GET UP AT NIGHT.

YOU GIVE MONEY.

NO.

IN THE MORNING, ANOTHER SEARCH, A MORE THOROUGH ONE. HE INSISTS ON STEALING MY SLEEPING BAG.

YOU GIVE THIS.

NO.

I'M GETTING SERIOUSLY FED UP.

MOST UNEXPECTEDLY, HE LEAVES THE DOOR OPEN WHEN HE GOES OUT.

WHAT IS THAT SUPPOSED TO MEAN? AM I FREE?

I ASSUME I AM.

THE GUY FROM THE INN. DOUBTLESS IN CAHOOTS WITH THE CORRUPT COP. BUT HE'S THE ONLY ONE HANDY.

WHERE CAN I FIND A CAR?

I HAVE ONE

HE AGREES TO TAKE ME TO CHITRAL IF I PAY FOR THE RIDE, MY TWO NIGHTS AT THE INN, AND MY MEALS. FIVE HUNDRED RUPEES. I OBVIOUSLY PONY UP. I EXPECT TO SEE THE COP SHOW UP ANY SECOND.

WE GET INTO THE CAR.

BUM BORET FADES INTO THE BACKGROUND.

GOOD RIDDANCE.

IT'S LATE MORNING WHEN WE PULL INTO CHITRAL. I GET DROPPED OFF AT THE FREEDOM MEDICINE HOUSE.

IT'S EMPTY.

THERE ARE NO NGO PEOPLE THERE AT THE MOMENT. FORTUNATELY, THERE'S AN AFGHAN GUARD WHO SPEAKS ENGLISH AND REMEMBERS SEEING ME ON MY WAY OVER.

I TELL HIM ABOUT MY MISHAP OF THE THREE PREVIOUS DAYS. HE OFFERS TO REPORT THE CORRUPT COP.

THIS MAN IS VERY BAD. I'LL GO TO THE POLICE MYSELF AND TELL THEM WHAT HE DID TO YOU.

HE OFFERS ME SOME TEA.

I'VE RUN OUT OF RUPEES. HE CHANGES ME 5,000 OF THEM FOR DOLLARS. THEN HE FINDS ME A TAXI FOR PESHAWAR. IT'LL MEAN A DOZEN HOURS ON THE ROAD AND WILL COST ME 1,600 RUPEES.

IN THE EARLY AFTERNOON I LEAVE CHITRAL IN THE FRONT OF A PICKUP TRUCK.

AS SOON AS WE LEAVE THE CITY WE HEAD UP A MOUNTAIN PASS. I SAVOR EVERY TURN OF THE WHEEL LEADING US TO THE TOP. IT'S GREAT BEING IN A CAR.

I SLEEP FOR THE REST OF THE TRIP. WE MAKE A FEW STOPS. EARLY THE NEXT MORNING WE GET TO PESHAWAR.

I'M BACK IN THE HEAT, THE BIG CITY, THE CROWDS, THE TRAFFIC. A WEIRD FEELING.

MSF HAS MOVED ITS DIGS FROM THE HOUSE I STAYED IN THAT SUMMER. THEY'RE NOW IN THE WHITE HOUSE, A LARGE COLONNADED MANSION IN A PARK, SHARED BY SEVERAL ORGANIZATIONS. I HEAD THERE.

I'M GREETED BY A GUY FROM AFRANE, THE FRENCH-AFGHAN FRIENDSHIP ASSOCIATION, WHO SAYS STRAIGHT OUT:

MAN, YOU STINK OF HORSE. I CAN TELL THAT YOU JUST GOT BACK FROM AFGHANISTAN.

MY FIRST SHOWER IN OVER THREE
MONTHS. I TRY TO GET RID OF THE
GHOST OF MY HORSE, BY VIGOROUSLY
SCRUBBING MY BODY AND HAIR WITH
SOAP (CAN'T FIND ANY SHAMPOO).

I'M COMING DOWN WITH FURUNCULOSIS:
I HAVE PAINFUL BOILS ON ONE EAR, ON MY
NECK, AND ON BOTH ARMS

THE MSF ADMINISTRATOR IN PESHAWAR
SHOWS UP. THERE HAVE BEEN RUMORS
WITHIN THE CARAVANS THAT
I DISAPPEARED ON THE WAY.

AREN'T YOU DEAD?

GUESS NOT.

HE CALLS MSF
HEADQUARTERS IN PARIS,
ON BOULEVARD
SAINT-MARCEL.

SINCE I'M THE ONLY ONE
TO HAVE RETURNED AT
THAT POINT, I GIVE A SHORT
REPORT ON THE MISSION
AND TALK A BIT ABOUT
WHAT I'VE SEEN
OF AFGHANISTAN.

MY VISA HAS EXPIRED. MY PASSPORT HAS TO GO THROUGH
ISLAMABAD FOR A VISA EXTENSION.

NO SPACE ON ANY PLANE FOR AT LEAST A WEEK.

OKAY.

VERY BRIEFLY, I CALL MY MOM.

EVERYTHING'S FINE. I'M COMING BACK IN ABOUT TEN DAYS.

YES, DON'T WORRY.

ME TOO.

THAT AFTERNOON I GO FOR A SPIN IN THE SADR BAZAAR.

MY PLAN IS TO GET A PROPER SHAVE FROM A REAL BARBER.

I FIND ONE WHO DOES A SHAMPOO, A SHAVE WITH A STRAIGHT
RAZOR, A HAIRCUT, MASSAGE, THE WORKS. HIS FINGERS HAVE
BARELY TOUCHED MY HAIR WHEN HE SAYS, WITH A LOOK OF
DISGUST AND DISAPPROVAL:

SOAP IS NOT GOOD FOR
CLEANING THE HAIR.

THERE. BEFORE GETTING MY PASSPORT BACK, I'M GETTING MY FACE BACK.

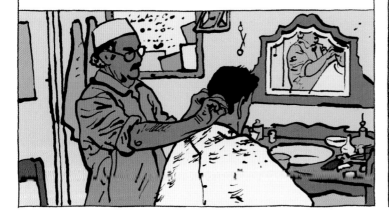

A BIT FARTHER, IN A KIND OF VARIETY STORE, I FIND THE AFTERSHAVE I USE IN FRANCE, "TABAC." I BUY A BOTTLE.

SIDE BY SIDE THERE ARE TWO INTERNATIONAL BOOKSHOPS, THE LONDON BOOK SHOP AND THE SAEED BOOK BANK. I HEAD IN.

THEY HAVE PILES OF *NATIONAL GEOGRAPHICS*, AND SOME NEWSPAPERS AND NEWS MAGAZINES FROM FRANCE, BUT NOT RECENT ONES. THERE ARE ALSO SOME AMERICAN PHOTOGRAPHY MAGAZINES. SOME THINGS TO LEAF THROUGH.

IN ALL THOSE PUBLICATIONS THERE ARE BIG BLACK MARKS MADE WITH A PERMANENT MARKER BY SOME CLERK FROM THE CENSORSHIP BUREAU, WHO WENT THROUGH EVERY PAGE OF EVERY ISSUE TO BLACK OUT REVEALING IMAGES OF WOMEN. A BIG JOB.

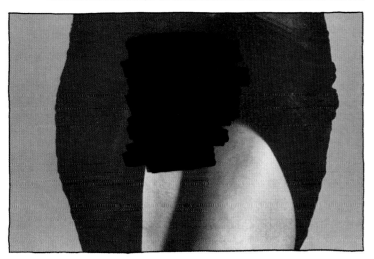

BACK AT THE WHITE HOUSE I EMPTY OUT MY BOTTLE OF "TABAC" IN THE SINK. I'VE BEEN GIVEN A COUNTERFEIT PRODUCT THAT STINKS OF GASOLINE.

THE NEXT DAY, JULIETTE AND JOHN SHOW UP. I REFUSED TO GO WITH THEM BECAUSE I WANTED TO GO FASTER AND, AFTER ALL MY TROUBLES, WE REACHED PESHAWAR ABOUT A DAY APART.

YOU KNOW WE SAW YOUR DEAD HORSE ON THE POJOL PASS?

I RECOGNIZED IT IMMEDIATELY. I WAS SICK WITH WORRY. I ASKED ALL THE PEOPLE WE MET, BUT NOBODY KNEW ANYTHING.

WE ENDED UP THINKING WE SHOULD'VE FLIPPED YOUR HORSE OVER. MAYBE THAT WE'RE LINGERING AT IT.

FORTUNATELY AIDER SHAH AND THE AMERICAN WOMAN IN BARG-E-MATAL EASED OUR MINDS.

DID SHE GET HER HUSBAND BACK? THAT JOURNALIST FROM ALSACE?

BELIEVE IT OR NOT, WE MET HIM ON THE WAY. HE WAS SICK, SUFFERING FROM A BLEEDING ULCER. WE TREATED HIM AS BEST WE COULD, AND HE CAME TO BARG-E-MATAL WITH US.

WILL HE PULL THROUGH?

OH YEAH. HE'S VERY TOUGH.

WHAT'S SORT OF FUNNY IS THAT RIGHT AFTER I ESCAPED FROM THE ROTTEN COP OF BUM BORET, JOHN AND JULIETTE FELL INTO HIS CLUTCHES.

GUESS WHAT THE BASTARD COOKED UP FOR US?

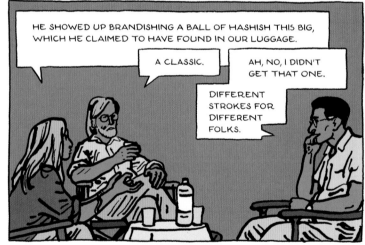

HE SHOWED UP BRANDISHING A BALL OF HASHISH THIS BIG, WHICH HE CLAIMED TO HAVE FOUND IN OUR LUGGAGE.

A CLASSIC.

AH, NO, I DIDN'T GET THAT ONE.

DIFFERENT STROKES FOR DIFFERENT FOLKS.

HE TOOK US AS WAR BOOTY TO CHITRAL.

FOR THE WHOLE LENGTH OF THE TRIP I WAS WONDERING IF I SHOULD SHOVE HIM OUT OF THE CAR.

ONCE WE GOT THERE I GAVE HIS CHIEFS SUCH AN EARFUL THAT THEY RELEASED US RIGHT AWAY AND GAVE HIM QUITE A DRESSING-DOWN IN FRONT OF US.

HAHA! REVENGE!

254

JOHN INSPECTS MY BOILS AND CAN'T RESIST THE TEMPTATION OF TAKING ANOTHER STAB AT THE ONE HE DIDN'T GET RID OF LAST TIME.

OW!

DON'T MOVE.

JULIETTE EXAMINES MY TEETH. NOT TOO BAD.

YOU SHOULD STILL GET A REAL CHECK-UP WHEN YOU GET BACK TO FRANCE.

OKAY.

MY OVERALL CONDITION ISN'T DEEMED ALARMING BY THE HEALTH COMMITTEE. I JUST HAVE TO FILL OUT A BIT BY EATING HEALTHY.

THE MSF ADMINISTRATOR LIKES PHOTOGRAPHY. HE GOES INTO THE CITY WITH ME, WITH HIS CAMERA AROUND HIS NECK. HE TAKES MY PORTRAIT WITH ONE OF MINE, SO I'LL BE ON SOME OF MY FILM.

WE DISCOVER A SPECIAL PLACE: AN OVERGROWN BRITISH CEMETERY SURROUNDED BY MILITARY BARRACKS, ON THE WALLS OF WHICH NEAT ROWS OF SOCKS ARE HUNG OUT TO DRY. I FIND THAT CEMETERY VERY MOVING. I COME BACK IN THE FOLLOWING DAYS.

255

DAYDREAMING IN THAT PLACE, I THINK ABOUT THE BEST AND WORST OF WHAT I'VE JUST EXPERIENCED IN AFGHANISTAN. AND I REALIZE SOMETHING: I FEEL LIKE GOING BACK.

HERE I AM ON THE BUS FROM PESHAWAR TO ISLAMABAD, ON MY WAY TO PICKING UP MY PASSPORT. I HAVE MY HEADPHONES ON, LISTENING TO A WALKMAN THAT I LUGGED AROUND EVERYWHERE IN AFGHANISTAN AND NEVER USED. I'M LISTENING TO THE FRENCH JAZZ SINGER MICHEL JONASZ.

"C'ÉTAIT LES VACANCES AU BORD DE LA MER AVEC MON PÈRE, MA SOEUR, MA MÈRE..."

IT'S FRIDAY. THE FRENCH EMBASSY IS CLOSED. I HAVE TO GO TO THE HOME OF AN EMPLOYEE OF THE PAKISTANI INTERIOR MINISTRY, WHO WILL GIVE ME THE DOCUMENT INFORMALLY.

IT'S A SMALL HOUSE IN A RESIDENTIAL NEIGHBORHOOD. HIS YOUNG SON OPENS THE DOOR.

DAD'S UPSTAIRS, IN HIS BEDROOM. HE LEADS ME UP.

THE GUY IS ACTUALLY IN BED.
MY PASSPORT IS THERE, ON THE NIGHTSTAND.

WEIRD.

THANK YOU.

BUT WHAT MATTERS IS THAT EVERYTHING IS DULY STAMPED.

"JOUEURS DE BLUES... ON EST LES JOUEURS DE BLUES..."

I HAVE MY TWO PLANE TICKETS, PESHAWAR-KARACHI AND KARACHI-PARIS. I'M LEAVING THE NEXT DAY.

257

BYE.

SEE YOU IN PARIS.

YES, IN PARIS.

MY RETURN TRIP IS MADE FEVERISH BY A HUGE BOIL THROBBING ON MY NECK.

I'M GLAD TO GO HOME. OBSESSED BY THE THOUGHT OF GETTING MY FILM DEVELOPED. AND SEEING THE RESULT, AT LONG LAST. ONE HUNDRED AND THIRTY ROLLS OF FILM. A BUNCH OF MONEY. BUT I HAVE TO WAIT FOR THE GREEN LIGHT FROM MSF BEFORE STARTING.

I GET TO PARIS ON THE EVE OF A WEEKEND. DOMINIQUE GETS MY TRAVEL DIARY. I PASS THROUGH MEAUX, VISITING SOME FRIENDS. THERE, I LINE UP MY ROLLS OF FILM LIKE HUNTING TROPHIES.

I HEAD FOR BLONVILLE, NORMANDY. I MEET UP WITH MY GRANDMA.

SEE BIENCHEN THE DOG.

AND MY MOM. SHE'S BEEN WORRIED.

COME WITH ME, IT'S TIME FOR HER WALK. AND YOU'LL TELL ME A BIT.

YES.

259

PLANCHE N° .... RÉF. AF 86. 129

SUJET .... Maman à Bbuille. Retour d' Afghanistan.

....

DATE .... Nov 86. .... BOITIER ...... Leica.

Portraits

Mrs. Lefèvre had to wait twenty years to find out, in this book, the details of Didier's trip. That day, on the beach of Blonville, as they walked Bienchen the dog, he served her the usual bromides that sons give their mothers: "It was great, Mom, and nothing bad happened to me." With the passing of time, even that bald-faced lie came to be mostly true.

In the year that followed the mission, Didier suffered from chronic furunculosis and lost fourteen teeth. These were direct consequences of his dreadful return, with its attendant exhaustion, lack of hygiene, malnutrition, and stress. On December 27, 1986, the French newspaper Libération published six of his photographs in a two-page spread. Of the four thousand photos he brought back, getting six published seems like a dizzyingly small fraction. But it was a privilege: many of his subsequent remarkable photo stories were never published. And the tale of his experience of the mission was reserved for close friends who wanted to hear it. His buddy Emmanuel Guibert was one of them, and thirteen years later he suggested to Didier that they make a book of it together.

Didier dug out the contact sheets from the boxes where they'd been sleeping, and his memory, spurred by the pictures, threaded back together the story you have just read. In all, Didier made eight trips to Afghanistan between 1986 and 2006—all of them interesting, none of them easy. A beautiful book of his pictures, Voyages en Afghanistan, was published by Ouest-France in 2002. He collaborated with newspapers and magazines, either on his own or through agencies, at different times. He enjoyed returning to the same places periodically, seeing how things changed, meeting up with people again.

He produced remarkable photographic documentaries on the postwar situation in Kosovo, the AIDS epidemic in Malawi and Cambodia, farming in the countries of the former Eastern bloc joining the European Union, and also the epic Paris-Roubaix cycling race, which he enjoyed covering each year in April. The success of The Photographer in the French-speaking world (about 250,000 copies have been sold to date), and a dawning international recognition thanks to several foreign translations, surprised and delighted Didier, as well as the other partners in this adventure. It provided an opportunity to gather together a good part of the team from 1986 and to share intense moments of friendship. In January 2007, Didier died of heart failure at home, at the age of 49, leaving behind his wife and two young children. His work and character, both of which were outstanding, remain mostly to be discovered.

Régis returned from this mission with Amrullah, the young mujahid who had been badly wounded in the face (see the entry about him below). In 1987, MSF sent him to Sri Lanka, where he met Constance, his future wife, an anesthesiologist. Later, in Herat, northern Afghanistan, they carried out "the most difficult and most beautiful mission in all of MSF's work in the country" (as Juliette described it).

Back in France, he was invited by Professor Philippe Dabadie to teach classes on "Medicine in a Sanitary Wasteland" at the University of Bordeaux II, as part of the program in Disaster Relief Medicine. In 1991, Régis worked in MSF's Human Resources department in Paris and moved toward fulfilling his dream of following in his father's footsteps by becoming a wine producer. In September 1991 he began to study oenology. A dilemma arose in 1992: he was offered a new Afghan mission when MSF began to return to the country, which was caught in the turmoil that followed the fall of the communist government, marked by rivalries among the mujahideen. His indecision did not last long, and Régis returned immediately to Afghanistan.

He finally earned his oenology degree in 1994. In 2000, he bought a vineyard near Bergerac, which he looks after with the care that he used to lavish on his patients. To thank him, each year that vineyard gives him delicious Pécharmant wine. Régis had been a Gascon of Badakshan, and he is also an Afghan of the Périgord, who still chews naswar chewing tobacco and plays rugby with as much gusto as others do buzkashi. Whenever he and Didier used to meet, they would invariably exchange some Rocher Suchard chocolates, remembering a moment which may have struck readers too.

Robert's mission lasted another year. He and Evelyne stayed at the Palandara hospital and weathered a particularly trying winter, during which he came down with dengue fever. Dengue is a viral infection that causes high fever, liver and kidney malfunction, and bouts of coma. Thanks to his strong constitution, to Evelyne's daily care, and to a good dose of sheer luck, he pulled through and went back to work. His feet froze on the return journey. He lost all his toenails, but fortunately none of his toes. Robert took over from Juliette as manager of Afghan missions and remained in Afghanistan or Pakistan until the end of 1989.

Back in France, he worked at the hospital of Chalon-sur-Saône. During the night of April 27 to 28, 1990, Frédéric Galland, an MSF logistician, was murdered in Palandara. It was a political crime, carried out by masked men. As a result, all MSF teams left Afghanistan for two years. Since that time, the Palandara hospital, which this book shows being built, has been abandoned. Robert himself went to retrieve the body of Frédéric Galland and brought him back to France.

Ten years later, Robert closed down his private doctor's practice in the city of Le Cheylard, near Lyon, and earned a baccalaureate degree in oenology in 2000. In 2004, he bought a vineyard next to the one owned by Régis, and the two friends teamed up to make wine. "It's hard to describe all that the Afghans gave us," Robert observed. "I reckon that thanks to them we're just a bit less dumb than we would've been."

At the end of 1988, Juliette left Afghanistan and Peshawar for the US. She joined John in Minneapolis, where they started a family and Juliette took a Master's degree in Public Health and Ethnomedicine. In 1989 she and Francis Charhon had the idea of starting a US arm of MSF. There were two births in 1991: Alexandra, the daughter of Juliette and John, and MSF-USA, of which Juliette was one of the four key players. MSF-USA recruits volunteers, educates the public as well as political and humanitarian leaders, collects private funding to preserve the organization's financial independence, and manages missions.

Juliette also became an associate professor of dental surgery at the University of Minnesota Hospital. In her spare time, she joined a team of animal biology researchers who tracked, on snowshoes, the hibernation patterns of polar bears in the forests of the far North. She left MSF-USA in 2002 and returned to France in 2003 to support her father during his illness and up to his death. Today, she has moved away from MSF, after having spent twenty-three years championing its cause. She is "her daughter's mother and her mother's daughter" and looks after both of them as she waits to see what new course suggests itself.

But whatever happens, each year in September she helps her buddies Robert and Régis harvest the grapes from their vineyards.

For a year in Peshawar, John helped draft a training manual for Afghan medical personnel with the five NGOs active on the ground at the time. At the end of 1988, he returned to the US and took up ER work again at a prestigious university hospital in Minneapolis, where was an assistant professor. He was also active within MSF-USA.

He no longer does much fishing, but he has become a keen rollerblader and he introduced his daughter Alexandra to the sport. Didier always told everyone around him that he wouldn't have hesitated one second before putting his life in John's hands.

Sylvie stayed in Afghanistan until September 1989, when she left to do a two and a half year mission in Zambia. She then ran a day-care centre in Lyon and was active with MSF's regional headquarters. She recently returned to fieldwork. She says she enjoyed rediscovering those familiar motions.

After her missions with MSF, Evelyne took a degree in pediatric nursing. She now works in Fontainebleau, near Paris, in a Maternal and Child Welfare center.

Odile took a seventeen-year break from her work as a nurse to raise her three children. She recently returned to work in a physical rehabilitation clinic near Aix-en-Provence.

Mahmad did not wish to have anything said about him. We'll just send a friendly thought his way and say he is fine.

The journalist from Alsace, now in his early eighties, has continued on his unique path. As but one example, he covered the Taliban's retreat to southern Afghanistan under pressure from the advancing US forces in October 2001, living among them.

We hadn't been able to gather any news of Michel and Ronald by the time of publication. If they read this book, in English, French, or Dutch, they should know that the whole team is expecting to have them over for a feast of palao and chorchoy.

After the Red Army's withdrawal in 1989, Palawan Iklil made use of the experience he had gained with MSF. He borrowed some money to buy a few trucks and set up a transport and logistics network between Chitral and Badakhshan.

Najmudin often came to visit Robert and Evelyne during their stay in Palandara in the winter of 86-87. Later, when Robert was stationed in Peshawar, he saw Najmudin a few more times, finding him "always friendly, always glad to meet up again," but more aloof, less comfortable in the big city than in his home village. There hasn't been any news of him since the end of the 1980s.

Robert also occasionally saw Abdul Jabar in Peshawar. The MSF staff's ties with him weren't as close as with Najmudin. We don't know what became of him.

265

Didier later met up again with Aider Shah in Barg-e-Matal, during a mission in October 1988. He showed the same fatherly hospitality. He hasn't been seen since that time.

Bassir Khan, a former schoolteacher, ruled the whole valley of Yaftal throughout the war against the Soviet Union and beyond, until the takeover by the Taliban. He was an ally of Ahmad Shah Massoud within the Jamiat-e-Islami party, but not without rivalry. He retired at the time of the establishment of the Northern Alliance and returned to Feyzabad, where he is believed to remain until now. He promoted the presence of the MSF teams and supported their work. That earned him the team's gratitude and even fondness. Régis describes him as a bon vivant. Didier had a harsher take on him. He remained angry with Bassir for having dumped an escort on him whose desertion nearly cost him his life.
Apparently, Bassir had the four men of the escort punished with a severe beating upon their return to Yaftal.

The Wakil, or representative, of Teshkan, was described by several members of the team as a shrewd man, with whom you had to know precisely what you wanted and stick firmly to your positions. He ruled with a strong hand one of the poorest valleys in the area. He was also a hard-boiled fighter who, despite a withered arm that was horribly painful in the wintertime, didn't shy away from rough games of buzkashi. He was murdered in 1989, shot in the back by Afghan rivals as he prayed, at Massoud's headquarters in Takhar province.

Upon his father's death, the Wakil's son took over interim command of the valley for a brief period, but he didn't have the stature to handle such responsibility. Power passed to another commander during an administrative reorganization of valleys.

The story of Amrullah is truly extraordinary. After having suffered an awful face wound and undergone an operation in Zaragandara, led by John, Robert and Régis, he was sent to France through the efforts of an association started by an anesthesiologist and a surgeon in Alès, in southern France. Régis brought him to France and took him to Alès, where he was warmly welcomed and underwent several more operations on his jaw. Thanks to the remarkable work already done in Zaragandara, in the minimal conditions that we saw, no bone grafts were needed. After a few months, Amrullah, who had been adopted by the people of Alès as one of them, returned to Badakhshan and was welcomed back there by Robert. He brought with him some money that had been collected by the association to fund several schools. Robert recalls that Amrullah did not tell the people of his village about what his stay in France was like. He preferred not to say anything.

The little boy who was wounded during the bombing of Püstuk and died a few hours later was not called Ahmad Jan, as Didier thought he heard. His name was Nazim Jan. He was three years old.

Didier's relationship with Dominique did not withstand the test of time. Nor did Didier's notebook, his diary of his return from Afghanistan. It disappeared during a move. This graphic novel would have been different if the authors had been able to draw on that document. Too bad, or so much the better. Still, if a reader finds it in some corner of France, Emmanuel would be grateful to hear about it. One thing that did survive is a small red spiral-bound notebook in which Didier kept track of the monies spent over the course of the return, especially the amounts extorted by the "wolf" and his men. The English-Dari dictionary also made it, which isn't bad, considering all it went through.

Kandinissa, the girl who was wounded in the same bombing by shrapnel fragments that cut her spine, died six months later of septic shock. Living conditions in her village did not allow for the constant care that she needed. She was about ten years old.

Despite the dressing-down he got from Juliette and his chiefs, the corrupt cop of Bum Boret continued to ply his little racketeering trade. Régis also fell into his clutches and Robert avoided him only narrowly a year later. So be warned.

Even though Madeleine and Jacques Fournot do not appear in this story, we could not conclude it without saluting them. It was thanks to them that their daughter Juliette came to know Afghanistan so deeply. The family settled there in the 1960s, a time of peace. Jacques, an engineer, worked on developing some of the rural regions of the country. His passionate interest in Afghanistan's arts and crafts, traditional industry, ways of life, and spirituality, in addition to his deep knowledge and fairness, won him the respect of many Afghans. Fifteen years later, in the midst of a war, just mentioning his name brought Juliette some crucial protections.

Most of the members of the MSF missions to Afghanistan met the Fournots either before leaving or upon their return, receiving wise advice, comforting talk, or a listening ear. "They gave us the keys to Afghanistan," explains Robert. All those who met this couple, and saw how they lived with their door and their hearts open to the world, felt that their lives were hugely enriched as a result. Our fond thoughts go to Jacques, who passed away in 2004, and we send our warm greetings to Madeleine.

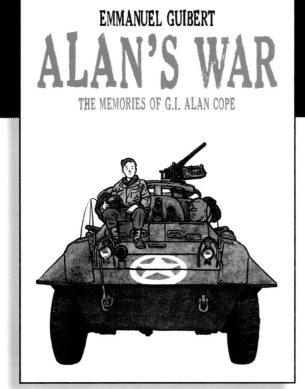

EMMANUEL GUIBERT

ALAN'S WAR

THE MEMORIES OF G.I. ALAN COPE

Alan's War
by Emmanuel Guibert

★ "This is one man's war memories, filled not with tales of larger-than-life heroism but with the chance encounters, tragic absurdities and small kindnesses experienced by a sheltered young soldier of uncommon intelligence, as recollected by an older man who has come to take stock of his life and reconsider the values by which he has lived it. He comes to question himself, his country and humanity in general, while retaining a humanitarian warmth and a deep appreciation for the arts. . . . This epic graphic memoir spans oceans and generations, with a narrative as engrossing as the artistry that illustrates it. . . . a volume that underscores the resonance and legacy of war."

— *Kirkus Reviews*, Starred Review

★ "Guibert writes and draws for American G.I. Alan Cope in this poignant and frank graphic memoir of a young soldier who was told to serve his country in WWII and how it changed him forever. . . . Together, Cope and Guibert forge a story that resonates with humanity. Guibert's illustrations capture the time period vividly. While the subject matter is familiar from many wartime memoirs, Guibert's fluid, simple but assured line-work captures the personalities of Cope and his friends, elevating the material to a far more affecting level."

Publishers Weekly, Starred Review

Notes for a War Story

by Gipi

"An inevitable story about a boy becoming a man under the most extreme conditions. Once [people] see themselves in Giuliano, they won't likely forget his memories."

— *School Library Journal*

"Challenging and provocative."

— *Bulletin of the Center for Children's Books*

"In this powerful graphic novel... Gipi uses deceptively crude black-and-white panels to portray a world sliding into chaos. Young men are left adrift as society unravels."

— *VOYA*

Deogratias
by J.P. Stassen

★ "The heartbreaking power of Deogratias is how it keeps the reader distant from the atrocities by showing the trivial cruelties of everyday life before and after the genocide. . . . There is no catharsis, only the realization that even justice turns its champion into a monster."

— *Publishers Weekly*, **Starred Review**

"The tragedy and international shame of the Rwandan genocide that took place in the 1990's Is realized in this fictional and symbolism studdod parable."

— *Booklist*

"One of the most intense, gripping graphic novels to date... a masterful work with vibrant, confident art, this book will stay with and haunt its readers."

School Library Journal

Laika
by Nick Abadzis

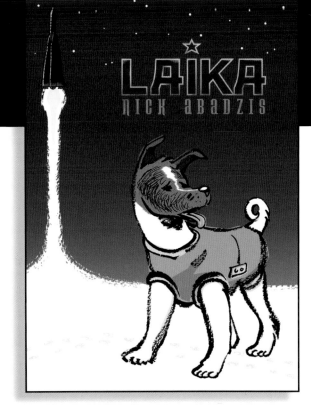

★ "Evincing the cruelty and sadness of her life, Laika's striving to be loved echoes, and the strong bond between man—or woman—and his best friend resound off every page of her journey. . . . a luminous masterpiece filled with pathos and poignancy."

— *Kirkus Reviews*, Starred Review

★ "Abadzis's tear-inducing and solidly researched graphic novel treatment of Laika's surpassingly tragic story is a standout."

— *Publishers Weekly*, Starred Review

★ "Abadzis's artwork genuinely captures the Cold War atmosphere.... Those with a special fondness for dogs may wish to have some tissues handy."

— *School Library Journal*, Starred Review

"Abadzis conjures the complex, scary period known as the Cold War."

—*The Boston Globe*

The Lost Colony
by Grady Klein

"Masterful political fantasy."

— *Booklist*

"An unusual take on American history and colonial experience..."

— *Kirkus Reviews*

"Like some fairy tale take on the Old South, peopled with fantastic characters and lightly leavened with satire, Klein's third Lost Colony volume is a treat from start to finish."

— *Publishers Weekly*

"A zany cast of slaves, ex-slaves, capitalists, opportunists, inventors, and just plain regular folk lead the way through this colorful and delightful tale. . . . chock full of insight into the controversies of the past."

—*VOYA*

First Second

New York & London

Le Photographe, tome 1 © Dupuis, 2003 – Guibert & Lefèvre.
Le Photographe, tome 2 © Dupuis, 2004 – Guibert & Lefèvre.
Le Photographe, tome 3 © Dupuis, 2006 – Guibert & Lefèvre.
English Translation copyright © 2009 by First Second

Published by First Second
First Second is an imprint of Roaring Brook Press,
a division of Holtzbrinck Publishing Holdings Limited Partnership
175 Fifth Avenue, New York, NY 10010

Distributed in Canada by H. B. Fenn and Company Ltd.
Distributed in the United Kingdom by Macmillan Children's Books, a division of Pan Macmillan.

Originally published in France under the titles *Le Photographe, tome 1* (2003),
Le Photographe, tome 2 (2004), and *Le Photographe, tome 3* (2006) by Dupuis.
www.dupuis.com - All rights reserved

Colorist: Lemercier
Design of American Edition: Danica Novgorodoff

Cataloging-in-Publication Data is on file at the Library of Congress.

ISBN-13: 978-1-59643-375-5
ISBN-10: 1-59643-375-2

First Second books are available for special promotions and premiums.
For details, contact: Director of Special Markets, Holtzbrinck Publishers.

FIRST

EDITION

First American Edition May 2009
Printed in China
1 3 5 7 9 10 8 6 4 2

BY ART WE LIVE

www.firstsecondbooks.com